The Many Faces
of Christology

The Many Faces of Christology

Tyron L. Inbody

Abingdon Press
Nashville

THE MANY FACES OF CHRISTOLOGY

Copyright © 2002 by Abingdon Press

All rights reserved.

This book is printed on recycled, acid-free paper.

Library of Congress Cataloging-in-Publication Data

Inbody, Tyron.
  The many faces of Christology / Tyron Inbody.
    p. cm.
Includes bibliographical references and index.
  ISBN 0-687-03003-X (pbk. : alk. paper)
  1. Jesus Christ—Person and offices. I. Title.
BT203 .I53 2002
232—dc21

2002003213

02 03 04 05 06 07 08 09 10 11—10 9 8 7 6 5 4 3 2 1

MANUFACTURED IN THE UNITED STATES OF AMERICA

Contents

Did Pilate Remember Jesus?

Anatole France, the witty, charming, and skeptical French novelist of the late nineteenth and early twentieth centuries, displays his gentle cynicism about human history—and about Jesus—in his short story about the encounter in old age between Aelius Lamia and Pontius Pilate.[1] Lamia, born in Italy of illustrious parents and resident of Rome at age 24 after studying philosophy in Athens, is accused of "engaging in criminal relations" with the wife of a man of consular rank. He is exiled by Tiberius Caesar to wander in exile throughout the eastern Mediterranean. When Tiberius died, Caius permitted Lamia to return to Rome. A wiser and a reformed man, he settles into writing about what he had seen during his distant travels. Eventually, however, the vexations of old age set in after his 20 years in Rome, and at 62 he retreats to the waters of Baiae, a resort for wealthy Romans, to seek relief for "an illness which proved in no slight degree troublesome."

One evening in Baiae he ascends to the summit overlooking the waves below. An elderly man of immense bulk passes him being carried on a litter. He immediately recognizes him as Pontius Pilate, the man with whom he had spent more than ten years as his guest and companion while Pilate was the procurator of Judea. Lively conversation immediately ensues as Pilate informs him that he now lives in Sicily, where in retirement he has estates and cultivates wheat for the market. He is passing through Baiae on his way to some sulphur springs on the Phlegraean plain to treat his gout. Pilate assures Lamia that, though he is ten years his senior, he has preserved his mental vigor and his memory is not in the least degree enfeebled. In their discussion Lamia recalls Pilate's plans to suppress a

Samaritan uprising as he was leaving for Cappadocia. Pilate laments that although his intentions had been honorable and his strategies restrained, the Samaritans succeeded in getting him expelled from Syria on the grounds that he had provoked them against Rome. "These occurrences are as vividly present to me as if they had happened yesterday," he tells Lamia. Although Pilate had returned to Rome in an effort to justify his actions against the Samaritans, he was ignored for reasons of intrigue, and through this "stroke of unmerited misfortune," he had withdrawn in retirement to his estates in Sicily. Recalling the Samaritan rebellion, Pilate indulges in a discussion of his low opinion of the Jews and his own self-justification and self-pity, ending their conversation that night with Pilate's self-indulgent reprise about his lack of honor at the hands of Rome.

Lamia and Pilate agree to have a more relaxed dinner the next night at Pilate's house, where they will talk more about Judea. Pilate begins by recounting how he had planned to provide Jerusalem with an aqueduct, a plan which the ingrates of Jerusalem forced him to stop because "whatever is of Roman origin is distasteful to the Jews." Although Lamia suggests to Pilate that he is not all that innocent because of his insensitivities to the Jews, Pilate simply shrugs his shoulders, displaying his ignorance of Judaism by claiming that the Jews actually have the Roman gods and Roman offerings. In the midst of his soliloquy, he confirms this ignorance by recalling the occasion when "some madman" proceeded to overturn the stalls bearing offerings to the Roman gods. Pilate's disdain for the Jews as ungrateful, contentious, and narrow-minded continues, as he argues that the Jews really wanted Rome to kill those with whom they disagreed, and so his own downfall is the responsibility of the Jews who engineered his recall to Rome. Indeed, he says, launching into a diatribe about his long-standing resentment and sinister foreboding about the Jews, they are dangerous and must be "exterminated" before they destroy Rome.

Lamia, less critical of the Jews, praises their mildness, simple manners, and faithfulness of heart, especially the Jewish women. "The Jewesses . . . I found extremely pleasing," he says. Pilate criticizes Lamia's womanizing, however, as a violation of the patrician view of the sacredness of marriage. Ignoring Pilate's admonitions, Lamia recalls in vivid detail "a Jewess at Jerusalem who used to dance," a woman who would have made Cleopatra grow pale with envy. He had followed her everywhere, but one day she disappeared and he saw her no more. Some months after he lost sight of her, he had learned by chance that she had attached herself to a small company of men and women who were followers of a young Galilean thaumaturgist (miracle worker). "His name was Jesus; he came from Nazareth, and he was crucified for some crime, I don't quite know what. Pontius, do you remember anything about the man?" Pontius Pilate contracted his brow, and his hand rose to his forehead in the attitude of one who probes the depths of memory. Then after a silence of some seconds: "Jesus?" he murmured, "Jesus—of Nazareth? I cannot call him to mind."[2]

Anatole France's short story can be interpreted in a number of ways. He may be suggesting that no one perceives the significance of any event while in the midst of it. Or France may be making a gentle but cynical attack on the importance of Jesus in world history. Twenty years after the events surrounding the crucifixion, not even a major participant in the event could recall the person or any details surrounding the event. The event was so inconsequential in his career as procurator and in the history of his times that only the vague recollection of some "troublemaker" still registers within the reliable memory of this major player. One scholar makes something of this point in his designation of Jesus as "a marginal Jew," meaning, in part, that Jesus in his own day "was at most a blip on the radar screen" in the estimation of the larger Greco-Roman world, evidenced by what Josephus, Tacitus, and Suetonius say about him.[3] One could, also, of course, interpret France's story as an even more cynical comment about history itself, and the relative lack of significant meaning any event has at the time of its occurrence or even thereafter.

However, one might also interpret this story as inadvertently making a decisive point about christology. Jesus may have no special significance to the man who condemned him to death on the cross, perhaps not because of his hard-heartedness, but because he did not have any reason to see him as anything other than a forgettable figure within other more significant events for Pilate's own life. Jesus of Nazareth is important as the Christ not because it was obvious to the people involved in the events that he was important, or to people of the first century or any other century following, but because some had the "eyes of faith" to see that there was some transcendent meaning about this person and the events surrounding his life and death.

Christology is not about Jesus of Nazareth as a victim of first-century Roman politics. There is no reason apart from a christological interpretation of his life and death to assume that Pilate would not have forgotten, almost completely, the incident involving Jesus of Nazareth, reliable as his memory might have been in old age. Christology is about the importance of Jesus of Nazareth, his person and work as the Christ, for those who have the "eyes of faith" to see who he was and why he was important for the life of the church. Christology is not simply a historical memory of Jesus; it is the interpretation of his significance and the grounds and nature of his significance for Christian faith and life. There can be no christology apart from the faith of the believer. Yet the faith of the church is tied intimately to this historical person from the first century. Although christology is about why and what one recalls about Jesus for the life of faith, that faith is inseparable from the historical figure of Jesus of Nazareth. That claim sets the context and agenda for this book, and is the explicit agenda for the first chapter. I will, subsequently, explore some of the many faces of christology which have followed from the double claim that Jesus is the Christ and that Christ is Jesus. All of the many faces of christology contain this double claim.

Context and Motivation for the Book

No one ever fully comprehends the assorted motivations for their work. Motives are always enmeshed together to push and pull one toward an objective. In the case of scholars, their subjects of interest and attention, their agendas, and their approaches are a complex blend of intellectual, professional, and biographical influences. At least that is certainly true of my interest in christology throughout the last decade. I was raised in a conservative evangelical church in northern Indiana in the late 1940s through the mid-1950s. The church was the most important thing in my life until I went to college in 1958. All my family life was focused primarily on church activities, and the most important people in my life, the Smiths and the Ables, essentially surrogate parents, were church families. I did not know what family and friends meant apart from my small, close-knit evangelical church about a half mile away from my house. Jesus Christ and a special relationship with him was the center of every worship service, not simply at the semi-annual two-week "revival meeting." Until later in my life, I felt inadequate as a Christian, even somewhat guilty, because I could not name a time or place where Jesus Christ "became real to me," and I never had a "born again experience" I could celebrate and promote. I tried, many times at many of these semi-annual meetings to get or to allow such an experience to happen, but it never "took." I was never sure I was a "real" Christian. I long admired, and even envied, those Christians who knew the reality of Christ without having to endure a sense of the inadequacy or illegitimacy of one's faith because it was not determined by a "born again experience."

However, at the same time I knew everything I believed most deeply and treasured was defined by the church, especially the hymns, which I still sing from memory without the benefit of a hymnal, and the preaching services. Once a quarter we had the eucharist—we called it "communion Sunday"—and although it was preceded by an evangelistic sermon, the last part of that service was like no other thirty minutes in the life of my church. I knew there I was a Christian, I knew I knew Jesus

Christ, and I knew that that reality was at the center of my view of the world, how I constructed it, what I valued, what I wanted to be and to be like. I wondered how could one be a Christian, whose very life is defined by that reality, and yet not a "real Christian" because there was no "born again experience" or life-shattering moment? My frustration about this dilemma, which existed for many years at the deepest level of my own religious sensibilities, is reflected upon theologically in my chapter on evangelical christology, where my critique of it nevertheless retains the evangelical conviction that the reality of Christ must be located at the core of one's being or else it is no reality at all. Although I have acquired many sacramental and postliberal views of Christian identity, I still am both modern and evangelical enough to remain convinced that if one knows God in Christ that knowledge must be "of" and not simply "about," must go to the depth of who one is, shaping all of one's life if it is genuine faith and belief. In that sense, I remain an evangelical to this day, even though the "depth" of that reality and the meaning of "the core of one's being" has been expanded greatly by the many other "faces of Christology" I have read, studied, and taught over the last forty years.

Unlike most students either then or today, college was the other "most important thing" in my life. If I ever had "a born again experience," it was not in my church but in college, as my four years in college, under the influence of Bob McBride and Marvin Henricks, deconstructed much of my former life and set me on the path of reconstructing every aspect of my new life. My college was a small, denominational school in University Heights in Indianapolis—the kind of place and time when new worlds were opened up to many adolescents raised in small midwestern towns. The experience remade me in ways that seem not to happen to most college students today. I never "lost" my faith in Paul Tillich's (German-American existentialist theologian, d. 1965) and Schubert Ogden's (American process theologian, b. 1928) senses of ultimate concern and confidence, but I lost many of my beliefs, including most of my inherited christology. Liberalism was alive in those times and places, even in small midwestern colleges, and I imbibed of it deeply. It was a time of faith as ultimate concern and confidence, and of doubt about the doctrines I had inherited. Basic questions about faith and reason and the reality of God were at the forefront, even as I went to seminary (where christological concerns were more about piety than belief). But this was especially true when I went to the bastion of liberal theology, the Divinity School of the University of Chicago, for my graduate work with Langdon Gilkey (University of Chicago theologian, b. 1919). Christology was put on my back burner, since those days at Chicago were focused more on matters of theological method and the question of the reality of God than on the major doctrines, such as christology. My preoccupations with theological method and God followed me into my first teaching appointment at Adrian College in Michigan. Indeed, during my seven years of teaching there, my closest colleague, an expert in the early church fathers, insisted (and still is a bit suspicious to this day) that I had no christology. This was true to the extent that I did not then read and discuss much christology, and that I was never a heart-felt or head-convinced follower of Karl Barth (Swiss neo-orthodox theologian, d. 1968) either in my method or the content of my theological doctrine.

However, when I moved back to my seminary to teach, a move which I welcomed even though I relished teaching in undergraduate college, I "rediscovered" christology, not only because my students had more interest in it than I did at that time, and not only because I had special responsibility to help them think through it for their own personal and professional reasons, but also because I discovered that further down than I had recognized, I could not evade this question for personal as well as theological reasons. I came at it more because christology was inescapable within the context of other theological questions I was asking, such as the questions about method and the reality of God, as well as the historical Jesus and the relation of Christianity to Judaism and the other religions— "the many faces of christology" which provided the outline for the following chapters—than because of speculation about christology as a distinct topic of theological reflection within a dogmatic system.

Furthermore, I encountered some practical catalysts which nudged me to consider christology anew. I immediately assumed responsibility to teach the course in systematic theology, a course which obviously required reflective thought about Jesus Christ, regardless of whether one assumed Barth's strategy of making christology the beginning and center point of all theology (Barthianism), or assumed christology to be the centerpiece of a systematic theology (liberal theology). Even if I did not teach systematic theology from a christocentric point of view, I found it impossible to teach the course without a christomorphic emphasis to each of the doctrines. Regardless of methodological questions, however, no course in systematic theology in a seminary could, or should, be taught without christology as central to the project, for theological as well as personal and professional reasons. Consequently, I shifted my work from primarily theological method, or, theology proper (the doctrine of God) to a more explicit concern with christology. At the same time, I was rediscovering how deep christology had been and, indeed, still was in my consideration of the issues of method and God. All of this conspired to compel me to raise anew the issue of christology in most of my courses, and, finally, to teach an entire course on christology throughout the past few years. In this process I discovered "the many faces of christology," both in the sense of the diversity of "guises" of Jesus Christ in the tradition and in the contemporary discussion, but also in the sense that it appears under many "disguises" as historical questions, as questions of method and perspective, and as questions of the relation of the many religions.

My interest was piqued by another practical consideration. I was appointed by my bishop to serve on the Board of Ordained Ministry of the North Indiana Conference of the United Methodist Church for an eight year term. I was shocked at how little most potential ordinands had thought about their answer to the christology question from our *Book of Discipline*, "What does it mean to say that Jesus Christ is Lord?" Furthermore, I was appalled at the vacuity of their christological statements, in part based on little knowledge of the Jesus question and even less about what was at stake in the history of the creeds. It was in this context I rediscovered the connection between a vacuous piety and an unformulated, even uninformed, set of beliefs. Consequently, with my new motivation to consider christology within the context of systematic theology joined with the need to do "remedial work" with ordinands in preparation for their ordination exams, I decided to devise a course in christology which would consider together scripture, the creedal tradition, and the various approaches and emphases of the major voices in theology today. In preparation for the course, and throughout numerous offerings of this well-subscribed course—the word got around quickly that the Board was very likely to ask the ordinand about their views on christology and baptism—I prepared papers on these topics which have gone through many revisions over the years. Professionally, then, the motivation and origins of this book are rooted in the convergence of my personal and professional reasons to reconsider christology after years of preoccupation with other issues. This book is not the story about my conversion to "christomonism" (Christ only). Although I have been influenced by Barth's thought, as will be evident in chapter two on the trinity, I have never been a true believer in an extreme christocentrism (detractors call it "christofascism"), although the conclusions of each of the eight chapters will show how "christomorphic" (Christ shaped) my theological conclusions are.

I am, then, and this book reflects this, something of an anomaly today. I am a blend of evangelicalism inherited from childhood and adolescence, of classical liberalism adopted during my college and graduate years, and of postliberal sensibilities which gradually have influenced me throughout the years of teaching in a denominational seminary. Most college and seminary students today do not inhabit all of these worlds sequentially as I have, for they do not live in a world which is as rich as the complex world of evangelicalism, liberalism, and postmodernism all wrapped up in one person. Being shaped, past and present, by all of them makes it impossible for me to adopt an ideological label. Although I have less and less sympathy with fundamentalist forms of Christianity, I increasingly am fascinated by the developments which have occurred among the new generation of evangelical theologians. I have a love/hate relationship with classical liberalism. I am convinced we are not and should not be beyond the Enlightenment, but I am also convinced about the weaknesses, even some of the demonic qualities, of classical liberalism. Not only do I not fit an ideological label; I am not even much interested in one anymore. So the book which follows is more my conversation with a number of voices or faces who are engaged in discussion of specific topics, problems, and movements which have christology at the center of their discussion. I am more interested in taking the discussion wherever I think it should go than I am in advocating ideological purity.

Thus, it will quickly become clear to the reader by reviewing the table of contents that I do not offer a self-contained and speculative christology proper as another addition to the bibliography of constructive christologies available today. Rather I offer a discussion of christological issues as they appear in the context of a wide range of theological problems, such as historical Jesus research, the meaning and role of the creeds in faith today, the relation of Christian faith to Judaism and the other religions, and dialogue with evangelicalism, feminism, and the liberation theologies. Christology as an isolated, speculative theological problem has never been a distinctive issue for me or interest of mine. Christology as it arises within the context of distinctly theological topics and problems and as it underlies the primary theological issues at the core of these discussions has been a particular interest. So, I explore christology as it appears through its many faces. Sometimes these faces appear as portraits, sometimes as masks, sometimes even as disguises of christology proper. But behind the portrait or mask or disguise is the central question for Christianity, namely, Dietrich Bonheoffer's (twentieth century German Christian martyr to Nazisim) question of "Who is Jesus Christ for us today?"[4] I am concerned with how Jesus as the Christ, the christological figure at the center of Christian faith, reflects, exhibits, inhabits, and incarnates the reality and purposes of God within the context of Christian faith today.

Nature of the Book

Each of the eight chapters consists of a description and an evaluation of one of the issues of christology, as well as some of the current literature on the topic, ending in the fifth section of each chapter with my conclusions and constructive arguments about this issue for christology. Although, as I noted, the format for the book is not "an essay in christology," the chapters together consist of the major topics which I would include in a book in the format of "an essay in christology" or the conclusions I would affirm in the chapter on christology in my systematic theology. If the reader wants something like an essay in constructive theology, the reader may review the fifth section of each of the eight chapters as my constructive christological statement. The book as a whole, however, is both a descriptive analysis of a wide range of the contemporary discussion of the many faces in christology and my conclusions and arguments about what is crucial to affirm about Jesus Christ for an adequate understanding and affirmation of Christian faith in our late modern or postmodern context.

Chapter one begins with the historical Jesus for a theological reason. Whatever else Christian faith is about, it is about faith in God. However, for Christians faith in God does not exist apart from faith in Jesus Christ. Faith in God is christomorphic; it is shaped by Jesus Christ. This faith that is shaped by christology entails the claim that Christ is connected with Jesus and Jesus is the Christ. The "Jesus" referred to in this claim is Jesus of Nazareth. Christology does not exist apart from this figure. However, in the modern world the figure of Jesus has become more and more problematic. Modern historical method has asked who he was, what he actually did and said, and what we can know about him. This chapter examines the status of that question at the end of the century, argues that there are theological reasons the question must be pursued, and shows the significance for christology of the content of our answer to that question. The chapter concludes with the dual claim that the object of christology and the content of christology is focused on Jesus, the eschatological prophet from Nazareth. The conclusions of this chapter will become crucial to the arguments in chapters four and five on the liberal and postliberal christologies.

Chapter two picks up with themes implicit in chapter one, specifically, the claim that this Jesus is the Christ, the image or Word or Wisdom or incarnation of God. The chapter begins with a discussion of how the Christian concept of God is shaped by christology, through the doctrine of the trinity, and how this important concept has become so controversial and yet important in the modern Christian world because of the problem of the relation of God to a suffering world. After introducing my argument of why the theistic concept of God must be revised today, the chapter moves to trace the developments of the christological controversy in the early church as it wends its way toward its formulation of dogmatic trinitarian and christological doctrine in the councils of Nicea (fourth century) and Chalcedon (fifth century). The chapter returns, then, to the reconsideration and reaffirmation of the concept of God as the triune God in late modern theology by moving christology to the center of theology proper in an effort to reconstruct the theistic concept of God. When christology becomes decisive for the shape of our concept of God, the classical theistic concept of God gives way to radical reconceptions of God and how God is related to the world. This chapter argues for a reconception of God in the light of the Christian doctrine of the trinity, which is at its core a christological claim.

Chapters three, four, and five explore christology from the point of view of major "types" or "perspectives" on theology today. Chapter three, on evangelical theology, argues that there is no distinctive evangelical christology proper; evangelicals claim to represent only biblical and creedal christology. What is distinctive is their soteriology, namely, their claim that there is one proper way to know God through Jesus Christ. I examine this epistemology in the light of modern sources and norms, and conclude that evangelicalism is a very modern form of christology. Although it is a form of biblical, creedal, and mystical christology, it also assumes a thoroughly modern form of epistemology. As such it runs the risk of becoming one more form of modern subjectivism or even a form of gnosticism. Chapter four explores two other types of christology which formulate christology in the context of the modern world, one, liberal christology, notably process christology, which attempts to interpret christology explicitly by adopting modern liberal problems and criteria, and postliberal christology, notably, African American and Latin American christologies, which attempt to interpret Jesus Christ in the light of the consequences and liabilities of modernity and of postliberal agendas and norms. The conclusions about Jesus in the first chapter become especially important in these two chapters, as Jesus' preaching and teaching of the kingdom of God becomes central in these christological constructions. Chapter five deals with another form of liberation theology, namely, feminist and womanist theology, and shows why christology is a central problem for many womanists and feminists, many of whom are engaged in an effort to reconstruct christology. This chapter ends with an argument for the significance of a wisdom christology for a postliberal christology.

Chapter six considers atonement theory. After summarizing six different theological interpretations of the cross which are still alive today, I focus on major criticisms of the satisfaction and substitutionary theories of atonement, arguing that these two theories in fact end up offering a sacralization of abuse. I review in the middle of the chapter what I think is the strongest case which can be made for these theories, but conclude that they are not finally redeemable. Assuming that the cross is central to any theology of the redemptive work of Christ, I offer at the end of this chapter the argument that the redemptive significance of the cross can be reinterpreted in a non-abusive way by showing how it unmasks the fundamental human condition of violence, how it is a part of the scope of the entire life and work of Christ, and how it is an essential moment in the

Christian interpretation of the identity and character of God. Here the conclusions in the final section of chapter two become decisive for a reinterpretation of the cross in chapter six.

Chapters seven and eight raise the question of the relation of Jesus Christ and Christianity to the non-Christian religions. Chapter seven considers the relation of Christianity and Judaism to be a special case in this larger question. The chapter is written with the significance of the holocaust for Christian theology continually in mind, and so begins with the questions of the relation of Jesus to the Judaism of his day, especially to the two questions of his relation to the Pharisees and "Who killed Jesus?" The chapter then moves on to argue that the persistent debate between Christianity and Judaism is not about Pharisaism, crucifixion, or even the resurrection, but rather the messiahship of Jesus, a debate within the Abrahamic faiths which Christians can "win" only by redefining messiahship through their eschatology. The chapter concludes by arguing that Judaism and Christianity are two versions of faithfulness to the God of the covenant through faithfulness to the Torah and to Christ.

Chapter eight enlarges the question of the relation of Christianity to all the religions, including the nontheistic religions. A new context and new attitudes demand that this question come to the forefront of the contemporary christological agenda. I review the three dominant "answers" to this question in the last two decades, namely, exclusivism, inclusism, and pluralism. The central argument for each theological position, the reasons for the position which is taken, and my critiques of each one of the three standard alternatives is presented. I conclude with a viewpoint which I think includes the truth there is in each one of the three but avoids the liabilities of each. I call my view confessional pluralism.

It is, of course, impossible to acknowledge, or even to recognize, all of the persons who have been influential in the formation of this book and its constructive arguments. First and foremost I want to recognize and to thank the many students who have taken my christology course over the last several years, who have read and critiqued earlier drafts of these chapters, and who continue to show me how important the question of christology is for Christian faith and life. There are also a number of colleagues who have read and responded to selected chapters or who have discussed some of these issues with me in the hallway or over lunch or in their home or mine, such as Andrew Park, Larry Welborn, Tom Boomershine, Kathy Farmer, Tom Dozeman, Carolyn Bohler, Jerry Stewardson, Ted Zaragoza, Kendall McCabe, Ed Zeiders, and Julie Carmean. I want to acknowledge and express my gratitude to the United Theological Seminary Board of Trustees for their generous sabbatical program which sets aside concentrated time for faculty to do the kind of reflection and revision needed to bring this material to publication. I also want to thank Michael Russell, my editor at Abingdon Press, who shepherded this manuscript through to its final publication, along with Kathy Armistead, Lynn Kauppi, and especially Terrie Livaudais, Production Editor, who worked with the manuscript at various stages of its preparation. Finally, but most important and with the deepest gratitude and affection, I want to thank Fran, my wife, who not only indulged me the time in my office or at our dinners with colleagues and friends to discuss these matters on occasion, but whose love and support makes such a project possible.

CHAPTER ONE

Jesus of Nazareth and Christology

Different people have different reasons for their interest in Jesus. Historians note him as one of the most influential figures in history. No one can give an account of Western art, literature, and music apart from him.[1] He has been the subject of numerous cinematic presentations over the last one hundred years.[2] Who he was, and who he came to be, is an essential ingredient of Western history and culture. In addition, one third of the world's population ascribes him as the object of their faith. For Christians, therefore, interest in him is theological even before it is historical. Jesus of Nazareth is Jesus the Christ, the object of the community's faith. The figure of Jesus Christ stands at the center of Christian identity and practice. Since this is a historical as well as a historic faith, the theologian is committed to resolving the puzzlement about the relation between Jesus of Nazareth and christology. In short, christology is an account of the significance of the historical Jesus for believing Christians. This chapter explores the figure of Jesus, and how and why that figure has been central to modern theological studies.

I. Three Approaches to Jesus

Christians do not believe in Jesus; they believe in Jesus Christ. They do not know anything more about Jesus of Nazareth than any secular historian knows about him through historical research. Christians believe this Jesus is the Christ, the One whom God raised from the dead, the incarnation of the second person of the triune God. Regardless of where one places oneself along the continuum of historical conclusions—from the claim that all we know is *that* Jesus of Nazareth is the one whom the church proclaimed (Rudolf Bultmann, German New Testament scholar and theologian, d. 1976), to the claim that Jesus of Nazareth is the Christ precisely as he is portrayed in the Gospels (evangelicalism)—Christians believe Jesus is the Christ, and the designation Christ refers to Jesus of Nazareth. This claim is what makes interest in Jesus christology and why christology is, willy nilly, implicated in the quest for the historical Jesus.

The grounds and content of our knowledge about this Jesus who is the object of faith are utterly controversial in contemporary christology. "Whose picture of Jesus?" is the preliminary question for any christology in the late modern world, especially for any "ascending" christology which begins "from below" with the Jesus of history. Once a christological claim is made, the Christian faces the tough question: "Whose Jesus?" is the grounds or object of any christological claim? Is the Jesus who is the object of faith and the subject of christology Jesus of Nazareth? Or is he the historical Jesus who is discovered within New Testament texts and reconstructed by modern historical methods? Or is he the Jesus of the kerygma (the church's preaching), the risen Christ who is the subject of the apostolic witness contained in the New Testament and in the life and liturgy of the church? Or is he the Jesus of the narrative itself, the one who is the subject of the received New Testament texts?

I have discovered in my classroom that no discussion of christology can proceed very far without recognizing three different approaches to the historical Jesus. The conclusion about who "Jesus" refers to marks one of the most substantive and controversial differences between premodern, modern, and postmodern approaches to christology. The assumptions, goals, programs, and conclusions about Jesus differ widely between these three contemporary approaches. It is important to notice that I am not here addressing the significance of Jesus for Christian life and faith, which is the subject of the remainder of this book. Here I am asking the prior question of who was the Jesus who is significant for the believer.

The Premodern Approach

Premodern Christianity (christology prior to the eighteenth century Enlightenment) presumed that Jesus of Nazareth, the portrait of Jesus in the four Gospels, and the Christ confessed in the orthodox creeds are indistinguishable. Christians assumed the *identity* between the individual from the first century and what the texts and the creeds claim about him. Jesus of Nazareth said, did, and was precisely what is recorded in the New Testament. He was the divine savior, who came into the world, who died for the sins of the world, and whose life and death opened up the possibility of eternal life for us all. As the divinely begotten Son of God, his life and message consisted primarily of inviting hearers to believe that what he proclaimed about himself as God was salvific.

This premodern assumption about the identity of Jesus of Nazareth, the scriptural narrative, and the creedal Christ is not restricted to Christians who lived before the Enlightenment. It is still the dominant view among many (indeed, probably most) contemporary Christians, including not only the typical lay person in the local church congregation, but also clergy, theological school students, and a significant cadre of conservative biblical scholars and theologians in the academy as well. Regardless of how modern most Christians are in their views of politics, economics, education, art, music, and even morality, many, if not the majority, are still premodern in their view of the Jesus who is the object of their faith.

The modern distinction between "Jesus" and "Christ" is, for the premodern Christian, not only an unimportant but even an unthinkable distinction. Premodern Christians assume the historical reliability of every element of the story about Jesus recorded in the four Gospels. Not only are there dogmatic reasons to assume that every word gives a reliable historical account of Jesus of Nazareth; there simply is no reason to doubt that the narratives are historically accurate records of what Jesus said and did, including what he said about himself. If one had been there on the spot with a camcorder, one would have recorded exactly what is written in the Gospels. The four Gospels are history and biography as well as theology. Read correctly, they report the historical facts about Jesus, what he said and did, who he eternally was and is and will be. Although some defenders of the premodern approach would grant that there are some minor problems of harmonization among the four Gospels, they nevertheless assume a premodern view that the gospels are history and biography, and that the Jesus of history and the Christ of faith are one and the same person.

The presupposition of the premodern view is summarized clearly in the recent claim that "the most reasonable answer to the question why the Gospels present Jesus as they do is because that is essentially who Jesus was. The Gospels faithfully preserve the memory that he left on his followers, that he was divinely legitimated and empowered to be God's Son and Servant."[3] Thus, the "pre" in premodern does not refer to a viewpoint chronologically prior to the modern historical-critical approach to scripture developed throughout the Enlightenment. It refers to a set of assumptions, a methodology, and set of conclusions held by the church prior to the modern historical-critical approach to Jesus in the last 200 years and still effective among most Christians in the modern and postmodern West.

The Modern Approach

The Enlightenment challenged this approach to Jesus. Modern theologians have had a difficult time subscribing to the premodern assumption about the identity of the historical Jesus and the creedal Christ, even the identify of Jesus of Nazareth and the Jesus of the New Testament narratives. The profound change which drastically altered our view of Jesus is the modern concept of historiography. A new understanding of historical knowledge, and so our attitude toward all documents from the past, emerged. This development had its impact on biblical scholarship and theology throughout the last 200 years.

The modern approach to historical documents has been shaped by three assumptions. First, we should bring a critical attitude to every document we read, because what is reported in any document may not necessarily be what actually happened. The historian cannot assume that any text from the past is to be taken at face value. There is a tendency of the human imagination, for a variety of reasons, to embellish or to "overinterpret" any historical event. The historian, therefore, must be skeptical about each claim in a historical text, and must either have rational reasons for accepting the claims of a text at face value or a method for determining what actually happened by reconstructing the facts of the past based on the evidence within the texts or from relevant data recovered from the context. "History is the past reconstructed interactively by the present through argued evidence in public discourse."[4]

Second, historical claims must be evaluated according to what we know to be possible in history. Modern historiography proposed to take a purely scientific approach to the events of history. "Material is more likely to be regarded as historically reliable if it does not require acceptance of ideas that contradict modern views of reality."[5] Miracles, exceptional cases, complete novelty, and events of supernatural origin and purpose give way to naturalistic explanations of the events of history. The decisive assumption which has come to dominate the modern worldview was stated most clearly by Cicero centuries ago. "For nothing can happen without cause; nothing happens that cannot happen, and when what was capable of happening has happened, it may not be interpreted as a miracle. Consequently there are no miracles. . . . We therefore draw this conclusion: what was incapable of happening never happened, and what was capable of happening is not a miracle."[6]

Third, this concept of historiography marks the watershed between the premodern and modern approaches to Jesus. Faith statements about the history and significance of Jesus are permissible, but "within the limits of reason alone" (that is, within the natural world). Theologians who have operated out of the guidelines of modern historiography, therefore, have had a hard time sustaining the premodern assumptions about Jesus. Belief in a supernatural origin, nature, and destiny of Jesus cannot be derived from historical knowledge within the realm of history. Any transcendent significance of Jesus must be grounded in a realm beyond historical knowledge, such as the realm of mythology, poetry, aesthetics, morality, spirituality, existential encounter, imagination, or narrative. The "problem of the historical Jesus," then, is a thoroughly modern problem, depending primarily on Enlightenment assumptions about the nature of historical knowledge and the relation of historical knowledge to faith and theology.

The Postmodern Approach

Postmodern theologians are uninterested in the question of the Jesus of history in the way modern theologians are. There are three reasons for this disinterest. First, the postmodern thinker has lost confidence in our ability to make any sharp distinction between "historical fact" and "interpretation" and "imaginative construction." Postmodern biblical scholars and theologians have been more or less skeptical about the possibility or importance of historical facts for the meaning and truth of any text. Indeed, in some extreme forms the notion of "historical fact" has lost any meaning at all. History is rearranged under the genre of fiction. The argument is not that fiction is false; it is, rather, that truth, at least the kind of truth by which we live our lives, is not based upon historical facts and knowledge but upon the meaning of constructed worldviews. For the postmodernist, the key to the meaning and truth about anything or anyone is the narrative itself, for all supposed knowledge is finally an interpretation of (a long series of) interpretations of images, metaphors, stories, and narratives. The truth of an idea or person lies wholly in the constructed symbolic significance of the idea, event, story, or person, not in its factual truth read directly off the pages.

Second, facts about Jesus of Nazareth are not important for christology. Since we have no access to pure historical facts, and especially to historical persons in all of their complexity and their context, christology rests on some other grounds than historical knowledge of the past. Indeed, the Jesus of history, or the historical Jesus, or the pre-Easter Jesus are not christology. Christology is about, and is based upon, the post-Easter Jesus, the Christ of faith, the kerygmatic Christ, or our experienced personal Lord and Savior. Regardless of whether one is premodern (and assumes the identity of Jesus and Christ) or postmodern (and distinguishes between Jesus and Christ), Jesus who is the Christ in the church's biblical texts and proclamation is the proper subject of christology.

Third, the identity and significance of Jesus is lashed to the story about him. What is important in christology is what believers have in front of them—the stories, the beliefs, and the testimonies—all known through the biblical texts. Thus, christology cannot be based on the modern assumptions about our ability to get behind the Bible to something or someone who lies behind its texts as a "truth" or "reality" more real than the stories themselves. Jesus is the Jesus of the narrative; there is no other Jesus. The quest for Jesus is the quest for "the story of a story, a story of which history is but a part, and sometimes but a shadow. . . . We just let the story take us wherever it is going."[7]

The basis for christology in the postmodern perspective, then, is the narrative of the New Testament canon, the New Testament texts, the stories about Jesus conveyed in the narrative itself. Faith in Jesus Christ is based on the stories we find in the texts themselves, not on a distilled kerygma (C. H. Dodd, British biblical scholar, d. 1973), the earliest Christian proclamation embedded within the texts (Bultmann and Ogden), or a critically discovered and reconstructed historical Jesus (the three quests for the historical Jesus). Our faith is built on the biblical story itself, not someone who stands behind or even within those texts. Faith arises from and depends upon the narratives as such, not on reconstructions or hypotheses about the historical person behind the texts. Most postmodernists simply are not interested in the quest of the historical Jesus, at least as grounds for christology, which, ironically, puts premodern and postmodern theologians close together in their approach to the critical questions, "who was Jesus?" and "what is significant about Jesus for christology?"

One excellent example of the postmodern approach is William Hamilton's "search for a post-historical Jesus." The modern quest for the historical Jesus, he believes, has come to an end. Though not a thorough deconstructionist in his view of history, Hamilton is nonetheless skeptical about the results of the modern quest for the historical Jesus. "We can know something about Jesus," he concedes, "but what we know is of little use to us in the late twentieth century."[8] The Jesus of history, therefore, is either invisible or irrelevant. Instead, the Gospels must be read as fictions,[9] and the Jesus we have before us is the Jesus we can turn to after we have determined that the historical method has given us very little. Specifically, we have the Jesus there before us in the texts. Our christology is based on these narratives about forgiveness, freedom, reconciliation, and refusal of privilege. They can be followed even if they are taken as fiction instead of history. What we work with in constructing christology are the texts of those who have written about Jesus

24

knowing full well that they were writing fiction. Furthermore, we should look not only to canonical texts, but the texts of other "poets" as well, such as novelists, imaginative biographers, playwrights, and journalists.[10] Even though we cannot say what is historical and what is not in the story of Jesus, we should not despair, for the Gospels give us a Jesus. Whether it is history or kerygma or fiction does not matter, for it carries a truth that can change human lives. As a postmodernist, Hamilton wants "to move beyond history to literature as its key to the New Testament."[11]

It is important to reiterate that all three of these orientations toward Jesus persist as living options at the beginning of the twenty-first century. The premodern assumptions guide contemporary fundamentalism, much evangelicalism, and, indeed, probably are the assumptions of the vast majority of "untyped" Christians who simply take their religion at face value. Postmodern strategies have emerged in the recent past, and so far, are confined to a small cadre in the academy, specifically, within the Society of Biblical Literature and the American Academy of Religion in esoteric forms. The modern project also persists at the end of the twentieth century, most notably in the persistence of the post-World War II second quest and the 1980s and '90s third quest for the historical Jesus. Although Albert Schweitzer (German scholar and missionary, d. 1965) put to bed, or even to death, the "liberal lives of Jesus" of the eighteenth and nineteenth centuries,[12] the project is alive and well today through the "new quest for the historical Jesus" in the '50s and the renewed version of the '80s and '90s.

II. The Three Modern Quests

Christianity, at least catholic Christianity, is an incarnational religion. It claims that in some sense God is incarnate in Jesus of Nazareth. Since the Enlightenment the premodern formulation of the meaning of that claim has become more problematic. However, regardless of how postmodern many of us have become in significant respects, the modern agenda cannot be wholly repudiated or even ignored without the incarnational nature of catholic Christian faith put in jeopardy. Therefore, even for some of us postmoderns, historical Jesus research remains necessary to the integrity of catholic faith. Although no definitive conclusions have been reached in the modern project, and no such conclusions seem possible in our postmodern world, the research must go on, I think, for historical, ethical, and theological reasons.[13] During the 200-year-old modern search for the historical Jesus, the quest has gone through three distinct phases.

The First Quest

The modern quest began with the work of Hermann Samuel Reimarus (1694-1768). His attempt to write a modern life of Jesus was published only posthumously by Lessing from 1774-1778 as the *Wolfenbuttel Fragments*. Reimarus argued that Jesus was a failed Jewish messianic prophet whose disciples stole his body and proclaimed his resurrection. The most important figure in the Enlightenment period, however, was David Frederick Strauss (1808-1875), who argued that a rigorous histori-cal-critical understanding of the Gospels requires both that supernatural-ist and rationalist approaches to the texts must give way to the mythical approach.[14] His approach to the Gospels understood them not as the record of eyewitnesses to the facts, but as fictitious representations of reli-gious ideas. These mythical representations are derived mainly from Jewish messianic expectations; the precise influence of Jesus' actual per-sonality and history is now irrecoverable. For Strauss, however, these rad-ical conclusions do not threaten faith, since faith's security lies not so much in the facts of the past as in ideal truths—truths, in fact, better upheld by the mythical than by the historical or creedal ideas.

Strauss's work was followed by a host of others, such as Joseph Ernst Renan (1823-1892), who argued that the four Gospels are legendary biog-raphies and therefore must be critically reviewed in order to sift the authentic material about Jesus from pious embellishment.[15] Jesus, a per-son of infinite charm and conscious of an intimate relation with God, began his ministry proclaiming a pleasing theology of love. A rebuff of him by the Jewish leadership was followed by his increasing apocalyptic emphasis, his radical alienation from the world, and his final martyrdom. Jesus himself, however, stands at the summit of the human race, the embodiment of humanity's purest idealism and the perfecter of the world's true religion.

Renan stands in the middle of a long line of nineteenth century lives of Jesus, a phase of the modern quest brought abruptly to its close at the beginning of the twentieth century by Schweitzer's *Quest*. Schweitzer concluded that the lives of Jesus over the previous 130 years generally failed because the content of their portrayal was Jesus as a man relevant to the modern world rather than a man of the first century who held vastly different views from ours. They were better accounts of the lives of the authors than of Jesus. Jesus himself was thoroughly a person of his own time in that he believed that history was about to come to a cata-clysmic end and that the Kingdom of God was about to be established. In short, Jesus preached and taught a "thoroughgoing eschatology." He could not be made into a modern person, even though Schweitzer himself believed that his spirit transcends his times and can inspire people today.

With Schweitzer, the first phase for the quest of the historical Jesus came to a close. Throughout most of the first half of the twentieth century, biblical scholars and theologians were not interested in continuing the quest of the historical Jesus. There were several reasons. At least to some extent the modern project was intimately connected with the establishment of bourgeois culture, and that culture seemed challenged if not doomed by World War I and World War II.[16] Furthermore, the scholarly assumptions of the twentieth century differ from those of the nineteenth. Nineteenth century critical scholars "assumed that the real 'Jesus of Nazareth' could be found by means of the newly-discovered historiography promising to narrate the past 'as it actually was.' Hence for the nineteenth century the two meanings of 'the historical Jesus' tended to coincide: 'Jesus of Nazareth as he actually was' coincided with 'the reconstruction of his biography by means of objective historical method.'"[17] Twentieth century New Testament scholars recognized, however, that the objective factual level of history upon which the nineteenth century operated is but one dimension of history and is not what is significant about history for christology. Theologians questioned the modern quest both as possible or legitimate. The only "historical Jesus" they could envision was the one available via nineteenth century reconstruction, and so the quest was abandoned in the first half of the twentieth century in favor of the preached Christ of the New Testament kerygma and the church's contemporary preaching and sacraments.

The original quest had largely rejected the kerygma as a falsification of the religion of Jesus. "For a moral reformer of the Victorian era is quite different from the message of divine salvation proclaimed by an eschatological sect of the Hellenistic world."[18] However, Bultmann considered the center of christology to be the kerygma, the proclamation about Jesus as the Christ, not the historical Jesus himself.[19] He set the agenda in post-World War II Europe and North America for the discussion about Jesus. His study came essentially to skeptical conclusions about our ability to know anything important about the historical Jesus. We can know a good bit about the history of the tradition of proclamation about Jesus, but little of the Jesus who is the subject of that proclamation. This gap, however, was not a major problem for Bultmann and his followers, because the important thing for christology is the proclamation of Jesus as the Christ. That was the christology of the earliest church and that is what modern christology should be built upon. Thus, Bultmann's skepticism about history did not terminate his theological work because such historical knowledge is neither possible nor the necessary grounds for christology. Christology is built upon, and continues to be, an existential interpretation of the kerygma of the church, not upon historically reliable information about the teachings, character, or self-understanding of Jesus of Nazareth. From the turn of the century to mid-century, then, the quest of the historical Jesus seemed to be dead.

The Second Quest

Bultmann's students, however, beginning with Ernst Kasemann's programmatic essay in 1953, "The Problem of the Historical Jesus,"[20] were not as skeptical as he was about our knowledge of Jesus, nor did they concur fully with his claim that knowledge about the historical Jesus is insignificant for christology. Their issue, in part, was a dispute about how skeptical one must be about the possibility of historical knowledge. They thought his thoroughgoing skepticism was unnecessary. Many of Bultmann's students believed we can get a reliable picture of Jesus of Nazareth. Their method, they conceded, did not lead them to "the objective facts" of Jesus. But the New Testament kerygma includes a certain kind of historical material, namely, "those sayings and scenes in which Jesus made his intention and understanding of existence most apparent to them."[21] Although the church did not preserve chronology and biography, it did preserve in the parables, in beatitudes and woes, in kingdom sayings, and in exorcisms "sufficient insight into Jesus' intention to encounter his historical action, and enough insight into the understanding of existence proposed in his intention to encounter his selfhood."[22]

The still-classic formulation of the new quest for the historical Jesus was Gunther Bornkamm's.[23] He began his study admitting that "no one is any longer in a position to write a life of Jesus."[24] The nature of the sources does not permit us to paint a biographical picture of the life of Jesus. Nevertheless, the traits and outline of his person and history are available within the texts.[25] The core of Jesus' message is, "The Kingdom of God is near." "All the conceptions and pictures in Jesus' message are directed with concentrated force on one thing only, and are contained in that one thing—that God will reign."[26] Beyond that, his real peculiarity lies in the directness with which he preaches, in the authority with which Jesus proclaims that the kingdom of God is near, and in his call for conversion. In his mission, the hidden dawn of the mystery of the kingdom of God appeared to all who have eyes to see and ears to hear. "All the beatitudes are directed towards the coming kingdom of God and are embraced in one idea, that God wills to be present with us and will be with us all, in as manifold and individual a way as our needs are manifold and individual."[27] God's future is God's call to the present, and the present is the time of decision in the light of God's future.

In Bornkamm's view, the reason Jesus set out with his disciples toward Jerusalem was to deliver this message of the coming kingdom of God and to summon the people to make a decision for the coming kingdom. Upon his death and resurrection, however, the proclaimer became the proclaimed. "Jesus' words and the gospel about Jesus Christ have become a unity."[28] Through an existentialist interpretation of existence represented in the teachings and actions of the historical Jesus, we can come to know both him and a new self-understanding through our knowledge of him as a result of our encounter with the kerygma of the church. This second quest for the historical Jesus remained powerful throughout the '50s and '60s, as long as existentialist interpretations of the post-war period held sway. But as enthusiasm for existentialism waned and postmodern orientation emerged, the second quest seemed to be dead in the waters by the early 1970s.

The Third Quest

Within a decade, by the early 1980s, a third phase of the modern quest suddenly appeared. At the center of this third quest is a renewed confidence that we can know with a high degree of probability the real Jesus. Dominated by such contemporary New Testament scholars as Marcus Borg, John Dominic Crossan, Burton Mack, Robert Funk, Gerd Theissen, Richard Horsley, and others, these third quest scholars believe we can locate Jesus in his original social setting by drawing on what we have learned about the ancient Near East in recent archeological studies, what we have learned about the ancient Hellenistic and Roman world in historical studies, and what we have learned about the ancient world in sociological and comparative anthropological studies. Added to this is a new set of textual resources which have recently been discovered, such as the extra-canonical gospels, especially *Q, The Gospel of Thomas* and *The Gospel of Peter.*[29]

As a result of these new methods and resources, a new portrait of Jesus has appeared in the last twenty years. Throughout most of the twentieth century, the predominant picture has been Jesus as an apocalyptic or eschatological figure who announced in his preaching, teaching, and deeds the immanent inbreaking of the kingdom of God. A morphed portrait has appeared. "According to this way of understanding Jesus, he may not have been an apocalyptic figure at all. In the Gospel of Thomas and the first version of Q, Jesus does not use apocalyptic images to announce the coming of God's kingdom, but rather declares that the kingdom is already a present reality. . . . While wandering from place to place, he uttered parables and clever sayings—sayings of wisdom—in order to make those around him confront a new and compelling vision of life."[30] Jesus is now variously pictured in some combination as Hellenistic cynic (the Greco-Roman form of the philosophy of world-negation), itinerant teacher of wisdom, gnostic, charismatic, countercultural sage who speaks in paradox, irony, and wit, a revolutionary advocate for the poor and against the wealthy, and an anti-temple and anti-Jewish-establishment reformer. By dismissing the passion narratives of the Gospels as misrepresentations by the early church of Jesus' mission and message to accommodate its own needs and interests during a period of persecution, and by recovering the hidden picture of the "original" Jesus and "the pure voice of the Gospel Jesus"[31] who stands behind the church's misrepresentation of him in its canonical texts, we now have an accurate picture of the Jesus of the first century and "the Gospel's soul" as "one of the primary revelations of life's sacredness."[32]

The most prominent, if not notorious, representatives of the third quest are various members of The Jesus Seminar, originally around 200 scholars who were involved in one way or another in the proceedings of a group founded in 1985 by Robert Funk.[33] Its climactic publication, so far, has been *The Five Gospels,* a product of about 74 members of the seminar. Although each member has their distinctive strokes in their portrait of Jesus, they construct a relatively common picture of Jesus as a first century Palestinian teacher of wisdom and social reform, not a first century Jewish eschatological prophet.

For most of the members of the Jesus Seminar, Q presents the unvarnished Jesus as he was in his own time, an itinerant cynic traveling among the towns of lower Galilee teaching countercultural wisdom and egalitarian ideology at the eastern edge of the Roman Empire. This Jesus stands in contrast to the first quest, where the Sermon on the Mount presented the pure and simple Jesus in his ethical teachings uncorrupted by the theological speculations of Paul and the emerging church, and the post-Schweitzer second quest, where the Kingdom of God as an immanent eschatological reality dominates the picture of Jesus. In this reconstruction, Jesus' original teachings, found in Q and the Gospel of Thomas, were deeply affected by the social stresses of the first century, intensified by Roman rule in Palestine. The original Jesus movement was one popular response in the first century to the economic and political oppression of the masses. Jesus' "religious type" was cynic and social reformer, not ethical moralist, as Adolf Harnack (German historian, d. 1921) envisioned, or apocalyptic prophet, as Schweitzer concluded, or eschatological proclaimer of the coming Kingdom of God, as Bornkamm imagined.[34] Jesus' "social type" was more like a barefoot Socrates (of whom there were many in Palestine in the first century), a gadfly on the social conventions of his day. Like the cynics, he argued that only God is king and so all else is relativized; he begged for a living; he was critical of all human law and the Roman *imperium*; and he was critical of the luxury, vice, and conventional morality and religion of the day.

Here I can review only two of the most public and prominent of this new cadre of third phase scholars. For Marcus Borg, the "real history" of Jesus is unlocked by the social sciences and the history of religions. The real Jesus was not an eschatological prophet (by which Borg means Jesus was not an apocalyptic predictor of the immanent end of the world), but rather a charismatic religious figure and a countercultural sage who founded a renewal movement within Judaism in first-century Palestine. More than the other members of the Jesus Seminar, Borg makes a great deal of Jesus' religious experience. Jesus was a charismatic figure, a Spirit-defined person. The foundation of his life was his "spirituality—his experiential awareness of Spirit."[35] Jesus was grounded in the world of the Spirit. "Jesus' relationship to the Spirit was the source of everything that he was."[36] He constantly pointed away from himself to God. His context, however, was more cosmopolitan than typically imagined, and he, his family, and his mission were all shaped by his membership in the *tekton*, the lower end of the peasant class in Palestine, people who had lost their land in the Roman reorganization of the peasant economy.

This spirit person was not a messianic figure, however, but a person of compassion and a teacher of wisdom, using the classic forms of wisdom speech, such as parables and aphorisms, to teach a subversive and alternative wisdom. He was also a social prophet, similar to the classical prophets in ancient Israel, criticizing the economic, political, and religious elites of his day, and advocating a social vision that was in conflict with the authorities of his day. Specifically, Jesus was a critic of the politics of holiness and an advocate for the politics of compassion. "For Jesus, compassion was more than a quality of God and an individual virtue: it was a social paradigm, the core value for life in community."[37] Whereas the politics of holiness meant the separation from everything unclean, and required a society structured around a purity system with sharp social boundaries, Jesus provided an alternative social vision: "a community shaped not by the ethos and politics of purity, but by the ethos and politics of compassion."[38] This was most apparent in his open table fellowship, which was perceived as a challenge to the purity system. As such he was the founder of a renewal or revitalization movement within Judaism. Thus, Jesus was not into eschatology but into wisdom ("this is the strongest consensus among today's Jesus scholars"[39]), and must be seen as a sage instead of an eschatological prophet. He was one of the world-subverting sages of first century Palestine who taught an alternative to the conventional wisdom. His aphorisms and parables, formed in the language of paradox and reversal, put us in touch with the voice of the pre-

Easter Jesus. "He directly attacked the central values of his social world's conventional wisdom: family, wealth, honor, purity, and religiosity."[40]

The second, and I think most engaging of the new Jesus scholars, is John Dominic Crossan, a post-Vatican II Irish Roman Catholic scholar now retired from DePaul University in Chicago. Crossan's sheer charm, wit, and cleverness are enough to make his portrait of Jesus compelling to us non-experts in Jesus studies. Depending on extra-canonical sources as of equal or greater value than the canon for reliable data about Jesus, and on social history and cross-cultural anthropology for uncovering the historical Jesus, Crossan sets Jesus in the context of the Greco Roman and Jewish culture of the first century, an empire with a highly stratified social class system of patronage operating within a framework of shame and honor. Jesus was a Jewish peasant in first-century Palestine, whose program was a countercultural egalitarianism resembling, though not necessarily derived from, the ancient cynic philosophers.[41] Jesus began as a follower of John the Baptist's version of peasant apocalypticism, but shifted his preaching of the kingdom to a kind of radical egalitarianism and absolute equality. Jesus' kingdom was, in fact, not a future place but a present life style which challenged temple prerogatives and privileges of exclusivism.

Contrary to the "apocalyptic eschatology" of the Baptist and the early church, Jesus' was a "sapiential eschatology," which "announces that God has given all human beings the wisdom to discern how, here and now in this world, one can so live that God's power, rule, and dominion are evidently present to all observers."[42] Unlike the apocalyptic eschatology of Q or the ascetical eschatology of the Gospel of Thomas, Jesus' kingdom, whose eschatology is available in the Common Sayings Tradition, was an "ethical eschatology." Directing his kingdom movement to the destitute and dispossessed peasants who were casualties of Antipas's urbanization and commercialization of Lower Galilee in the 20s, the "heart of his program" (most clearly apparent in the canon in Mark 6:7-13) was "not about heaven but about earth. It is about divine justice here below."[43] The basic elements in his program within the first century context of the complete dislocation of peasant life, family support, and village security were itineracy, eating with those who receive, and healing the sick. The kingdom he announced was not his monopoly, a kingdom in which disciples were related to and defined by him, but rather it was a "companionship of empowerment" available to all who had courage enough to accept it.[44]

His ministry turns out to be primarily a vision for a radical lifestyle challenging established structure and hierarchical power. "For Jesus, the Kingdom of God is a community of radical or unbrokered equality in which individuals are in direct contact with one another and with God, unmediated by any established brokers or fixed locations."[45] Crossan's

Jesus was a Mediterranean Jewish peasant Cynic, who flouted the basic codes of propriety and decency, custom and convention, and who preached inclusiveness and equality. He was noninstitutional and nonpatriarchal; his kingdom consisted of an open table where everyone accepts everyone else, a kind of "open commensality." His preaching, teaching, and healing were a populist attack upon civilization itself in the form of a countercultural lifestyle. Without knapsack and staff, he was what a Jewish Cynic looked like.

III. An Appraisal of the Third Quest

Each quest and each quester has been subjected to severe criticisms. Indeed, we enter into what seems to be an overwhelming gallery of portraits. Virtually no reconstruction of Jesus offered by any scholar has been widely accepted or remained uncontradicted by another scholar. In the light of this fact, the third quest leaves the theologian who appeals to Jesus in their christological construction with two questions, one unique and one recurring. I want to be candid in recognizing that my appraisals arise within the context of my theological agenda. I have already acknowledged my theological reasons for maintaining the necessity of the modern historical quest in formulating a christology. My questions relate to how a theologian who affirms the necessity of the historical Jesus for any christology is to evaluate the portraits of the Jesus of the third quest for christology. First, the third quest has posed a new problem of what sources and norms one should use in christological construction. Second, the third quest has only heightened the recurring problem of the role of the perspective of the historian in all Jesus research.

First, in the recent literature on Jesus, the primary controversial question has not been the conclusions of each study. Before the third quest, there was debate about how to interpret one's sources, but no debate about which sources one should use. Now we face the preliminary question of what texts are most useful for our knowledge about Jesus. The answer to that question depends significantly on how one dates the non-canonical sources and understands them in relation to the canonical Gospels. Are some of the non-canonical sources the earliest and most unvarnished records of the real Jesus, or are they a competitive alternative to catholic Christianity from the early years of the Jesus movement?[46] In all premodern and modern christologies, the assumption was universally held that knowledge about Jesus depends almost wholly on the New Testament canon, and specifically the four Gospels (or if one was thoroughly modern, on the synoptic Gospels). With the discovery of the Nag Hammadi texts in Egypt in 1945, however, the question of what sources we are to use for our knowledge about Jesus has become a central historical issue. Since the discovery of these more than fifty so-called apocryphal Gospels,[47] most notably the Gospel of Thomas,[48] determination about which sources are to be used and what these sources say about the historical Jesus have become decisive for christology.

One's solution to this quandary sets the theologian on a path toward either a more catholic or a more gnostic christology. The predicament is this: the Jesus of the extra-canonical literature is not primarily the Jesus of the four Gospels, especially the synoptic Gospels. The non-canonical Jesus is more a teacher of wisdom than either the divine Son of God of the premodern view or the eschatological prophet of the modern reconstructions. If these non-canonical texts are not only alternative views of Jesus but are also earlier than the canonical Gospels, we have significant historical evidence that the historical Jesus was significantly different from both the Jesus of the New Testament canon and the reconstructed Jesus of the first two quests. Furthermore, if they are the earliest and most unvarnished records, these new texts give us hints about how to read the four canonical Gospels themselves in a new light, so that Q and the Gospel of Thomas become decisive for the reconstruction of Jesus of Nazareth. The Jesus of the canonical Gospels becomes more and more to be seen as the theological revision of earlier Jesus material, the result of the political, religious, and theological agendas of the canonical Gospel writers.

I am not qualified to evaluate either the dating of the materials or the details of this picture of the historical Jesus. Much more expert opinion than mine has been offered. E. P. Sanders[49] and Leander Keck[50] have provided critiques from the mainstream viewpoint; two significant conservative critiques have been published by Luke Timothy Johnson[51] and Ben Witherington III.[52] My own conclusion is that some of the reconstruction of the third quest has only the slightest historical evidence, and is based on imaginative reconstructions spun from a spool of thin threads, even lint. More concretely specified, I can scarcely imagine how one can expurgate either Jewish piety or Jewish eschatology from Jesus of Nazareth and substitute Roman cynicism or gnostic wisdom in its place. The conclusion that those who were contemporary with him and those who immediately followed him were pious and eschatological Jews, while he was neither, stretches not only the evidence but credulity as well. How the church could have so thoroughly misunderstood or maliciously misrepresented him in favor of their alternative agenda which had little connection with his is beyond my boggle point. It is, of course, possible, but is it plausible? The Jesus we have before us is a Jewish eschatologist (though not necessarily an apocalypticist), regardless of how much Schweitzer and all who follow him did not like such a figure, and regardless of how embarrassing or problematic or unmodern any species of the genus eschatology is today.

Second, this preliminary problem is, of course, much more complicated than stated so far. No one interprets Jesus, or the relevant data, apart from their own presuppositions and needs. Obviously, it is difficult to uncover one's own presuppositions with honesty and accuracy. That is perhaps best done by one's critics, or analyst, or students, or spouse. But the reconstructed Jesus in all three phases of the modern quest is indebted at least as much to the social location of the historian as to the text themselves or any other historical evidence. Indeed, the real problem is how to know—or how one can even believe—that one's picture of Jesus is more than a mirror reflection of one's own prejudices, interests, and needs. Schweitzer showed how the Jesus of the first phase of the quest was primarily a product of the assumptions and agenda of the liberal, bourgeois, moralistic culture of Western Europe and North America in the nineteenth century. Current critics, such as Giorgi and Koester, have shown how much all three phrases are tied to the rise, challenge to, and current triumph of capitalist culture.[53] To what degree does the historian look down into the well of history and see their own reflection?

The significance of the existentialism of post World War I and World War II Europe for the reconstructed Jesus of the second quest seems clear to us at the beginning of a new century. Likewise, it seems to me that one learns as much in Jesus Seminar books about the scholar's own social, educational, and political agendas as one learns about the historical Jesus. The Jesus of these books is significantly a portrait of the kind of persons admired by alienated intellectual elites in our universities, colleges, and seminaries, who, in the safety of their settings, fancy themselves as sort of countercultural cynics or ironists in the waning days of late capitalism in the West. Jesus is the kind of figure they imagine themselves to be or wish they were. Their portraits of Jesus mirror the dominant alienated consciousness and agenda of ironic sophistication of academics, in short, the cultural assumptions of the contemporary North American academy. "Crossan's peasant Cynic who preaches inclusiveness and equality fits perfectly within the idealized ethos of the late-twentieth-century academic: he is nonpatriarchal and noninstitutional; his kingdom consists of an open table where everyone accepts everyone else."[54]

However, every critic could offer the same critique of every biblical scholar and theologian and the portrait of Jesus they work with at every point along the continuum. Furthermore, powerful as the role of perspective is in historical reconstruction, there is an option between the certainty of a positivistic view of historical study and the skepticism of a narcissistic or solipsistic view of history. There is a view of history in which the past and present interact with each other in such ways that a reconstruction is possible through "argued evidence in public discourse."[55] Therefore, I do believe evidence and public arguments about plausibility are appropriate and make portraits of Jesus more or less credible.

Within this context I think there is much in the work of Borg and Crossan which is significant for a christology which begins from below with the historical Jesus. Their interpretation of the kind of Judaism, and especially the complexity of the eschatology, that undergirds Jesus' preaching and teaching about the kingdom of God is convincing and important for christology. The existentialist eschatology of the second quest must be rethought in the light of the political or ethical eschatology of the wisdom tradition. However, it seems to me they underplay the significance of eschatology in Jesus. The predominant evidence is that Jesus' life and ministry is defined primarily within the context of Judaism and eschatology, influenced as it is by the sagacious traditions. It is related primarily to his understanding of the eschatological kingdom of God. In short, Jesus is thoroughly Jewish and thoroughly eschatological (though eschatology has yet to be defined, and cannot simply be identified with Schweitzer's apocalypticism). I think the evidence is that Jesus' eschatology was much richer, more complex, than Schweitzer's apocalypticism and the second quest's existentialism. But how one can talk about the historical Jesus, his life and his death, apart from Jewish eschatology as decisive and definitive is, frankly, beyond my boggle point.

IV. A Consensus Portrait of Jesus?

Is there, then, a consensus portrait of Jesus among modern scholars? Anyone who knows anything about contemporary biblical scholarship knows it is delusional to speak about a consensus portrait of Jesus. All we non-experts can do is to survey the literature, try to detect widely shared if not common themes, and select what seems to be the most plausible portrait within the broad range of portraits. Thus, in suggesting a "consensus portrait," I do not take that to mean that anyone has certainty about the historical Jesus but that this is who he appears to be as a historical figure to those constructing a portrait of him as a real person, all the while acknowledging the theological agenda of some kind of catholic christology. I think there are four common brush strokes for the historical Jesus which appear in one degree or another in the portrait of most scholars, including the more conservative Witherington and N. T. Wright, the more radical Crossan and Borg, and the more moderate John Meier, Raymond Brown, Paula Fredriksen, and E. P. Sanders.[56]

1. Jesus was a Jewish eschatological prophet. Jesus went to Jerusalem to preach the immanent kingdom of God through his words and deeds.

Although his proclamation of the coming kingdom does not center on himself and his own role, it is probable he thought he had something to do with its coming. Although his preaching was not a political program or a moral ideology in the strict sense, but rather had something to do with God's dawning new age in Israel's history, his prophetic preaching and deeds, especially with respect to the Temple, brought down the wrath of a few in the religious and political establishment in Jerusalem and led to his death by the Romans on the grounds of political subversion. His untimely death produced disillusionment in his followers, for the messiah of God's new age could not be put to such an ignominious death.

2. *Jesus was a Jewish eschatological teacher.* Jesus taught the irruption of the kingdom of God in the present time. The center of his teaching is the proclamation and description of the kingdom of God among his hearers. The kingdom, he thought, was already present but also immanent in the near future (the degree to be which he was an apocalypticist is highly doubtful, though not undebatable). Primarily through parables he taught what the reign of God was like and that God's reign both was unexpected and present. His sayings and teaching, such as the Sermon on the Mount, were not primarily ethics but characteristics of what human relationships are like when the reign of God is accomplished. The radical demands of his teachings did not provide conditions for entrance into the kingdom but signs of the presence of the kingdom.

3. *Jesus was a Jewish eschatological healer.* The most characteristic miracles in the synoptics are healings, especially exorcisms. Hardly anyone then or now can be skeptical that these healings occurred (at least the exorcisms; the other two types, viz., resuscitation and nature miracles are surely the tendency of the tradition to heighten the miracles even more), and that these were one of Jesus' characteristic activities. The issue is how to interpret them then and now. Are they the work of the devil or of God? Some understood them to be signs of the power of God's immanent kingdom. They were signs that the eschatological kingdom was breaking in or was now being inaugurated in the healings of Jesus.

4. *Jesus was a Jewish eschatological sage.* There is increasing evidence that Jesus was also a representative of Jewish wisdom as well as Jewish prophetism. The most convincing and constructive contribution by recent scholars to the portrait of Jesus as a Jewish eschatological prophet has been the addition of a sapiential (wisdom) or ethical/political component to Jesus' eschatology. In some ways Jesus was a prophetic sapiential sage.[57] Jesus' mode of public discourse used one or another form of wisdom speech, including riddles, parables, aphorisms, personifications, and beatitudes, in contrast to John the Baptist who was a more traditional apocalyptic prophet. Jesus' itinerant ministry, his rejection by the leadership in Jerusalem, his creation theology, his views of a counter order of

society for righting of wrongs, his acts and consequences scheme all point to his involvement in the wisdom tradition of Israel, all of which would have had implications for religious, political, and economic reform in Judaism and in Palestine.

Following his resurrection and Pentecost, some followers of this crucified prophet, preacher, teacher, and sage confessed him to be the Christ. Both the presence and the character of God's inbreaking reign were connected with what he said and did. "He who formerly had been the bearer of the message was drawn into it and became its essential *content*. The proclaimer became the proclaimed."[58] Some of his followers understood this post-Easter Jesus, whose teaching and life were connected to the pre-Easter Jesus, to be the power and presence of God in such a decisive way that they confessed him to be God incarnate. He now is Jesus Christ. His confessors began to make christological claims. But it was this Jesus, the Jew from Nazareth, whom these Christians confessed as Christ.

V. Significance of the Historical Jesus for Christology Proper

One can, of course, be a historian, even a New Testament scholar, without having to make any commitment about the religious implications of one's research and conclusions. However, the moment one steps over the line to ask what significance the Jesus one has discovered has for one's own faith or for the faith of the Christian church, one is speaking as a theologian. One's historical research and conclusions become christology proper.

It is important, again, for me to be candid at the conclusion of this chapter. If I did not think the modern quest is central to christology, I would not begin with the "quest for the historical Jesus." As a theologian I accept the modern quest. Indeed, I insist on its necessity for three reasons. First, it must be pursued for historical reasons. Regardless of how uncertain the "consensus portrait" offered above of the eschatological preacher, teacher, healer, and sage proves to be, the Christian gospel has something to do with the historical Jesus. "In that the kerygma contains historical elements, it is entirely proper and necessary to inquire concerning the relation of the Jesus of history and the Christ of faith."[59] What Christians mean by God, the Word of God, the nature of God, and the activity of God has something decisively to do with the historical Jesus. On the basis of the above summary, I think that the continuity between the historical Jesus of the modern quest and the Christ of the church's kerygma is precisely their common focus on the dawning of the reign of God in what he said and did, and what the church said about him in relation to that reign.

Second, "Christianity's own claims necessitate historical study of Jesus. Specifically, the doctrine of the Incarnation . . . begs the historical question. By confessing this doctrine, the church 'lays upon itself the obligation to do history.' Otherwise, Christians will be docetists, believing in Jesus only as a divine figure, not as the human (historical) representation of God."[60] Christology is not a proclamation about a mythical figure but rather about the soteriological significance of a historical person. Thus, "it is the concern of the kerygma for the historicity of Jesus which necessitates a new quest. For how can the indispensable historicity of Jesus be affirmed, while at the same time maintaining the irrelevance of what a historical encounter with him would mean, once this has become a real possibility due to the rise of modern historiography?"[61] The kerygma claims to mediate a faith encounter with a historical person, and so a specific understanding of his life, mediated through a contemporary understanding of history, is as important for christology as an existential encounter mediated through the preaching of the church. The quest of the historical Jesus is essential because the Christian "is committed to a *kerygma* which locates its saving event in a historical person to whom a second avenue of access is provided by the rise of scientific historiography since the enlightenment."[62]

Third, it must be pursued for reasons of Christian life and practice. The historical Jesus is decisive for the Christian because the historical Jesus also shapes the Christian life and praxis. Christology is not only proclamation about Jesus as the Christ in the light of his cross, resurrection, and exaltation. It is also a way of life embodying his particular kind of praxis. The content of the Christian life is not wide open to simply any interpretation. If it turned out, say, that Jesus was really a political revolutionary who wanted to kill as many Romans as possible, or that he was dragged screaming and kicking to the cross, it would radically alter the Christian way of life. The way Christians are to live is connected to Jesus' way of life, and thus the search for the historical Jesus and the kind of eschatological reign he preached, taught, and enacted is decisive for the shape of the Christian life. "One should attempt historical reconstructions of Jesus' life and practice not simply as a moral example but also as an individual historical communicative and critical praxis."[63] The historical Jesus available in the modern quest both deconstructs false or distorted or inadequate ways of living and provides a positive picture of Christian love, forgiveness, and justice. This feature of the modern quest will come more into focus in several of the many faces of christology described in the following chapters.

This theological agenda, however, does not end the theological and practical decisions which must be made in the light of contemporary research. One of the key decision points staked out by the third quest is between those who see a reconstructed Jesus pointing toward a more "catholic" incarnational christology and those who see it pointing toward a more "gnostic" sagacious christology. "Catholic" christologies have always made the historical events of the passion, cross, and resurrection of Jesus, as well as his teachings, central to their christology. Although premodern and modern catholic Christians may differ on what his significance consisted of, and how to formulate that doctrinally, they concurred that the Jesus of history and the history of Jesus of the canon, which consisted centrally of the passion narrative taken more or less "straight" from the canonical texts, provided the ground and shape of the religious faith and life of believers.

This "catholic" christology has since the second century stood in conflict with other christologies, most notably "gnostic" christologies. Some participants in the third quest have revived this ancient debate and it is not simply a debate about historical scholarship. There is a theological agenda as much at stake in this form of the third quest as there is in the more "catholic" forms. The third quest portrait of Jesus, based partly on the extra-canonical Gospels, and the canonical Gospels interpreted in the light of Nag Hammadi texts, implies a more "gnostic" christology than a "catholic" christology. Jesus is primarily a teacher of wisdom, and what he teaches is a different interpretation of the kingdom of God than what "catholic" Christians read in the canon.

The *Gospel of Thomas* is the clearest example, although Burton Mack interprets Q as similar to Thomas in its recollections of a gnostic Jesus. In that Gospel, Jesus and Judas Thomas are twins, and the secret gospel of Jesus to Thomas is that he, too, is a Christ. Jesus is a teacher of gnosis, literally translated as knowledge, but perhaps better translated as insight—knowledge which communicates wisdom or spiritual enlightenment. What is crucial about Jesus is that he teaches his followers the good news that the kingdom of God is a state of self-discovery in which the individual comes to know oneself, at the deepest level, and thereby comes to know God or that God is in them. "The statement is meant to say, in effect, that 'you, the reader, are the twin brother of Christ; when you recognize the divine within you, then you come to see, as Thomas does, that you are Jesus and, so to speak, identical twins."[64] The relationship between Jesus and the disciple is transcended in than moment, and the follower becomes not a Christian but a Christ. The enlightened one now knows that he or she is not to follow Jesus and his way or to imitate him, nor is the believer to depend on Jesus for anything. They are to go into themselves and find that they are and have always been a Christ. There is no "distance" between ourselves and God; there is only a "discovery" of our own divinity to be made.[65] The key is that "gnostic" interpretations of Jesus stresses discovering an immanent divinity within ourselves rather than relying on a relationship between anyone or anything outside ourselves.

The remainder of this book is a description of the many faces of catholic christology. Catholic christology is primarily about the importance of Jesus for our salvation. The Jesus of christology is also Jesus as we need him or want him to be within the contexts of our own contemporary religious, moral, and social agendas (whether they be fundamentalist, evangelical, liberal, feminist, liberationist, countercultural, or libertarian). I suggest here a principle I will exhibit many times throughout the book, "the Inbody principle of christological construction." Not one of us in our christology, no matter how fundamentalist, evangelical, creedal, liberal, scholarly, revolutionary, or cynical, will ever permit our image of Jesus to be anything more or anything less than we find necessary for salvation, whether salvation be pardon from sin, or reunion with God, or sanctification, existential decision, gnostic enlightenment, or postmodern irony! Even though Jesus is more than a "litmus test" for our own religious sensibilities and needs, or a "Rorschach blot" into which we can project any image whatsoever we admire or idealize or long for, I believe any Jesus we select from the canon or reconstruct from the texts will be shaped, guided, and guarded by our own various religious, political, and theological agendas. Christology proper is the interpretation of Jesus and the significance and meaning of Jesus for the faith and life of the believer.

How, then, does one make the transition from talk about Jesus of Nazareth to talk about Jesus Christ? Two types of claims are entailed in making that transition: claims are made about Jesus Christ by the church, and claims are made about God in Jesus Christ. The first thing is to recognize that an early group of believers proclaimed they knew him to be still alive among them. The second is to recognize that they made claims about God in the light of this experience of Jesus as the risen Christ.

In the first move, a few, and then many, "saw" him as present to and among them. Jesus in some recognizable "form" appeared among them. They recognized him with their eyes or in their mind's eye as still present among them in a new but recognizable mode, some in a spiritual vision (Paul), some in some sort of physical presence (Emmaus), and some in a rather direct physical form (the women at the tomb). They claimed the power of his continuing presence in the life of some followers after he had been put to death. They inaugurated a first level confessions about themselves and the life of their community as a community in which Jesus continued to be present in some powerful way.

But they also made claims about God, not just about their experience of the proclaimer of God's kingdom. The proclaimer became the proclaimed. Through a series of verbs, they made claims about what God had done with him. God raised Jesus from the dead; as resurrected life, God *trans-*

formed the crucified Jesus into the first fruits of the new age to come; God *confirmed* him in the resurrection and at Pentecost as a new work of God for the consummation of the creation; God *exalted* Jesus to God's right hand after his death; God *vindicated* Jesus' life and death in his resurrection as the inauguration of the new age to come on earth as it is in heaven. Within a short period of time, and especially over the long period of time from the Gospel of John to the creeds of Nicea and Chalcedon, the church moved to an even stronger verb: in some sense, the meaning to be worked out over a long period of time, the strongest claim possible is made: Jesus *incarnated* God, and, finally, is God. How that happened, and what such a claim does and does not mean then and now, are the subjects of the next chapter. But here it is important to recognize that any ascending christology from below entails, simultaneously, claims about the believer and about God, and these claims are focused on the figure of Jesus.

CHAPTER TWO

Jesus Christ and the Identity of God: The Christological Creeds of Yesterday and Today

The purpose of this chapter is to focus on the significance of christology for the enigma of God and human suffering. I am interested, specifically, in what the ecumenical creeds affirm about the identity of God, the character of God, and the mode of divine power in relation to oppression and injustice. I am not as much interested in esoteric formulations about the intra-trinitarian life of the Godhead as I am in the way the doctrine of the triune God addresses human problems of anguish and inequality. Just as I focused on the historical Jesus as a proclaimer of the reign of God, its nearness and its character in what he said and did, I now focus on the significance of Jesus Christ for our understanding of God in relation to suffering and injustice. My argument is that the fourth and fifth century creeds affirm concepts of the identity of God, the character of God, and the mode of divine power which can in the twenty-first century address precisely these fundamental human problems. Thus, my discussion of christological dogma will focus on soteriology instead of on speculation about the Godhead. My discussion hinges on the assumption that soteriology was at the center in the early debates and continues to be the reason Christians affirm the triune God today.

I. The Concept of God in Late Modernity

Christians have always claimed to be monotheists. They inherited their concept of one God from Judaism; they stood in contrast to the polytheism of Greco-Roman paganism. Christians eventually developed a distinctive concept of God known as "theism," a doctrine about the identity and qualities of the one God. God means "a person without a body (i.e., a spirit), present everywhere, the creator and sustainer of the universe, a free agent, able to do everything (omnipotent), knowing all things, perfectly good, a source of moral obligation, immutable, eternal, a necessary being, holy, and worthy of worship."[1] Variations of this theism are still alive today in the piety of most Western Christians and in systematic theology. Across a wide spectrum of British and North American philosophers of religion and theologians, belief in God is equivalent to belief in theism. The God of philosophy, theology, and piety is the theistic God. God is the sovereign monarch because he is the omnipotent power of the universe, whose omnipotence is to be thought of either as inscrutable but direct through determinate cause, such as predestination and election, or more indirectly as the hidden but ultimate determiner of the world, the primary cause who works indirectly in and through secondary causes and effects of nature and through human freedom. Human suffering and injustice are interpreted within the context of classical theism.[2]

This concept of God, however, is under attack today, not only from outside the Christian community but from inside as well. From outside, such a God is dismissed as a mistaken or unnecessary principle of interpretation, an illusion of experience or perception, or a key concept in an ideology of alienation and oppression, suffering, and injustice. From inside, however, the theistic God also is dismissed as not the biblical or Christian God at all. One can detect inside assaults on theism from at least five different sources. First, although British and North American theologians continue to debate the truth or falsity of theism, few Continental theologians in the 150 years since Immanuel Kant (German philosopher, d. 1804), either in the liberal or neo-orthodox tradition, would consider themselves theists or even take their bearings from theism.[3] Second, in North American philosophy of religion and theology, a major gulf exists between the American Philosophical Association, and its theological associates, The Society of Christian Philosophers, on the one hand, and the Philosophy of Religion and the Theology and Religious Reflection Sections of the American Academy of Religion, on the other hand. In the former, the question of the meaning and truth of theism is at the center of the debate, whereas in the latter, the question of the meaning of any language about God, theistic or not, is the focus. Third, most postliberal theologians in North America are highly critical of theism. They tend to see theism as a distinct product of modernity (Theodore Jennings, Stanley Hauerwas).[4] Since modernity is waning, and properly so because of its hegemonic consequences, theism exits along with it, to be replaced by a concept of God formulated more on the basis of Wittgensteinian language usage, phenomenology of experience, or postmodern narrative theory than on metaphysics.[5] Fourth, many of Barth's successors in Germany, such as Jurgen Moltmann, Dorothy Soelle, and Johannes Metz, have been highly critical of theism on biblical, theological, and political grounds. Finally, an entire range of critiques based on a postmodern hermeneutics of suspicion, including deconstructionism, poststructuralism, historicism, feminism, Black and Latin American liberation theologies, have focused on the ideological, exploitive, and repressive character and consequences of theism throughout the modern period.

A common criticism of monotheism occurs throughout all five of these censures of theism and has caused biblical hermeneutics, philosophy of religion, and systematic theology to rethink the concept of God. As the Western world enters a late modern or postmodern phase, we have come to see how monotheism, through the concept of theism, and particularly through the notion of omnipotent power, has had repressive consequences throughout human history. The common criticism of the theistic idea of power has been that by denying (predestination) or minimizing (election) human freedom in favor of divine power and causality, theism denied or minimized human agency and therefore undercut human freedom and responsibility to be agents of history. In our late modern period, however, two related but somewhat new themes are common to the "ideology critique" of monotheism. These both go beyond the early modern criticism that monotheism is a threat to human agency. The first late modern criticism is that monotheistic religion is a major source of violence in human history, and the second is that monotheism is a totalizing concept and therefore is exclusive, repressive, and destructive not so much of human agency as such but of "difference" and "otherness" within human agency. In short, it has served as cause and ideological justification of human suffering and injustice.

The first criticism is well formulated by Regina Schwartz. She argues that monotheism (exclusive worship) is linked to collective identity within the context of the tragic principle of scarcity (embodied in the biblical story of Cain), and that monotheism (one Deity) is closely linked to the biblical principle of oneness (one land, one people, one nation). Monotheism, with its requirement of exclusive allegiance, demands exclusion. Arguing that identity formation itself is an act of violence, Schwartz says, "this God who excludes some and prefers others, who casts some out, is a monotheistic God—monotheistic not only because he demands allegiance to himself alone but also because he confers his favor on one alone."[6] Monotheism is a myth that grounds particular identity in universal transcendence, and it forges identity antithetically, that is, against "the other." Schwartz, it must be noted, means by monotheism, henotheism or "monolatry," the myth of a people whose identity is constituted by a particular god or God to the exclusion of the other.[7] The story of Cain shows how monotheism, by its principle of exclusion, sacralizes violence.

Other late modern critics of monotheism have argued, however, that it is the very idea of monotheism itself that is the problem, not simply monotheism as henotheism distorted into monolatry. Monotheism by its very nature is the impulse to drive or to pull everything into the One, and once that dynamic is in motion, the consequence is to absorb everything into or under one mono-reality. Monotheism is a totalizing notion, thereby subordinating, devaluing, and finally extinguishing all differences. The idea of monotheism consumes and eliminates polytheism and even henotheism, thereby eliminating plurality by subsuming it under or consuming it into a principle of monism. All difference, as in genuine pluralism, is ultimately extinguished. Once the monistic principle is in motion, the political and cultural implications ignite in a dynamic that totalizes all reality within one vision and one "system," ultimately eliminating all difference and otherness. In short, monotheism is by definition the ontological, and then political, elimination of "the other."

Both of these are very powerful critiques. But there is another option here, and it cannot be dismissed out of hand. Some Western theologians argue that monotheism is not a principle of exclusion but precisely the opposite, the principle of transcendence which functions as a principle of prophetic criticism of all finite loyalties and the inclusion of all diversity within the one God. Specifically, because the monotheistic God is wholly transcendent, the concept of God serves as a principle of relativity of all finite reality and the inclusion, instead of exclusion, of all within or under the transcending One. When all finite and partial values are made relative by the principle of monotheism, all finite and partial values and loyalties are made provisional and not proper sacralized objects of loyalty.

One of the best representatives of this claim is H. Richard Niebuhr with his idea of "radical monotheism." The chief rival to monotheism, he argues, is henotheism, and henotheism is an inherently oppressive belief because it locates ultimate value, trust, and loyalty in a finite society, either cultural or religious, which is closed and all-consuming. As Schwartz admits, henotheism as monotheism or monoltry is the problem, because it makes something which is finite ultimate and all-consuming. Thoroughgoing monotheism, or "radical monotheism," is neither the closed society nor the principle of such a society but is rather the principle of being itself, the One beyond the many. In it the principle of being is identified with the principle of value, and vice versa. Although radical monotheism is a principle and thus an abstract reality, "radical monotheism dethrones all absolutes short of the principle of being itself. At the same time it reverences every relative existent."[8] Monotheism is the principle of "the One beyond the many . . . the principle of being itself and loyalty to its cause."[9]

It is not my purpose to try to revolve this fundamental debate about monotheism as a totalizing principle of negation of the many versus monotheism as a critical principle of relativization of all finite being. It is, rather, my purpose to argue that theism long ago dethroned the Trinity as the primary framework for Christian thinking about God, and that that deposition contributes dynamics to human suffering and injustice which the doctrine of the triune God shaped by christology does not permit. Theism identified God as the Monarch in whom divine causality and omnipotent power are the primary characteristics. As an alternative to theism, I argue in the remainder of this chapter that the Christian concept of the triune God describes a God who addresses precisely the soteriological needs of late modernity. I will return to the contemporary significance of the concept of the triune God after grounding it in the linguistic formulations of the fourth and fifth century christological controversy. I explore the significance of trinitarian doctrine for suffering and injustice, first by showing how this was the primary issue at stake in the formation of the first two ecumenical creeds, and, second, by showing how a christology which leads to the doctrine of the triune God is the answer to our contemporary search for solidarity and justice.

II. Antiochene and Alexandrian Christologies[10]

Jesus as the resurrected Christ was soon worshiped as the presence of God through the power of the Spirit in the life of the church. Through recitation, proclamation, and sacrament the Christian participated proleptically (by anticipation) in the new reign of God. Christian life was defined by Jesus Christ, the first term of the appellation referring to the inauguration of the life of God for us in Jesus of Nazareth, the second term referring to our empowerment through our participation in Jesus vindicated and present as Christ. The proclaimer had become the proclaimed, the historical Jesus had become the Christ, the remembrance of the historical Jesus had become christology. As Christians began to worship Jesus, however, they became nervous about saying that Jesus was divine. As Jewish monotheists, such a claim sounded too much like affirming two Gods. Especially when Jewish monotheism was supplemented by the Greek philosophical tradition as the church moved West and adopted much of its language and assumptions, Christians made an alliance with a tradition that taught that the divine is eternal and immutable and therefore cannot suffer and change (apatheia). How could a human being, especially a crucified human being, be divine? There was something very unGodly about it all.

The debate about how to formulate high claims about Jesus Christ within a montheistic framework simmered among theologians through-out the seond and third centuries. Generally speaking, some form of sub-ordinationism prevailed among second and third century theologians such as Justin Martyr, Mileto of Sardis, Irenaeus of Lyons, Tertullian of Carthage, and Origin of Alexandria. However, once the final siege to stamp out the church failed, and the debates about what to do with apos-tates during the persecution were resolved, debates about christology became the center of attention (and the centerpiece in the efforts of the emperors in the fourth century to unify the empire). For a century and a half the controversy raged, predominant in the East, but involving the West as well. The controversy was about biblical hermeneutics, the pre-eminence of ecclesiastical sees (a geographical center for a bishop), empire politics and unity, high-profile personality conflicts, speculation about the identity of the Godhead, and the soteriological significance of Jesus Christ for human life. The last factor is the focus on my account of the two coun-cils of Nicea and Chalcedon.

By the early second century, many Gnostic Christians had solved the embarrassing problem of Jesus and God-talk by concluding that Jesus Christ had not really been a human being at all, but instead he had only appeared to be (docetism, "to seem") human. However, Christians who believed that Christ's suffering and death on the cross had saved them from sin and death feared that if Christ only "seemed" to suffer and die, then they could only "seem" to be saved by his death and ressurrection.[11] Perhaps, alternatively, he was not divine at all but simply a great person, a prophet, a teacher, or perhaps even an angel. This option, however, was equally problematic for the majority. Both the New Testament claims and their own religious needs and experiences made neither interpretation adequate to account for the salvation from sin and death they experienced in Jesus Christ. By the late second century, then, most Christians who had come to grapple with the question, Who was this man? concluded, on the basis of their experience and their worship, he was a human being, but he was also Lord, Christ, and Son of God, more and more exalting him in their thinking. This language of humanity and divinity, however, did not settle anything; it simply laid the foundation for the two-hundred-year debate to follow.

One line of development to follow in trying to unite these two claims that he was human and also God was to move "from below" (his human-ity) to "above" (his divinity). Most clearly seen in the Synoptic Gospels, there is a movement from the teachings and stories of and about Jesus to claims that the reign, power, and purposes of God are incarnate in his life, death, and resurrection. Such a movement from Jesus to Christ has been called by contemporary christologists an "ascending christology," by which we mean a movement from the man Jesus of Nazareth to the view of him as the incarnate Word (Logos) or Wisdom (Sophia) of God. The strategy developed in the first chapter lays the groundwork for modern christolgies which move in this direction.

Antioch in Syria was the primary source of the "man" (anthropos, or human)/Word (logos) type of christology, or christology from below, or ascending christology. Based on John 2:19, Jesus the human being is "assumed" by the Word. The human psychology of Jesus is stressed in such a way that he is affirmed to be a "man" (a human being, a biological, psychological, and moral person) in the full sense of the word. Their tendency, then, was to speak of a moral (more than a metaphysical) union between God and the human Jesus. The stress for Antiochenes (adherents to this theory), therefore, tends to be on a duality within the full reality of Jesus Christ, that is, the human and divine elements are separate and not to be confused or mingled together. Antiochenes are even sometimes accused of a dualistic christology, in which one can only speak of the man Jesus and the indwelling Word of God but not of the one person. Behind this view stands Aristotle's view of a human being as a psycho/physical unity; therefore, the duality of the human and the divine had to be stressed within this framework. Salvation, consequently, is viewed more as a restoration of lost human integrity, or, in our modern language, more as humanization than as deification.

There developed, also, a strategy to talk of the God-human relation in Jesus Christ which moved in the opposite direction, the "descending" direction, from the Word of God who is itself God to the Word made flesh in or as the man Jesus. This movement was affected by the tendencies toward gnosticism in the early church, tendencies which were deep in the Hellenistic culture into which the church had moved. Such a movement focused on the transcendence of the Word and in its extreme forms tended to bypass (if not downright deny) his real existence in the realm of history. The clearest New Testament example of this descending movement in christology is the Gospel of John, which starts with the claim that the Word was God (John 1) and stresses that the Word did indeed become flesh (incarnate) in or as Jesus. This descending christology moves from the Word to the flesh, a strategy some historians call "logos-sarx (Word-flesh) christologies."

Alexandria in Egypt was the primary source of the Word *(logos)*/flesh *(sarx)* type of christology, or christology from above, or descending christology. Based on John 1:14, Christ is the Word made flesh *(sarx)*. The human soul of Jesus Christ is not stressed, or is even denied, for example, by Apollinaris (fourth century), for whom the Word takes the place of the human soul of Jesus. It is almost as if Jesus was flesh—*sarx*—(in a formal sense, or in the sense that he was embodied or entwined in flesh or "has" flesh), but is not human in the sense that he is a whole human person *(anthropos)*. The tendency of Alexandrians is to speak of a *union* of the divine and human in Jesus Christ, analogous with that which obtains between the body and the soul of any human being. Stress is on the unity of Jesus as Word and flesh. Behind this view stands Plato's instead of Aristotle's conception of human nature, namely, spirit inhabiting an alien flesh. Salvation is viewed more as a process of deification instead of full humanization. Critics argue that the Alexandrian stress on the unity tends to jeopardize any continuing distinction between the two natures and so plays down, or ignores, or eliminates, or denies real humanity.

III. Main Players in the Fourth-Century Drama: Phase One

The location of Nicea and Chalcedon underscores the extent to which the christological debates were located in the Eastern Church. These two church councils which declared the orthodox christological formulas occurred in what is today known as Turkey. Specifically, they occurred in and around what is today Istanbul, then known as Constantinople, and prior to that, Byzantium. Constantinople was then, and is today, the geographical spot where East meets West. Watching it loom larger and larger as one sails into the harbor through the Bosporus is one of the most awesome sights a travel can encounter. Nicea, today known as Iznik, is located on the coast about forty miles southeast of Istanbul; and Chalcedon, today known as Kadikoy, faces Istanbul about five miles across the mouth of the Bosporus (which connects the Sea of Marmara and the Black Sea) and is today primarily a residential district of Istanbul.

"The christological controversy" consists of two main phases. During the first phase, culminating with the Councils of Nicea (325 CE) and Constantinople (381 CE), the issue was the real humanity and the real divinity of Jesus Christ. Most Christians believed that Jesus Christ was divine as well as human, and at the same time they believed there was only one God. Did their claim mean Jesus Christ was simply identified with the one God? Well, not exactly; indeed, not at all. The New Testament repeatedly distinguished between the Father and the Son, and Christians remained hard-core monotheists. Jesus as the Christ cannot simply be identified with the God of whom Jesus spoke and to whom he prayed as the Father. But if Christ is divine but is not the Father, then are there two Gods? The orthodox theologians argued that one can distinguish between Christ and God but one cannot separate the two. The debate was about how one could do this. Richard Norris formulates the main issue of the first phase of the controversy in terms of two distinct questions: 1) What is the nature and identity of the heavenly "power" which is said to have become incarnate in or as Jesus? and 2) What is the church to make of the denials of Jesus' "flesh," that is, his ordinary human nature?[12] This debate constitutes phase one of "the christological controversy."

While the West had adopted Tertullian's unexplained formula of "one substance, three persons" by the beginning of the third century, the situation was much less stable and unanimous in the East. The Eastern Greek-speaking Empire boasted three great metropolises: Alexandria, Antioch, and Constantinople. The former was the most populous and civilized region on earth with about a million souls spread out over ten miles along the Mediterranean coast, while the Latin West was a cultural and economic backwater, and Rome herself was a city in sad decline.[13] The two main players throughout most of the fourth century were two Alexandrians, Arius (a presbyter) and Athanasius (a bishop). Arius worked out of the Alexandrian Word/flesh scheme described above. Using the familiar Stoic term Logos (the word, mind, power, deed, reason, structure, and purpose of God[14]) to defend the faith, he viewed the Word as "less than" God because God, before creation, had uttered the Word to make "him" (or in the Wisdom literature of the Hebrew Bible, especially in Proverbs, "her") an agent of creation. This subordinationist tendency had earlier been characteristic of Justin Martyr, Tertullian, Origin, and Clement of Alexandria. The tendency of this teaching was worked out explicitly by Arius, a presbyter living in Alexandria around 300 CE, whom history has cast as the villain in our story.

Arius's teaching is almost uniformly presented as a claim about the necessity of conceiving the Son as subordinate to the Father for strictly theological reasons. He is represented as a radical monotheist who believed there was only one God, and this God was so distinct from every element of the creation that no part of the creation could "embody" God. Starting from the top down, the exclusive attributes of God the unoriginate are delineated, the origination of the son follows, and then the relation of that creaturely son to God and the rest of the created order is described. His agenda presumably was to protect the absoluteness and unity of God.[15] Arius believed no direct analogy can exist between the sovereignly free Creator who operates by his will and the creatures who exist at his pleasure.[16] No matter how exalted the Son becomes, he was a perfected creature whose nature always remained creaturely and whose position was subordinate to the Father. There is first God the creator, and then there are creatures, who are from God only in the sense they are by his will and not out of his substance.[17] Although the Son was a creature, he existed before time; nowhere does Arius suggest the Son's beginning was marked by the birth or baptism of Jesus of Nazareth.[18] But Arius distinguishes between God and the Father; God only receives the name Father upon the creation of the Son before all time.[19]

No sharper contrast exists between Arius and his critic, Athanasius, than the manner in which each understood the biblical term "begetting." Is the term an essentialist/genetic or a relational/adoptive category? Does Christ's sonship belong to him by virtue of his nature or essence or, like all creatures who come to call God Father, by adoption? Father and Son are not essentialist words in Arius's vocabulary, but pertain to priority of importance, sequence of time, and quality of relationship. Arius fears essentialist or substantial linkage between the Father and Son will blur or destroy the kind of relationship that exists between the Father and the Son. The relationship of the Son to the Father is transactional rather than genetic. "'Bringing into being' or 'creating' has less to do with genetic laws or ontological categories than with the willed actions of the sovereign God; and existence, by implication, is defined not by the 'stable state' dictated by one's nature but by the events—each having its own 'when'—which signal the creature's election into a relationship of promise."[20]

When Arius spoke of Christ, he thought of a being called into existence by the divine will, a creature finite in knowledge and morally changeable (perfectible), whom God foreknew would not sin but would be the perfect creature. Perfection is understood as community of will and covenantal obedience rather than renovation of creaturely essence.[21] By steady choice, this creature found favor with God, who foreknew his fidelity. "God's chosen one possessed sonship by virtue of his performance as an obedient creature and by virtue of God's grace, which both anticipated and rewarded his efforts."[22] Jesus was a creature who could have sinned had he so chosen, but who never actually did. He was created precisely because he was of a kind to be obedient and so became a Son.[23]

As contemporary church historians Robert Gregg and Dennis Groh have shown, Arius is most intelligible when his version of monotheism and subordinationism are viewed as a soteriology rather than a cosmology. What is at stake are two views about the content, shape, and dynamics of salvation. Arius's concern was to explicate the closest possible links between Christ and fellow creatures. "It is not the Arian plan to demote Christ in order to clear space and secure preeminence for the high God; rather, he is the one upon whom sonship is conferred, his election being a signal of the salvation accessible to other creatures."[24] Does salvation feature the eternal, consubstantial Son of the Father, whose descent arrests us from perishability, or is the Son one among creatures, the foreordained and faithful servant who brings himself to perfection by discipline and exemplifies the relationship to be had with the Father by all other creatures?[25]

At the center of Arius's soteriology is a redeemer, obedient to his creator's will, whose life of virtue modeled perfect creaturehood and hence the path of salvation for all Christians.[26] His central point is that Christ gains and holds his sonship in the same way as other creatures. The believer is mirrored in his portrait of Christ as the one who advanced toward God, winning the prize through ethical choices and improvement and progress. "Seeing redemption in a creature, they beheld the shape of their own redemption."[27] Salvation depended not on their ability to know the Father's essence and to enjoy ontic identity, but upon the dynamic of command and obedience (using biblical covenantal language), upon the transactions of will which constitute the sons and daughters of God.[28] It is the sonship to be held by all believers which is being proclaimed. "What is predicated of the redeemer must be predicated of the redeemed."[29] Just as Christ persevered in the good by the exercise of his will and was chosen as Son, so, also, Christians claimed to be able to become sons and daughters of God.

Arius's Alexandrian bishop, Athanasius, had a different view of things. Athanasius took his monotheism as seriously as Arius. God is an unchangeable being infinitely superior to any creature. He granted that for the Creator to become human and submit to the power of creatures must seem humiliating. But that was the only way to save humankind from moral and physical extinction. In order to free us from sin and death, God did the unthinkable. God descended into human flesh. Out of his infinite love for us, he became the man Jesus that we might gain eternal life.[30] So Athanasius drew the closest possible links between the Father and the Son by emphasizing the ontological and essential common nature between Father and Son. Nature (essentialist) language rose above and interpreted language of will (voluntarist). "The key to both Christology and salvation lay in understanding the implications of the knowable properties (not divine planning and willing) which characterize the Son and undergirded our salvation."[31] In interpreting the scriptural language of "begetting," Athanasius chose the biological meaning of the term son (Isaac, son of Jacob) over the adoptive meaning of sonship (where son was circumlocution for believer). For him, Christ was a Son by nature; all others were sons and daughters by adoption.

Why was it necessary to assert the ontologically prior category of essence over the transactional language of adoption? As for Arius,

Athanasius's answer was also soteriological. Unless the Son is Son by nature, he cannot possess the attributes of the divine nature (immortality) which are necessary for our salvation. Christology and soteriology are answers to the problems of human nature (finitude) rather than of the human situation (sin).[32] What we predicate about human nature as physical beings is the key to salvation, not the human situation of willing relationships between Father and adopted son. For Athanasius, the primary human problem is death, mortality, and corruption, threats which are no longer external to human nature but now an essential part of it because of sin and the fall. The believer, by the grace of the incarnation of the immortal divine nature in Christ, can now through the resurrection rejuvenate our fallen human nature and restore our immortality. Not only death but continuing corruption after death can be reversed. "Christ has given to us a physical nature redeemed from corruption by making available to human nature a grace that is irreversible."[33] Grace moves us from the realm of changeability to unchangeability. This can happen only when our nature is brought into contact with the divine nature. As Gregg and Groh summarize Athanasius's soteriology: "The Athanasian Christology was founded in a theology of the differences between divine and human nature. By linking the Christ essentially and eternally to God, Athanasius insures that the incarnation will bring the divine nature into contact with human nature. . . . By our participation in him and through the flesh which he has renewed, grace has been made irreversibly available to the cosmos and to human persons. In short, the universe and the life in grace have become stabilized in the very structure of things."[34] The choice was between a grace which had come to provide entry into a stabilized order of redeemed creation and a grace which had come to empower people for moral advance in a transactional universe.[35]

The Council of Nicea (325 CE) sided with Athanasius. It dispelled any hint at subordinationism, condemning Arius's teaching as heresy. Meeting in early June with more than 250 bishops, almost all from the Eastern Empire, this council was the largest gathering of Christian leaders up to that time.[36] The bishops affirmed the Word, or Son, was eternally begotten (or born from) the same substance of the Father, not a creature created out of nothing ("begotten, not made"). The Son comes out of the Father's substance as a child comes out of its parents' substance. If the Son was created and not (eternally) begotten, then the Son was on the wrong side of the time/eternity line and could not be divine and therefore could not save us by our "putting on the immortality" of divinity. Furthermore, the Son was declared to be "of the same substance" (*homoousios*) with the Father, not "of similar substance" (*homoousios*). Finally, the Word of God became flesh; it did not pretend to be flesh; it did not seem to be flesh; it did not enter into a human being; it became flesh. Most important, however, it is essential to see why this is such an issue with the bishops. They agreed with Athanasius that "if the works of the Logos' Godhead had not been done by means of the body, humanity would not have been divinized. Furthermore, if the properties of the flesh had not been reckoned to the Logos, humanity would not have been completely liberated from them."[37]

It is important to note here that while Nicea affirmed the relation between the Father and the Son as one of substance, it never defined or even described what that "substance" is. Whatever "Godness" is, both the Father and the Son (and the Spirit) as equal "participants" in the Godhead share in it equally and fully. Subsequently, then, we are told what the relation of the incarnate Son is to us: for our sake and our salvation he was made flesh. At its core the argument was soteriological. The Council's decision became the touchstone for all orthodox christology.

Throughout the fourth century, Arianism was at least as popular as the doctrine that Jesus is God. Indeed, not only had the leadership of the church in Constantinople been in Arian hands for over forty years, but the majority of Christians in that city were still Arian rather than Nicene in their sympathies.[38] Since the history of the controversy was always tied to Empire politics—Athanasius was condemned by church councils and exiled from Alexandria no less than five times—the fate of the controversy continued to be tied to Empire politics following the death of Constantine in 330 CE, for "by appealing to the Roman state for support, bishops and theologians had tied their fortunes to the outcome of the struggle between Constans, emperor of the Nicene West, and Constantius, Arian ruler of the East."[39] Constantius convened at least nine Church councils between 351 CE and 360 CE, most of them in the West.[40] The struggle continued until, exhausted and threatened by the Goths on the frontier, the Empire settled on a reaffirmation of the Nicene Creed at Constantinople in 381 CE.

The debate continued, however, even after Athanasius's position triumphed. Someone had to explain how the Father and the Son could be "of the same substance" yet not identical. What was needed was something the Nicene Creed alone could not supply, viz., a doctrine explaining how God could be one and yet consist of two or three separate entities. The problem was easier to deal with in the West. The West had been satisfied with their formula since Tertullian. Furthermore, since the Latin language has no definite article, there was no way to make the distinction that the Greek language can make between God and god, so there was basis for widely discrepant understandings.[41] The task of saving the creed from being a mere empty formula fell to three Cappadocians from northern Turkey: Basil, Gregory of Nyssa, and Gregory of Nazianzus. These Cappadocians saved *homoousios* theology by making a *terminological* distinction; they clarified or redefined key words. Athanasius used "essence" (*ousia*) and "being" (*hypostasis*) interchangeably. Their secret was to distinguish clearly between essence and being. While the Father and the Son (and the Spirit) were "of the same substance" or essence (*homoousia*), there were three hypostases or beings (*hypostasis*) between them. "The Father, the Son, and the Holy Spirit are three separate beings, each with its own individual characteristics—they are three hypostases. But they are one and the same in essence—they are *homoousias*."[42] The unity and the tripartite division of the Godhead could now be explained.

In ordinary language, *ousia* and *hypostases* were both translated as "substance," as, indeed, Nicea had done. But the Cappadocians made a subtle distinction between these two words which can be grasped by way of an analogy. "Consider three people: Peter, Mary, and John. Each of them is a particular individual (a *hypostasis*), but the three of them are all human beings; they share the same essence or substance (*ousia*) of humanity. If you point to Peter and ask, 'What is that?' there are two accurate and appropriate answers to the question simultaneously: 'That is Peter" (a particular individual or hypostasis) and 'That is a human being' (a substance or ousia). Similarly, Christ is 'the Son' (hypostasis) and 'God' (*ousia*)—a different *hypostasis* than the Father, but, nevertheless, 'of the same substance' (*homoousios*), as the Nicene Creed has said."[43] Christianity became a distinct and distinctive form of monotheism. The problem that both sides in the debate had not grasped was this: whoever presented a detailed explanation of the relationship between the Father and the Son could easily be accused of heresy, for it was difficult, if not impossible, to describe Jesus' relationship to God in a way that did not seem either to deny his humanity (Sabellianism) or to question his divinity (extreme Arianism).[44]

The Cappadocians had developed ideas which made it possible for the moderate Arians and Nicene Christians eventually to unite. Although the formula succeeded in thwarting Arianism, the price paid for the breach between economy and essence, however, was "a de-emphasis on the details of the economy of redemption, and a weakening of the soteriological basis for the Christian doctrine of God."[45] Our question, then, in the final section, is how to interpret Nicene language when soteriology is once again moved back into the center of christological debate and trinitarian discussion. One can, of course, interpret the use of any "non-ousia" language in christology as "arian," and thereby reject as inadequate the economic doctrines of the trinity to be discussed in the last section of this chapter, as well as any christology which interprets the incarnation in the language of will, purpose, spirit, activity, presence, grace, or initial aims of God, thereby making most modern forms of christology "arian" or "heretical." But that only raises, it does not answer, the question of whether a full doctrine of incarnation (it is truly God who is involved in our salvation) is possible apart from substantialist categories. That, of course, will be at the heart of the problem of several of the subsequent christologies my survey will address, especially in chapters four and five.

IV. Main Players in the Fifth-Century Drama: Phase Two

After having declared the full divinity and full humanity of Jesus Christ in the decision at Nicea/Constantinople, the church was left, nevertheless, with the question of how they belong together. How could he be both at the same time? Were Christ's divine and human natures totally fused, or were they two separate natures somehow integrated into one Person? Were not humanity and divinity so different in kind that no one could be both with full integrity at the same time? Would not subjection to the finitude of time and space compromise the divinity of God, and would not possessing the qualities of divinity compromise the complete humanity of a genuine human being? "In the Greek-speaking lands, the end of the Arian controversy triggered nearly a century of intense conflict over this question, with the Alexandrians taking the view that there was one nature only in Christ, and the Antiochenes insisting that there were two."[46] The debate centered again in the two great cities of Alexandria in Egypt and Antioch in Syria. The logos-flesh christology of Alexandria, pushed to its extreme, became "Apollinarianism," while the two natures christology of Antioch, pushed to its extreme, became "Nestorianism." The church had to decide between these two or offer an alternative.

Apollinaris, a proponent of the Word/flesh type of christology from above, clearly denied that Christ had a human soul. The human soul was replaced by the Word. For Christ to have a human soul would imply that he was sinful, or at least subject to the movements of temptation. Ordinary human beings have a body and a mind. Christ had a human body, but in him the divine mind, the Logos, replaced his human mind. Apollinaris argued this on the basis of a distinction he made between flesh and human being: "He may be proclaimed as flesh because of his union with the flesh, yet according to the apostle he is not a human being."[47] His claim was that neither is changed by this replacement. However, his claim was that God is his spirit or intellect, and so Apollinaris's explicit claim was that he is not a real person: "He is not a human being but is like a human being, since is not co-essential with humanity in his highest parts."[48] When Theodore, the great theologian of Antioch, claimed that Christ had a human mind as well as a human body,

Apollinaris responded by trying to compromise, conceding that Christ had a human mind in its "lower parts" (fears and emotions), but in its "higher parts" (reason) the human reason was replaced by the divine reason. But for Theodore, if that were the case, then Christ could only redeem that part of the human being and not all of it, so Christ, he argued, must be fully human in all respects if he is to redeem the whole human being. Finally, then, Apollinaris claimed that Christ was merely clothed in flesh.[49]

Nestorius, a Constantinople partirach, and a member of the Antiochene school, claimed that the unity and the distinction within Christ are to be sought on different levels. His main problem was in looking more to Christ as a name applied to the two natures together than to the Eternal Son who personally unites a human nature to himself. The eternal Son was himself not really born in human flesh but he assumed human flesh. The human being Mary gave birth to was an instrument of the Godhead, a temple, a garment, in which the Logos dwelt. There are two natures, but they are not united in one person. Although Nestorius united them in worship, he could not unite them in person. The two natures simply existed side by side, not united in one person.

The Council of Chalcedon, held in 451 CE, had 600 bishops from the churches in attendance. The first half of the council's creed affirms of the one Lord, Jesus Christ, that he is both God and human: truly God and truly human, perfect in his divinity and in his humanity, consubstantial to the Father and to us, begotten of the Father and of Mary. That is, there were two natures, human and divine, which coexist in one person, and the oneness of the person makes it approporiate to apply the predicates of either nature to the other. The second half of the creed stresses the one selfsame Christ, affirming the unity of the person, namely, two natures without any commingling or change, division or separation. Thus the orthodox formulation is that Jesus Christ is two natures, there being no commingling or change of the natures which continue to be preserved in their specific character (against Alexandrian monophysites), and one person, there being no division of separation of the natures which are united in one person (against Antiochene Nestorians).

Chalcedon never answered in its creedal formula the metaphysical and the theological questions which remained following the adoption of the formula. Rather, it is most appropriate to interpret the language of the Chalcedonian formula in terms of its function in the church, viz., it is essentially a rule of christological language. Jesus is one subject, who is properly spoken of both as God—the divine Logos—and as a human being. To give an accurate account of him if one is to speak with the orthodox church, one must talk in two ways about him (human and divine) simultaneously. Both accounts are necessary. The formula dictates not a christology as such (a metaphysical and theological explanation of how the claims can be held together), but rather provides the formal outline and the formal language which are the criteria for a proper christological language and an adequate soteriolgy if one is going to affirm a christology within the orthodox church. In Christ there is one thing, a person, the divine Word who existed from all eternity (Ephesus, 431 CE). In Christ there are two things, two natures, divine and human (Chalcedon, 451 CE).

By and large, most modern Christians have avoided theological debates and definitions about anything, especially christology. Only when theologians interfere with popular piety do they arouse opposition, and only when Christians feel their salvation is threatened do they permit or require theologians to try to offer clear definitions and formulas. Here, however, at least in the fourth and fifth centuries, is a case where a proper formula for affirming and understanding salvation was at stake, for claiming anything less than what was claimed jeopardized the possibility of the salvation which they had experienced in Jesus Christ. Both full humanity and full divinity must be affirmed or salvation was not possible. Although substantialist language was used to affirm an orthodox christology, recognition of the soteriological rather than the metaphysical purpose of the language must be stressed, leaving open the question of whether substantialist rather than interpersonal or relational language is appropriate or adequate to affirm "God was in Christ reconciling the world to Himself." The soteriological issue, at the core of the Arius/Athanasius debate, was settled linguistically with the use of substantialist language. The soteriological issue arises again, in contemporary interpretations of the triune God and in the christologies which are described below, and again in chapters four and five, where our soteriological concerns about suffering and justice are closer to Arius's search for perfectibility than to Athanasius's search for imperishability.

V. Defining the Triune God Christologically Today

According to the principle of christological construction I proposed in chapter one, christology always is normed by soteriological requirements. However, religion clearly confronts a wide range of fundamental human needs. Paul Tillich sees the predominant need in the ancient world to be anxiety about death, in the medieval world to be anxiety about guilt, and in the modern world to be anxiety about meaninglessness.[50] In the late modern and postmodern world, however, the threats of human suffering and injustice are at the forefront of our felt needs, although obviously the threat of death, guilt, and meaninglessness has not vanished. Just as an answer to the menace of perishability set the boundary for adequate language in the fourth- and fifth-century christological debates, so an answer to suffering and injustice must set the boundaries for an adequate chris-tology today.[51] This requirement has initiated a thorough reinterpretation of God today. The Christian story of God with us and for us in Jesus Christ through the power of the Spirit moves suffering, transforming love, and interpersonal relatedness to the heart of God and our contemporary needs.

In contemporary theology, therefore, talk about God has shifted from "essential nature" of the Godhead to "the gospel story" of God with us. Although the language of the trinity has never been lost to liturgy, popu-lar piety, and devotional literature, the conclusion of much twentieth cen-tury theology is that "Chalcedon speaks of his divinity in a rather formal and abstract manner that fails to bear the imprint of the gospel narra-tive."[52] The substantialist language of the creed remains a conceptual problem for modern Christians. Although it is the "linguistic rule" by which the church speaks, is not such speaking conceptually obscure? How can one speak of "two natures" while speaking of "one person"? The contemporary perception is that as long as "person" and "nature" are understood in terms of the categories of substance, there is no way out of the impasse. However, the "narrative does not invite us to think first of what everyone knows about divinity to be and then to recognize in Jesus the presence of divinity."[53] Rather, it asks us to rethink the meaning of humanity and divinity "by depicting the actions and sufferings of the humble servant who gave his life unconditionally for the renewal of the world."[54] Contemporary trinitarian theology has followed this shift of focus. "The only solution is to interpret the personal identity of Jesus Christ by means of the more dynamic categories of history and narra-tive. . . . 'God was in Christ' is not a statement about Jesus' being; it is a confession that his history and his identity are a part of the history and identity of God. That entails an ontological claim about the relation between God and Jesus of Nazareth; the use of history and narrative rather than the concept of being (or "being") as categories for the inter-pretation of personal identity does not mean a surrender to subjectivity."[55]

This theological revolution which reconceives the identity and nature of God was at the core christological. Trinitarian thought is not primarily speculation about the number or interrelationships within the Godhead. The concept of the triune God originates in, is motivated by, and is related to God's salvation of the world. The doctrine of the trinity is an effort to understand the economy of God's work for the salvation of the creation, asking only subsequently what is implied by that salvation about the identity of God. Contemporary trinitarian discussion, therefore, has been focused primarily on soteriological and christological concerns. One might even argue that Barth's theology, which inaugurated this revolu-tion, was the most thoroughgoing christocentric theology the West has ever produced. Whether or not this is the case, christology is at the center of this reconception of God, which not only refocuses the identity of God as triunity instead of theistic, but thoroughly reshapes the classical Christian understanding of the character and attributes of God.

Such a reconception of God, then, has radical implication for our notion of divine power. As I suggested in the opening section of this chapter, the soteriological issues of suffering and injustice force us to ask how the Christian concept of God either exacerbates or answers these problems. That question focuses primarily on the meaning of divine power, and whether that power is to be thought of in terms of the monotheistic idea of God the Monarch/Father or the triune identity. Reconsideration of the concept of power formulated in the light of the idea of the triune God prompts us to recognize to what extent our notion of divine power has been determined by the assumptions of classical theism, which has always defined the divine power around concepts of divine sovereignty and omnipotence instead of christology. Consequently, the soteriological issue is what triune sovereignty means and how it engages the problems of suffering and justice.

In its most basic meaning in monotheism, divine sovereignty indicates that God "cares" and "embraces" all of human history,[56] that "God's sovereign freedom is able to will changes within the contingencies of history."[57] However, divine sovereignty carries an even more determinate meaning in classical theism. Sovereignty implies a determinateness to the divine will that is usually conceived as determination, even if the determination is hidden behind or within the distinction between primary and secondary causality. Sovereignty means omnipotence, and omnipotence means that the God who is the absolutely autonomous and wholly free creator of the world is the ultimate determinate cause of everything that happens. Biblical and theological notions of divine sovereignty have come to means "omnicausality," God the sole (ultimate) cause of both good and evil.[58] Consequently, God is above and beyond all of the suffering of the world *(apatheia)*, and the world in its structures and happenings is the will of God. Nothing happens that is not the will of God. The question that lies behind contemporary trinitarian discussion is whether this idea of God, and the power of God, is what is implied by the triune identity of God.

The concept of the triunity of God offers a radically new idea of divine power. The key to this shift is the recognition that God is not named and described by theistic speculation or definition but rather by the God who comes to be with us in Jesus Christ through the power of the Spirit. This shift means that christology and pneumatology are essential to the very meaning of the term God. The Christian God is neither the theistic God nor God the Monarch/Father. The term God means the trinitarian essence (essentialist trinity) and activity (economic trinity) as creation (creator and providential ruler), redemption (the cross and resurrection of Christ), and consummation (incorporation into the life of the Spirit).[59] Christology is not added onto a concept of God known prior to and apart from Jesus Christ and the Spirit. Christology is essential to the very meaning of the term God. When one begins with christology and the doctrine of the triunity of God, with the economy of God and the identity of God as triune, the power of God gets redefined and the relationship of the power of God to human suffering and injustice gets thoroughly rethought. The triune God does not *cause* human suffering. Rather, God in Christ through the cross and resurrection *identifies with* and *transforms* human suffering. God does not will human injustice and suffering. I will illustrate this theme by focusing on two contemporary reconceptions of the triune God which show the direct bearing of christological and trinitarian doctrine on the issues of suffering and justice.

The trinitarian theology of Jurgen Moltmann (b. 1926) has special significance for our understanding of the suffering of God and human suffering. He has been one of the most influential advocates among contemporary theologians in interpreting God's power in the cross and resurrection in relation to human suffering and injustice. His work focuses primarily on the consequences of a theology of the crucified Christ for "a revolution in the concept of God." We must, he argues, understand the being of God from the death of Jesus. He seeks to avoid the interpretation of the cross as an abuse and punishment by moving the cross from soteriology (the punishment of the Son for our sins) to theology (a statement about God in Godself: "the cross stands at the heart of the trinitarian being of God"). "The fault of earlier Protestant theology was that it did not look at the cross in the context of the relationship of the Son to the Father, but related it directly to mankind as an expiatory death for sin."[60]

Christian faith, then, stands against a theistic concept of God. The doctrine of the trinity speaks of God in relation to the incarnation and the death of Jesus. God suffered in the suffering of Jesus; God died on the cross of Christ, so that we might live and rise in God's future. God and suffering are not contradictions in a christological perspective as they are in a theistic one, for God's being is in suffering, and suffering is in God's being because God is love.

Moltmann does claim that God is not changeable, but that is a simile. That is, God is not changeable as creatures are changeable. Although not changeable in every respect, then, God is, nevertheless, free to change Godself, free to allow Godself to be changed by others of God's own free will. Furthermore, God does not suffer like creatures; creatures suffer unwillingly, but God voluntarily opens Godself to the possibility of being affected by another. Such suffering, however, is not a deficiency in God's being, but is intrinsic to the being of God because God suffers out of the fullness of God's being, that is, God's love. In other words, in God's case, this is an active, not a passive, suffering.

A trinitarian theology of the cross, then, provides a unique concept of God. In trinitarian thought, the death of Jesus says something about the being of God. "To understand what happened between Jesus and his God and Father on the cross, it is necessary to talk in trinitarian terms. The Son suffers dying, the Father suffers the death of the Son. The grief of the Father here is just as important as the death of the Son. The Fatherlessness of the Son is matched by the Sonlessness of the Father, and if God has constituted himself as the Father of Jesus Christ, then he also suffers the death of his Fatherhood in the death of the Son. . . . The Son suffers in his love being forsaken by the Father as he dies. The Father suffers in his love the grief of the death of the Son."[61] All the suffering of the world is encompassed in the affliction of the Son, the grief of the Father, and the comfort of the Spirit. Moltmann concludes, then, with a new concept of God. "I think that the unity of the dialectical history of Father and Son and Spirit in the cross on Golgotha, full of tension as it is, can be described so to speak retrospectively as 'God.'"[62] In one of his subsequent books, he says, "If God the Father was in Christ, the Son, this means that Christ's sufferings are God's sufferings, too, and then God too experiences death on the cross. . . . In Christ's God-forsakenness, God goes out of himself, forsakes his heaven and is in Christ himself, is there, present, in order to become the God and Father of the forsaken."[63]

What is key, for Moltmann, is that the Godforsakenness of the cross involves the Father as well as the Son,[64] so that the passion of Jesus is brought into the very center of what Christians mean by God. The Father and the Son experience the crucifixion differently. The Son suffers the agony of Godforsakenness, Moltmann claims, while the Father suffers the grief of the loss of the Son,[65] thus saving himself in the strict sense from the two ancient heresies of patripassionism and theopaschitism. Nevertheless, we have here an explicit repudiation of theism in favor of a theology of the suffering of God on the cross of Jesus Christ. In the end, whatever Christians mean by God and by the work of God in the death and resurrection of Christ, the power of God is defined by the crucified one who was raised by God and the one raised by the God who was crucified. The pain, suffering, and sorrow of the cross as well as the vindication of the crucified one stands at the very heart of what Christians mean by God. Suffering is not caused by God; it is taken into the very heart of God in Christ and transformed into a "theology of hope" for a free and open future.

Catherine LaCugna's recent trinitarian theology has special significance for our contemporary concerns about human suffering and injustice. She, also, presents a compelling case for the doctrine of the trinity as the Christian way to speak about God. "The doctrine of the Trinity is the summary statement of faith in the God of Jesus Christ."[66] As a "trinitarian monotheist" she also argues that theism is not the Christian doctrine of God primarily because it is a non-soteriological doctrine of God. Furthermore, the trinity is not primarily a doctrine about the nature of God, the inner life of God, God in isolation from everything other than God, or the self-relatedness of the Father and the Son and the Holy Spirit apart from us. Rather, it is about the economy of God, the economy of salvation, the self-communication of God, what it means to be part of the life of God through Jesus Christ in the Spirit. It is rooted in the experience of being saved by God through Christ in the power of the Spirit.

In the end, economic and essential doctrines are related, for the mystery of God and the mystery of salvation are inseparable. "The unity of *theologia* (theology) and *oikonomia* (economy) shows that the fundamental issue in trinitarian theology is not the inner working of the 'immanent' trinity, but the question of how the trinitarian pattern of salvation history is to be correlated with the eternal being of God."[67] So the trinity is about the shared life of God with the life of the creatures, the communion of God for us in the economy of redemption. In the end, a central theme of trinitarian theology is the relation between this economy and the eternal being of God. It is an attempt to understand the mystery of God on the basis of what is revealed about God in the economy of redemption. There is an essential connection between the threefold pattern of salvation history and the eternal being and identity of God.

Therefore, LaCugna's metaphysics is based on and reflective of the economy of salvation, not vice versa. She relates the being of God and the economy of God through what she calls an "ontology of persons in communion,"[68] a life shared by God and the creatures. "Trinitarian ontology affirms instead that persons, not substance, is the ultimate ontological category because it is the person of the Father, not the substance of the Godhead, who as Unorginate Origin is the cause *(aitia)* of everything that is."[69] Reconciling the doctrine of the trinity in the light of the mystery of salvation, then, the doctrine of God originates in the events of salvation, namely, redemption through Jesus Christ and the sending of the Spirit, which reveal the nature of the ineffable God. This does not mean the trinity exists only in our experience, but must belong to God in Godself, or else we would do away with God's self-communication.[70] There is an essential unity though not a strict identity between divine essence and divine energies, so we should not fix on the mystery of God in Godself but on the mystery of God's activity in creation, human personality, and history, since it is there and nowhere else that the essence of God is revealed.[71] "To speak about God in immanent trinitarian terms is nothing more than to speak about God's life with us in the economy of Christ and the Spirit."[72] What God is is what God shows Godself to be, and the essence of God is permanently unknowable as it is in itself.

This reconception of the trinity is a practical doctrine with radical consequences for Christian life. Since the subject matter of the trinity is the shared life of God and creatures, what is said about God in the light of the economy of salvation has consequences for creatures. What is said about the divine economy "dictates the shape of our experience of that life and our reflection on that experience."[73] It does not give us pragmatic principles for easy solutions to violence and injustice, but it gives us a framework for reflecting on the nature of human persons, on the relationships between humankind and other creatures, and on the relationship between God and ourselves. "Entering into the life of God means entering in the deepest way possible into the economy, into the life of Jesus Christ, into the life of the Spirit, into the life of others."[74] It is to enter into the life of love and communion with others. It leads to the life of orthopraxis, doing what is true. "The truth about both God and ourselves is that we were meant to exist as persons in communion in a common household, living as persons from and for others, not persons in isolation with withdrawal or self-centeredness."[75]

Existence is a mystery, then, of co-mingling persons, divine and human, in a common household within a common economy. It is to live life where God's life rules, to live within the reign of God, where life is governed for the sake of communion. It is a radical re-ordering of existence, where attachments, family, worship, anxieties, and ways of relating to each other are shaped by the life of God in Jesus Christ and his reign. "Living trinitarian faith means living God's life: living from and for God, from and for others."[76] It means to live within God's reign, God's (mon)arche. "The key to God's reign, and to the form of life appropriate to that reign, lies in Jesus Christ and in the nature of the 'monarch,' the one whose rule governs."[77]

In most of Christianity the divine monarchy is identified with theism, the reign of God is understood as the rule of God the Father, engendering all the various sorts of subordinationism in our life together. But in trinitarian monotheism, or in a trinitarian understanding of the divine monarchy, where Christ is affirmed to be equal with God (in *ousia*), the theoretical and practical significance of the move from theism to trinitarianism is radical. "The whole point of the original doctrine of the Trinity was that God (God's *ousia*) simply does not exist except as three persons. Vice versa, the divine persons are not other than the divine *ousia;* they are the ousia."[78] When persons take precedence over substance, everything gets radically transformed. When monarchy belongs not to one person alone (Father) as the exclusion (subordination) to others, but belongs also to other persons (Son and Holy Spirit) through self-communication, where the arche is shared by more than one person, the political implications are radical and transformative. "The primacy of communion among equals, not the primacy of one over the other, is the hallmark of the reign of the God of Jesus Christ."[79]

We have, then, what might be called a "trinitarian politics," where the reign of God is defined by God's self-revelation in Jesus Christ. Jesus is the meaning and culmination of God's reign. He announces God's rule; he inaugurates it in the qualities and characteristics about him described in chapter one. In the theistic notion of monarchy, projected onto earthly monarchs, God was used to justify all kinds of dominating hierarchy, religious, moral, sexual, and political. In trinitarian monotheism, "God's arche is the shared rule of equal persons in communion, not domination by some persons over others."[80] God's Fatherhood, God's Godness, must be thought of relationally, one person in relationship with another. God's arche is the arche of love and communion among persons. "The reconception of God's monarchy from a trinitarian perspective was potentially the most far-reaching and radical theological and political fruit of the doctrine of the Trinity."[81]

The point I want to make about the revival of the trinitarian identity of God, then, is that when one takes the life, ministry, cross, and resurrection of Jesus Christ as decisive for the concept of God, one has theological grounds for affirming the transformation of human suffering and the establishment of justice at the very heart of what we mean by God and God's power. Put in another way, anyone who takes christology seriously, and especially normatively, who takes the cross and resurrection as central in identifying and describing the activity of God, will speak about the suffering and transforming God whose nature and mode of activity is to will and to work for the transformation of human suffering and the establishment of justice.

The debate among Christians today is in part whether theism or trinitarianism is the proper way to name and describe God and how God works for our redemption of suffering and injustice. I have argued that the immutable and unrelated God of theism is inadequate for salvation, and, furthermore, in some ways underwrites much human suffering and injustice. The only God who can save is the God who is dynamic and related to the world, and that requires some form of trinitarian thinking. But even if one agrees, that does not settle all christological issues. The problem of precisely how normative is the language of trinitarian dogma (Nicea and Chalcedon) remains. If one adopts a dynamic and relational view of God, as contemporary trinitarian and process theologians do, the fourth century controversy between the language of essence

(Athanasius's substance) and the language of relationship (Arius's willing) is revived.

How essential is essentialist language? How adequate is relational language? That question will be implicit in the faces of christology I will explore in chapters four and five. Here I want to argue that the dynamic, relational, "revelation of God in history" language of the trinitarian doctrine of God is central to a Christian doctrine of God, and that christological language is faithful to trinitarian doctrine if it articulates the claim that it is "truly"or "really" God who is present and active, whether that be the substance of the Godhead or the activity of the transforming God or the presence of the relational God. Of course, that re-opens the fourth century debate about the language of substance and willing. But my claim is that even if one finds too many objections to the substance language too compelling to retain it and finds the language of presence, activity, relationship, "mighty acts," or some such language to be more appropriate on biblical and experiential grounds, the final criterion, according to scripture, Athanasius, the ecumenical creeds, and our contemporary experience, is the claim that it is "really" or "truly" or "fully" God who is at work in Jesus Christ for the transformation of the world from suffering and injustice to the life of justice and beatitude.

CHAPTER THREE

Evangelical Christology

"Evangelical" is both an adjective and a noun. I begin by establishing the theological map I will use in this chapter. Evangelical refers, in the first place, to the *evangelion* (the evangel), the gospel, the New Testament. An evangelical Christian is one whose faith is grounded in and measured by the New Testament witness to Jesus Christ, a use of the term which would mark most Christians as evangelical. The term refers, in its second meaning, to European Protestantism, specifically, to the scholastic heritage of the Lutheran Reformers,[1] which understands itself as a return to the New Testament witness so distinct from "catholic" Christianity where the emphasis is on the authority of scripture and tradition. The term refers, in its third place, to a religious-cultural phenomenon distinctive to many North American Christians. American evangelicalism is a broad and nearly indefinable movement within many Protestant denominations and independent churches following the Civil War and still powerful within contemporary Protestantism. Evangelicalism is identified with the view of salvation and the doctrinal beliefs represented in the American revivalistic tradition. This view of salvation and its corresponding beliefs is held by most Evangelicals as well as by Pentecostals and charismatics. "We shall call it the revivalistic interpretation of salvation."[2] I use the term in this third sense throughout this chapter.

Evangelicals constitute between one-fifth and one-third of the American population, depending on which survey you read.[3] The content of North American Evangelical faith is deeply rooted in the Reformation, especially Calvinism; in northern European Pietism and British Puritanism, especially Anglo-American Methodism;[4] and in American Puritanism and the Baptist sects, especially the First (eighteenth century) and Second (nineteenth century) Great Awakenings. Doctrinally, evangelicals adhere to belief in the sovereignty of God; the authority of the Bible as the inerrant Word of God, which serves as the source for our knowledge of God and our guide for Christian living; the divinity of Christ, both as God incarnate and the Lord and savior of sinful humanity; belief in the efficacy of the life, death, and physical resurrection of Jesus, which was the substitutionary atonement for the salvation of the individual soul; salvation by grace through faith; and the personal return of Christ. Behaviorally, evangelicalism is typified by an individual personal conversion through a highly subjective experience of spiritual salvation; "scriptural holiness"; and a conviction of the necessity of evangelism which actively attempts to convert all nonbelievers to evangelical experience and beliefs.[5] Contemporary North American evangelicalism includes the Baptist tradition, the Holiness-Pentecostal tradition, the Anabaptist tradition, and some forms of the Reformed-Confessional tradition. "What they all share, true to the spirit of the Reformation, is a restorationist approach to religion."[6]

I. Redundancy of the Idea of an Evangelical Christology

There is a sense, however, in which a chapter on evangelical christology is redundant. The reason is this: insofar as we have an accurate picture of orthodox christology, we already have an adequate understanding of what evangelical Christians think proper christological doctrine is. While christology is based on scripture alone, Nicea and Chalcedon give *the* proper and adequate account of scripture, or at least it provides the beginning point and norm for what scripture claims and means about Jesus Christ. What is distinctive about evangelicalism is not its theological doctrine but its spiritual ethos. It is a creative brew of Reformed emphasis on right doctrine and Pietistic concern for true religion, the religion of the heart. "Evangelicalism is basically Christian orthodoxy, as set out in the ecumenical creeds, with a particular emphasis on the need for the personal assmiliation and appropriation of faith and a marked reluctance to allow any matters of lesser importance get in the way of the proclamation and application of the gospel."[7] The key to evangelicalism is Jesus Christ as an experienced reality in the life of the believer. "In terms of the substance of this belief, it corresponds to historic Christian orthodoxy down the ages."[8]

There are, to be sure, some subtle differences among evangelical theologians about what Scripture properly interpreted by Nicea and Chalcedon means. Recently, Douglas Jacobsen and Frederick Schmidt have shown that in the 1980s changes were evident among some evan-

70

gelical theologians, "especially in the realm of christology." The major distinctions were between those who represent the "custodial core" and those at the "penumbra" of evangelicalism.[9] The former see themselves as inheritors of something they have no right to alter as well as self-appointed antimodernist custodians who define the norms and social boundaries of belief (such as Trinity Divinity School, Baker Books publishing house, and the Evangelical Theological Society). The "penumbra" are more amenable to the modern academy, and include "'private' evangelicals (James Dunn)," "'hyphenated' evangelicals" (Anabaptist-evangelicals and charismatic-evangelicals), and "non-aligned" (T. F. Torrance, b. 1913; Louis Berkhof, b. 1873; and Gabriel Fackre, b. 1926) evangelicals.

Developments within the custodial realm confine christology to the orthodox creeds. "Few if any . . . would argue as G. C. Berkhower (b. 1903) did earlier that Chalcedon represents the final complete and unenlargable statement of who Christ is. What they do argue is that Chalcedon cannot be transgressed."[10] A slightly more flexible layer argues that evangelical christology is simply the continuation of historic christology, although that does not mean every line or word is beyond criticism. They primarily hold that orthodoxy is the continuation of the christology of the New Testament and that Christians must grant explicit theological authority to the creedal tradition of the church catholic. At the "liberal fringe" of the custodians, contemporary evangelicals such as David Wells and Clark Pinnock "speak simultaneously of affirming Chalcedon and of getting down to 'the hard work of theological definition which we ought to be doing for ourselves.'"[11] Chalcedon becomes the beginning instead of the end of christological discussion, as evangelicals listen to what others have to say about christology.[12]

At the penumbra, such as anabaptists, pentecostals, and charismatic evangelicals, one finds everything from the extreme right wing (evangelicals must conform to a fully orthodox and largely fundamentalist and Calvinistic understanding of christology), to others who argue these traditions should adopt an explicit adoptionist christology. Most fall in the middle range by affirming Chalcedon and going not only behind it but beyond it, frequently critiquing the ontological categories of the creeds.[13] The last group which is part of this evangelical penumbra is a group of mainstream theologians who have arrived at more or less evangelical conclusions, such as Hendrikus Berkhof (b. 1914), Brian Hebblethwaite (b. 1939), Fackre, and Torrance. These theologians share the conviction about a real and unique incarnation of God in Jesus of Nazareth, the need to combine an approach to christology from above and below, and a need for Christians to admit, respect, and come to terms with the Jewishness of Jesus.[14]

Subtle differences notwithstanding, my claim about the orthodoxy of evangelicalism is based partially on the grounds that I know of no christology written by an evangelical theologian which intends to be anything less or anything more than a statement about what the Bible clearly teaches, and the christology which has been declared by the church since the fourth and fifth centuries, to be dogma. What Nicea confesses in the doctrine of the Trinity (one substance, three persons) and what Chalcedon formulates in the doctrine of the hypostatic union (one person, two natures), is precisely what scripture teaches about Jesus Christ. Evangelicals understand this to be the proper interpretation of what God revealed in the Scripture to be the truth about him. Insofar as our understandings of the conclusions of the christological controversy are an accurate interpretation of what these two councils said about Jesus Christ, they provide the doctrine about Jesus Christ which is taken to be normative and is to be taught by all evangelical Christians. Any interpretation of incarnation which uses the language of will, purpose, spirit, activity, presence, grace, or initial aims instead of substance is regarded as heretical. "All such [non-creedal] christologies have something in common. They seek a functional equivalent of Chalcedon by finding in the human life of Jesus a unique divine presence, a normative divine revelation, a decisive saving action. But none of them wishes to say that Jesus is God in the ontological sense that orthodoxy has demanded."[15] What the scriptures clearly teach as normative Christian faith is what the councils of Nicea and Chalcedon declared to be the faith of the Christian Church.

In short, I know of no unique or even distinctive evangelical christology. Regardless of whether these two councils are merely repeating what scripture directly and unequivocally teaches or are interpreting what is implied in scripture in a contextual but faithful way,[16] evangelical christology is explicitly the christology of Nicea and Chalcedon. As conservative evangelical theologian John Walls says in asking what is "the Christian message," "the answer which suggests itself most readily is that the essential things are set forth in the ecumenical creeds. . . . It has been the confidence of Christians for centuries that the church, under the guidance of the Holy Spirit, correctly understood and stated the meaning of God's revelation in the creeds . . . [Christians accept] the creeds as definitive statements of essential Christian doctrine."[17] When compared to these two dogmas from the tradition, there is nothing novel or unique about christological doctrine which has been written by a self-avowed, practicing evangelical. The evangelical Christian simply reaffirms what true Christians "in all times and places" before and after 325 CE and 458 CE have believed to be the truth about Jesus Christ revealed by God in the Scriptures. Insofar as any christology departs from these two explicit dogmas, it cannot qualify as evangelical christology.

It is true that North American evangelical Christians usually do not appeal directly to these dogmas in the same way that Orthodox, Roman Catholic, or "confessional" Protestant Christians who have creeds do, such as Lutheran and Reformed Christians. Nevertheless, the content of these two creeds, whether memorized in catechism classes (which is very unlikely) or learned more indirectly through preaching, teaching, liturgy, and especially hymns, is assumed to be the clear and infallible teaching of Scripture. Anything other than this is "nonbiblical," and so is not evangelical Christian doctrine about Jesus Christ. Perhaps one of the best representatives of this evangelical intention is presented by the United Methodist theologian, Thomas Oden, who adopts as one of his guidelines his intent never to innovate or add anything new doctrinally to "classical Christianity" or "ancient ecumenical orthodoxy," by which he means the first seven ecumenical councils.[18] Pleading for "the aesthetic beauty of retrogression," he wants to return to the classic Christian exegesis of the first five centuries.[19]

Among evangelical christologies, then, one can note the creeds as at least the necessary beginning point if not the normative claims, and often the proper language for christology as such, alongside other typical evangelical themes such as respect for the authority of the biblical text, concern for lived piety, and commitment to evangelism. It is difficult to find an evangelical theologian who would not begin and norm christology according to the language of Nicea and Chalcedon. I will illustrate my claim. In two significant books about evangelicals by evangelicals, viz., Bernard Ramm's work on Reformed evangelicalism[20] and Donald Bloesch's on Reformed and pietistic evangelicalism,[21] *christology is not even mentioned,* let alone discussed, as one of the "hallmarks" (Bloesch) or distinctive doctrines of the "heritage"(Ramm) of evangelical faith. Why is such an important doctrine in the historic Christian tradition missing from two books which claim to be describing what is distinctive about evangelical faith and doctrine? Why does not Bloesch so much as mention christology in his study?[22] The only remotely christological doctrines that are identified as "hallmarks" of evangelicalism are the substitutionary theory of atonement and personal return of Christ! The same question can be asked of Ramm's study. Christology is not mentioned in chapters 1-5, chapters locating evangelicalism within the Christian West, the Reformation, and Protestant scholasticism. It is not until pages 142-143 that he mentions christology, and then simply says, "Evangelical theology is christological and incarnational"![23]

I suggest that both of these authors so thoroughly assume the accuracy and adequacy, and indeed the undisputable normativeness, of the orthodox christological creeds as definitive of Christian faith and belief that it is not even worth mentioning them among the most self-identifying doctrines of evangelical Christian faith.[24] Some things are so obvious to the believers that it never even occurs to them to be worth mentioning! Like Oden, writing in the 1990s instead of the 1970s, Alister McGrath, a British Anglican evangelical, does think it worth mentioning that "in terms of the substance of this belief [in Jesus Christ], it [evangelicalism] corresponds to historic Christian orthodoxy down through the ages."[25]

II. Knowing God and Ourselves in a Particular Way

Why, then, isolate evangelical christology as one of "the many faces of christology"? One of the reasons is strategic. There are large numbers of evangelical Christians in North America who stress religious experience, such as rebirth (Baptists), assurance and holiness (Methodists), and charismatic gifts (Pentecostals) more than the historic Christian beliefs ("the Vincencian canon").[26] Although we have very few fundamentalists within the student body at the seminary where I teach, I have a large group of students who clearly identify themselves as evangelical Christians in one of these traditions. Their "face of christology" should be seen along with the other faces which enrich contemporary christology.

Another reason for including this "face of christology," however, is this: although evangelical Christians have nothing unique to teach about christological doctrine, there are nevertheless other themes characteristic of evangelical theology, especially soteriology, which they distinctively contribute to the understanding of Christology in the modern period. It is evangelical soteriology, and most notably evangelical *piety*, not evangelical *doctrine*, that is its unique contribution to christology. And this emphasis has been an insightful response to "the collapse of the house of authority" in the modern world. In evangelicalism, it is a particular way of experiencing Jesus that is crucial. A personal conversion or a personal experience of Jesus Christ is normative. This is more than a tingling sensation or a warm glow. Faith begins "when the sense of communion is so real, and the feeling of another personal reality is so overwhelming, that the only way to describe it is to say that one has been confronted by another, independent 'Thou.'"[27]

Both the Calvinistic type of evangelicals, Reformed Christians, for example, for whom divine sovereignty and correct doctrine tend to play dominant roles (such as James Boice[28] and Bernard Ramm), and the pietistic type of evangelicals, revivalists and methodists, for whom the experience of conversion and holiness tends to play a more important role than sound doctrine, have emphasized that the chief end of each human being is knowing God and knowing oneself (derived directly from Calvin's sixteenth-century *Institutes*). However, this primary purpose is interpreted in a distinctive way by evangelicals. One cannot know God or oneself without knowing Jesus Christ *in a particular way* (viz., personally, directly, and intimately in one's heart instead of in one's head).[29] Apart from this there is merely "an almost Christian" instead of "an altogether Christian,"[30] or, even worse, no Christian at all. Apart from a distinct experience of rebirth and assurance, one cannot truly know either God or oneself. "Knowing him also involves a personal encounter, an exclusive relationship, a permanent union, and a transformed life."[31]

Although there are many thoroughly modern, liberal, Enlightenment themes in all forms of North American evangelicalism (such as individuality, freedom, autonomy, subjectivity, decision, the quest for certainty, and so forth), at its best Protestant evangelicalism has simultaneously held that because of the deep fissure between God and us and within ourselves, we cannot know either God or ourselves (even or especially our liberal selves as autonomous, free, and fulfilled agents!) apart from being made alive (both by and in) Jesus Christ in a deeply personal and intimate way. Modern liberal themes at the core of evangelicalism notwithstanding, the intention of evangelical Christians has always been to claim that our chief end is knowing God and ourselves truly, and that this end is unattainable apart from knowing Jesus Christ *in a particular way*. One cannot know God or ourselves through inherited tradition, through ritual participation in a community, or through any other mediator. These have all disappeared with "the collapse of the house of authority." One can only know God and oneself through the direct and personal knowledge of an immediate experience. All else falls short of filling the void of true knowledge once the acids of modernity have eaten away all the other external objective grounds of knowledge and authority.

III. Evangelicalism and the Mystical Traditions

To be sure, this theme about the basis of authentic knowledge of God and ourselves did not arise with modern evangelicalism. Most Christians in most ages, including Orthodox, Roman Catholic, and Protestant Christians from the Reformation era to the present, whether scholastic, pietistic, puritan, liberal, modernist, or neo-orthodox, have faithfully represented some version of this Christian claim. But all three of these branches of Christianity have taken a variety of paths in formulating and seeking strategies to fulfill this goal, including confessional (creedal), liturgical (preaching or sacraments), axiological (ethical), and mystical (deification) forms of participating in and exhibiting true faith. What is noteworthy about evangelical Christians is that they have represented *one distinctive form of the mystical tradition*, namely, the tradition that upholds a conscious, immediate, personal experience of God or God through Christ as the truest and usually the only form of knowledge. The distinctive form of the mystical tradition represented in evangelicalism serves as the spiritual, liturgical, and theological core of this form of Christian faith.

It is important to note that the mystical tradition throughout the history of Christianity has been multifaceted, and some of its forms have been explicitly rejected by evangelicalism.[32] What is common to mysticism is the claim that there is a special sort of direct, immediate, and intuitive experience and knowledge of God which is essentially different from ordinary knowledge about ourselves and the world. Glenn Chesnut, however, shows that there have been at least three different forms of the mystical tradition.[33] First, there is the "pure" mystical tradition, which includes such persons as Meister Eckhart (d. 1327), John Tauler (d. 1361), St. Teresa of Avila (d. 1582), and Jacob Boehme (d. 1624). In "pure" mysticism, one eagages in an ecstatic rapture of the soul in God, a pure love and direct union, or at least communion, between the soul and God. This type of mysticism has also had some more christological versions, including such diverse forms as Orthodox worship, the Jesus Prayer, the medieval search for the Holy Grail, Piers Plowman, and Dante (d. 1321).

Second, there is a tradition of nature mysticism, apprehending God directly in and through the finite world. Primary examples, of course, are idealistic versions in the work of Wordsworth and the Romantic tradition in poetry in Europe and in the American transcendentalist movement in literature. Nature mysticism is also found in the theologies where a sense of creaturliness and the interdependence of the human and the natural processes are emphasized, such as in the earlier theology of Henry Nelson Wieman and Bernard Meland.[34] There are also threads of one or both of these forms of nature mysticism in the ecology movement today.[35]

But the tradition of direct, immediate knowledge of God or Christ or Jesus has a distinctly modern Protestant form, viz., North American evangelical Christianity. Salvation by faith alone is thought of not so much in terms of justification and imputed righteousness through divine grace (as in the Protestant Reformers), but rather in terms of a direct, immediate awareness of God as a loving and forgiving God (assurance) and Christ or Jesus as an immediate and constant companion in one's heart or by one's side. Saving faith is mystical knowledge of immediate union and continuing companionship with Jesus in one's heart. The person who has "been saved" knows that God or Christ or Jesus loves her or him with a direct, intuitive awareness that goes beyond the bonds of any kind of "normal" knowledge, including the "normal" religious knowledge in the means of grace provided by the church, such as reading Scripture, reciting creeds, participating in the liturgy, or any other kind of ecclesial mediation.

In the modern world, beginning with eighteenth century European pietism, including English and North American Wesleyanism, and particularly the nineteenth century revivalist movements, pietistic mysticism has been the key in shaping this modern North American version of christology. It is significant to note that Albrecht Ritschl, an expert on pietism, maintained that the themes of medieval mysticism reappeared in Protestantism through pietism.[36] Wesleyanism in England and North America countered the Enlightenment attack on Christianity not primarily by appeal to ancient authorities or to philosophical argument or, even in the final analysis, to the authority of the Bible, but with a direct, immediate, personal, and assuring experience of Christ as a loving savior (known through a new birth of the spiritual sensibilities as a result of prevenient, justifying, and sanctifying grace).

By way of the religion of the American frontier, especially from 1800 onward, this sort of evangelical faith or mystical experience, known by the code word of "revivalism," became the dominant form of Christianity in North America, at least until the great immigration movements of the late nineteenth and twentieth centuries began the shift toward a more pluralistic religious populace. The believer was expected to have "a conversion experience" through which the person comes to know Christ or Jesus in a direct, immediate, and personal way in order to be saved from the wrath to come. The person who so experiences Christ or Jesus this way feels the sudden, overwhelming force of a direct, personal awareness, beyond sense experience or human words, of God's or Christ's or Jesus' love for her or him personally. At the center of evangelical christology, then, and the most distinguishing marks of it as a christology, is this immediate mystical experience of love, acceptance, assurance, intimacy, and companionship. Although, as I have argued, evangelicalism offers nothing novel in terms of formal christology, it offers *through its soteriology* a distinctively modern version of the mystical tradition of immediate experience of Christ. When all else in the modern world fails as a basis for sure knowledge, or at least is susceptible to skepticism, this re-formed version of the mystical tradition offers the grounds for sure knowledge. If the church and the tradition cannot secure the true knowledge of salvation through its preaching and sacraments, then this form of the mystical tradition can provide secure, certain, and unassailable knowledge of God and of ourselves.

The difference between much of the tradition and modern evangelicals is that evangelicals assume the religious need of humans before God is not so much the need to "put on immortality" (Athanasius , d. 377), or to be "released from bondage" (Irenaeus, d. 90, to John of Damascus, d. 749) or even "to be forgiven" (Luther, d. 1546)—all mediated through the ministries of the church—but rather is to have a particular kind of experience of encounter and appropriation of Christ within one's inner life, viz., to be "born again" in an immediate and direct experience of God or Christ or Jesus as a loving and present companion in one's inner life. This kind of christology is not only compelling to many North American Christians since the eighteenth century, but is increasingly compelling to multitudes of Christians beyond the North American Protestant context, including North American Roman Catholics, Latin American, Russian, and African Christians.

IV. Evangelicalism and Modernity

Although modernization is not a mere transplanting of European institutions to other parts of the world, it nevertheless began in Europe and spread outward.[37] Sociologically, modernization is usually considered synonymous with development. It refers to that period in the history of a society "that is characterized by institutional and cultural concomitants of a technologically induced economic growth."[38] Modernization affects all of society, including economic, political, and social systems. Economically it takes the form of industrialization. Politically, many types of systems are compatible with it as long as they allow reasonably stable economic and social development. Socially, various forms of organization are compatible as long as they permit the necessary changes in personality, norms, social relations, and institutions from premodern societies. Most basically the difference between modern and traditional society is between action that is prescribed, where the individual is expected to behave in a specific way, and action which is chosen, where an individual selects her or his own course of action. In prescribed action, an individual expresses a collective act, whereas action by choice requires a fully individualized self. "The central meaning of secularization is that choice, as a deliberate act, requires persons endowed with sufficiently individualized minds to be aware of alternatives."[39] In short, modernity requires "its own type of personality structure, one capable of self-guidance and decision-making, with some capacity to confront change."[40]

Modernity refers to the period when the West was modernized in the above sense, the period that began with the European Renaissance in the sixteenth century, and came to fruition from the eighteenth century Enlightenment to late twentieth century American culture. Specifically, it refers to these guiding assumptions and primary projects of the cultural leaders of the Western world throughout this period. Modern, of course, can mean merely recent or the present, in which case every era is modern. At the beginning of "the Modern era," however, the appellation was used as a flattering term to refer to the party of "Moderns" in eighteenth-century Europe, who thought of themselves in distinction from the "Ancients" and "Medievals" as doing something historically new, hence inaugurating a new era of thought and life (for example, the French philosopher, Voltaire, d. 1778).[41] It is clear from our vantage point that the Renaissance humanists and the Protestant Reformers did not think of themselves as moderns; they were, at their core, restorationists, seeking to revive ancient modes of thought and civilization. But this was not true of the Moderns throughout the Enlightenment who looked to the present and future for their hope.

Most fundamentally, modernity, embodied foremost in the ideals of the Enlightenment, is a worldview, a body of attitudes and ideas.[42] Its key feature for our purposes was its reconception of knowledge, its search for the foundations of truth.[43] Knowledge is achieved through critical reason, conceived by rationalists as a deductive power of the mind and by empiricists as an inductive, or experimental, power of the mind.[44] This concept of knowledge underwrote the Enlightenment quest for certainty, for literal and objectifying thought, for direct representation of reality in language, for comprehensiveness, and for certain imperatives for practical action, most notably the quest for individual human freedom and the demand to create history.

Enlightenment thinkers held a mechanistic view of nature, and they sought the rational control of data, single meanings, universal claims for truth, objective interpretation, and a sensationalist doctrine of perception. They were devoted to the development of science and technology, to secularization, and to the belief that individuals and society should move toward such goals. Human nature, they believed, is not fixed but is malleable. Socially, Enlightenment modernity involved individualism, dualism, anthropocentrism, substantialism, Eurocentrism, unilinear progress, centralization, and the domination of nature. Meaning, value, and confidence finally were located in human subjectivity, the autonomous, self-consciously knowing and acting human "subject." In addition to the hard sciences, modernity developed new historical methods that led to a historical consciousness that tried to recognize change, novelty, and differences between periods and cultures.

In the area of religion, modernity entails "the collapse of the house of authority."[45] In premodern Christian societies, scripture and tradition were the objective foundations of religious belief and practice. In modern Christian faith, which has essentially been an effort to come to terms with the outlook of the Enlightenment, a critical and skeptical attitude toward traditional Christian dogmas, a positive attitude toward radical biblical criticism, a new understanding of history and the natural sciences, and stress on ethical rather than doctrinal dimensions of faith gained ascendency.

In the area of epistemology, modernity has been the effort to re-establish a grounds of authority. This is the primary feature of modern liberal theology, whereas orthodoxy, traditionalism, evangelicalism, and fundamentalism have been efforts to retain the authority of scripture and tradition. The essence of modern liberal theology is the effort to establish the grounds of authority on some other basis than either of these.[46] "Theological liberalism is a form of religious thought that establishes religious inquiry on the basis of a norm other than the authority of tradition. . . . The defining trait of the liberal character is a will to be liberated from the coercion of external controls and a consequent concern for inner motivation."[47] Initiated by Descartes (d. 1650), modernity as a form of consciousness presupposed confidence in human reason, the primacy of the person, the immanence of God, and meliorism, the belief that human beings were improvable and improving. Throughout its first phase, Descartes and Newton (d. 1727), its architects, and Locke (d. 1704), its master builder, represented rationalistic methods as the means to get to the reasonable core which was the essence of Christianity. Kant (d. 1804) and Schleiermacher (d. 1834), at the end of the eighteenth and beginning of the nineteenth century, embodied romantic forms of modernity, emphasizing the uniqueness of the individual and access to its concrete reality through individual experience. It its modernist phase, modern liberal theology, grounded in Darwin and built by Shailer Mathews (d. 1941) and Henry Nelson Wieman (d. 1975), discovered through evolutionary theory the significance of historical time and the notion of progress.[48]

My argument is that evangelicalism in the United States since the late nineteenth and early twentieth century "accommodates, resists, and legitimates"[49] many of these characteristics of modernity. Thoroughly modern persons will resist or protest against the discontents of modernity when they reach a certain level, especially the anomie resulting from massive deinstitutionalization in the private sphere and the alienation from the overinstiutionalized structures in the public sphere.[50] What is important in my argument is that resistance to modernity can take a religious as well as a political and cultural forms. Drawing on the themes of revivalism, millennialism, and holiness teachings, evangelicalism formed a "subcultural identity" of Protestant faith[51] rooted in the beginnings of the disestablishment of American Protestantism, 1890-1919, the entrenchment of fundamentalism as a cognitive minority, 1919-1942, and the neo-evangelicalism and reconstruction of conservative Protestantism, 1942-1980.[52] In its key presuppositions and strategy, even though not in all the details of its contents, evangelicalism is primarily one modern response to the dissatisfactions of modernity.

Although it is in some respects, then, a vital alternative to modern beliefs, it is, also, epistemologically of one piece and an embodiment of modern liberal culture. It is of a piece both in the sense that it accepts, willy nilly, the modern agenda about how one knows what one knows.[53] Even though it claims to be loyal to the belief that divine revelation is objective, and that objective revelation is encased infallibly in the scripture properly interpreted by the creedal tradition, it can sustain this belief only half-way, and so simultaneously accepts the modern strategy for how to respond to the collapse of the house of authority. In this sense evangelicalism is very modern. Furthermore, its strategy is liberal to the core. It shares fully the modern *turn to the subject* as the *grounds of authority* for authentic knowledge. Whereas modern liberalism has been a running debate about where within the subject the grounds of authority ultimately lies—in the mind or intellect (rationalism), in the senses (empiricism), in the heart or intuition (romanticism), in the stomach (marxism), or in the id (freudianism)—evangelicalism has cast its lot wholly with one of these thoroughly modern epistemologies. One knows the truth through, in, and on the basis of the authority of inner experience ("the heart").

Although one side of evangelicalism still appeals to the premodern sense of the objective (even infallible) truths of the scripture, in another sense it roots even the authority of the scripture in the subject—the witness of the Spirit to our spirit that we are children of God and that the teachings of the scripture are true.[54] Simultaneously and reciprocally, evangelicalism appeals, on the one hand, to the objective truth of scripture and tradition, and, on the other, to the authenticity and authority of the inner life of the knowing subject, the ultimate authority of the born again experience, the experience of Jesus in the heart of the knower. In the end, evangelicalism is a liberal religious epistemology in which the authority of the subject, and especially the subjective life of the subject, is the grounds of authority. The objective truth of Christian faith is rooted in the subjective life of the believer. No less than the liberal Christian does the evangelical Christian appeal to the authority of the subject in the face of the collapse of the house of authority. Evangelicalism, in short, is a very modern strategy. It not only recognizes in its bones the challenge of modernity to belief and action which is prescribed; it subscribes to the modern commitment to the grounds of authority as the subjective life of the believer.

In one sense, then, evangelicalism is a deep challenge to modernity. It retains the premodern focus on the authority of scripture and tradition in contrast to the primary status modern liberalism gives to experience and reason.[55] "Liberal Christian theologies in North America have generally maintained that religious beliefs are fallible and thus to be held tentatively, that reason and experience in some combination provide the fundamental tests of belief, that divine and human realities are continuous rather than oppositional, and that central to Christianity is its ethical dimension, social as well as personal."[56] In apparent sharp contrast, evangelicalism posits the priority and normativeness of scripture and tradition in the face of modernity. It acknowledges the supernatural origins and transcendental foundations of belief and behavior, rooted in scripture and properly interpreted by the creedal tradition of the church. In specific, it promotes as essential to Christian identity some of the most problematic beliefs and practices of modern liberal culture, and it identifies those beliefs and practices as precisely the beliefs and practices which identify the evangelical. Thus, it chooses those beliefs most likely to offend modern secular culture—virgin birth, bodily resurrection, infallible scripture, and so forth, and names those as the beliefs which identify evangelical Christians. In this sense evangelicalism marks itself off from liberalism.

But in its epistemology, it is modern liberalism at its core. Evangelicals know that, willy nilly, no modern person can simply assume the authority of prescribed behavior and beliefs. One cannot inherit one's family's or community's faith. Faith must be self-chosen, internalized, and confirmed in the inner life for it to be genuine and authoritative.

> For moderns—perhaps especially modern Americans—the ultimate criteria of identity and lifestyle validity is individual choice. It is by choosing a product, a mate, a lifestyle, or an identity that one makes it one's very own, personal, special, and meaningful—not "merely" something one inherits or assumes. In the value-epistemology of modern American culture, to believe, to want, or to do something simply because that is what one's parents believe, or what one's friends want, or what somebody else does is considered inferior and unauthentic. It is not enough simply to assume mindlessly the religion of one's family, to absorb uncritically the outlook of one's neighborhood, to follow by default the career path that somebody else has laid out. That is parochial, acquiescent, and artificial. Rather, every such thing must be personalized and substantiated through individual choice. And even if (as is often the case) one chooses what one was already inheriting or assuming, it is only through the observance of individual choice—whether actual or ritualized—that it becomes "real" and personally meaningful. If the primary socially normative basis of modern identity-legitimation is individual choice, then we should find that moderns having to choose their religion makes the religion they choose no less real or authentic to them. For, according to the cultural epistemology, personal choice is the fundamental basis of identity validity.[57]

Evangelicalism ultimately locates authority within the subject herself, and in this sense it is liberal to the core. Indeed, as I shall argue below, the intense individualism and subjectivism of much modern evangelicalism puts evangelicals right at the center of our modern "habits of the heart," where the culture of therapy or narcissism triumph in the realm of religion as much as in other elements of our liberal culture. As much as evangelicals appeal to the authority of scripture and tradition, it is not the authority of tradition as tradition which is epistemologically normative. It may be the content of scripture and tradition which are internalized in the subject, but it is the authority of the subject herself which authenticates, even makes true, the object of faith. The inner life of the subject predominates, illuminates, authenticates. And that epistemology is the absolute center of modern liberal culture.

Thus, there is a strange convergence between the conclusions drawn by the "new quest" scholars described in chapter one and evangelicalism. In terms of the most crucial question about the implications of the quest of the historical Jesus for christology, many of the scholars of the new quest, especially phase two, and evangelicals converge. They concur on the relative unimportance of Jesus for a christology of the kerygma (second quest) or of the heart (evangelicalism). The lack of interest in the historical Jesus as the grounds for christology proffered by theologians since Martin Kahler's distinction between the "so-called historical Jesus" and "the kerygmatic Christ,"[58] which was central to the existentialist christologies growing out of the post-World War II second quest for the historical Jesus, is also characteristic of modern evangelicalism, especially at the popular level, as well. For example, although evangelist Billy Graham exhorts Christians to accept as straightforward the historical accuracy of the New Testament reports about Jesus, in his preaching "Graham summons individuals to be born again, to enter into personal relationship with Jesus, to ask him to come into their hearts as their personal Lord and Savior. The focus of his faith, in other words, appears to be the risen, spiritual Christ that Schweitzer and Bultmann also confessed. Despite Graham's insistence that the biblical accounts are historically accurate, one has to wonder whether it would ultimately make much difference for his theology whether they were or not."[59] In my own teaching experience, I am amazed at the shock of many evangelical students when I ask them "what Jesus" they experience in their hearts. Clearly it is not the historical Jesus of Nazareth as a first-century homunculus residing in their hearts. It is Jesus as the risen Christ who resides there within the experience of the believer.

V. A Critique of Evangelical Christology

Although evangelicalism is a modern religious movement, responding to the crisis of modernity with the collapse of the house of authority by reconstituting the tradition through a personal decision to appropriate it within the inner life of the believer, it is, as I have argued, a complex form of modernity. It is not quintessential modernity. Evangelicalism understands itself to be based on, and constituted by, the Bible and the orthodox traditions of the church. As we have seen, most evangelicals claim that their version of Christianity simply is historic Christianity. The content of evangelical faith is derived from the Bible, and most believe the meaning and truth of the Bible has been faithfully interpreted by the orthodox tradition of the church, which usually means the early creeds now interpreted by the great Protestant reformers. There is no self-conscious attempt to accommodate modernity. In this sense, evangelical experience is not the source for some new version of the Christian tradition, but is rather simply the medium through which one appropriates and confirms the content which comes to one objectively from outside oneself. Experience is not the source and norm for Christian belief and practice; experience is the medium for appropriation and confirms what is known from the Bible and the tradition. In this sense evangelicalism is profoundly non-modern, a premodern alternative to the content of the beliefs of the Enlightenment and liberal Christianity.

At the same time, evangelical christology is always under the threat to become more modern than it claims or intends to be. The more weight that is given to the evangelical mystical experience, the more the danger arises that evangelicalism becomes just one more form of modernity, and even more offensively, a liberal form of modernity which grounds the meaning and truth of religious beliefs and practice altogether in the autonomous and inner experience of the believer, or even that the experience itself becomes the object of faith. This danger is recognized by conservative evangelical theologian Jerry Walls in his defense of the creeds and the "ontological reference" of the truth content of the creeds for Christian identity when he says, "For it is not clear whether the essential subject matter for Christian doctrine is God, or our response to God."[60] One of the reasons, I think, that the terms God, Father, Jesus Christ, Christ, and Jesus can so easily be used indiscriminately or interchangeably in evangelical christology is not because it is a sophisticated christological doctrine of *communication of idioms* (what can be said of his humanity can be said of his divinity, and vice versa). Rather it is because it is not the *object* of the experience—God as Trinity, or God as Father, the first person of the Trinity, or Christ as the incarnate second person of the Trinity, or Jesus as the risen Christ—that is crucial to or definitive of the experience, but *the nature of the experience itself* as overwhelming, vivid, and self-confirming which makes it authentic, efficacious, and therefore divine. The experience itself becomes the means of grace, and in extreme cases, the meaning of grace. Its witness to experience is what makes evangelical christology interesting, distinctive, powerful, and compelling, not its witness to and confirmation of the Jesus of the New Testament or the orthodox christological creeds of the church.

The evangelical experience and interpretation of Jesus Christ, then, are not expressed so much in creedal form as in personal confessions, gospel songs, and sentimental art. For example, the evangelical Christ is identified through personal witness, called the "personal testimony," through songs and hymns, most notably by singing the gospel songs of Fanny J. Crosby or "praise songs," most notably in the quintessential evangelical song, "In the Garden," and through popular art, such as the classic reverential Hollywood movie about Jesus, "The Greatest Story Ever Told," but perhaps most notably in the studio classic, "Head of Christ," which hangs on the walls of many evangelical homes. David Morgan says, for instance, "Millions have recognized in Sallman's picture the personal savior whose intimacy and tenderness is at the heart of their devotional experience. . . . Sallman's image of the personal savior appeals to those who long for the communal experience of face-to-face relationships. Sallman's image is intimate, like the portrait of a family member or a loved one."[61]

However, here is the rub. An uncomfortable tension exists at the heart of evangelicalism precisely at the point of what is distinctive about it. On the one hand, it intends to be an orthodox Protestant christology in its doctrine (Nicea, Chalcedon, Westminster Confession, Book of Concord, 39 Articles, or even "The Fundamentals"), and at one level, it is exactly that. No evangelical would do with these doctrines what liberal Protestants do (for example, Schleiermacher, the nineteenth-century liberal Protestant theologian, removed his discussion of the Trinity to an appendix in his *Christian Faith*, on the grounds that there is no basis in the experience of redemption in Christ to affirm such a doctrine). Evangelicals, unlike liberals, would never think of denying, doubting, or even questioning the truth or adequacy of any of these christological formulations.[62]

On the other hand, evangelical christology is experiential and mystical at its core, not doctrinal or theological or sacramental. Evangelicalism has institutionalized a type of experience, a kind of Christ-mysticism, to the point that it expects, even requires, all "true Christians" to be of this type and to have this kind of experience. This "other hand," ironically, has tended to push many evangelicals over the edge toward an extreme individualism and subjectivism, a religious version of the modern liberalism based on the autonomous authority of the inner, subjective experience of the person, the very liberalism evangelicals so much despise and claim to be an alternative to. When that happens, either intentionally or unintentionally, the creeds and sacraments become less important, or unimportant, and distractive, even alien to authentic Christian faith, which now is based on a certain kind of inner experience and not on external authorities or other sources of any kind. Finally, in some extreme cases, this kind of mysticism can lead even to a form of gnosticism, as has been argued in detail in Harold Bloom's and Philip Lee's studies, both protests against the Protestant "exaltation of the elite self as against community."[63] Many of the same characteristics of the gnosticism of the second century, which was opposed by Irenaeus (specifically, the promise of salvation by knowledge rather than by faith; stress upon secret or hidden, as against open and available revelation; disregard and devaluation of nature in favor of the pure, free, and unencumbered spirit; and concentration upon the radical individuality of the self) reassert themselves as much in Protestant evangelicalism as in Christian gnosticism or even New Age gnosticism.

As James Hunter has shown, the "new generation" of evangelicals has gone beyond the harsh self-denial and rigorous self-discipline of ascetic Protestantism. Since the mid-1960s, evangelicals have been one more (sub)cultural movement toward the accentuation of subjectivity and the virtual veneration of the self, directed toward self-understanding, self-improvement, and self-fulfillment. Visit any "Christian" or "Family" bookstore near your local shopping center if you have any doubt about this. "Though it might be supposed that Evangelicalism would be more resistant to change along these lines, traditional assumptions about the self appear to have weakened substantially here as well. There are, in fact, strong indications that a total reversal has taken place in the Evangelical conception of the nature and value of the self."[64]

A similar critique is offered by Yale postliberal theologian Paul Holmer when he argues that in evangelical religion subjectivity replaces the process of actually becoming Christian. "It is as if the evangelicals' interest in having a converted, sin-forgiven new life in Christ, with all its biblical vividness, is seriously diverted by too much emphasis upon one subjective power at the expense of all the other powers and capacities. . . . Surely it is an oversimplified psychological account which would allow us to think that believing would produce loving and hoping. Why not loving producing in some cases the believing?"[65] And Gary Dorrien, Professor and Chair of Religious Studies at Kalamazoo College, although speaking of the evangelical preoccupation with truth and inerrancy instead of the turn to the subject, nevertheless speaks of evangelicals as "antimodernist modernizers" because of their adoption of the agenda and guidlelines of modern epistemology.[66]

The dilemma so many evangelicals face in straddling th fence between the orthodox christology of the tradition they claim to uphold and the modern evangelical piety of an immediate, subjective, and private experience they so sanction has been described in some other recent sociological and literary analyses of American religion. "American religion," if there is such a thing, has been deeply shaped in all its forms by the kind of evangelicalism I have been describing. Robert Bellah and colleagues call the kind of American faith described here, devoid of any creeds or contact with a normative tradition at all, the religion of "individualism," or, as he otherwise designates it, "Sheilism," "just my own little voice."[67] Their samples include typical Americans across the theological spectrum.

In a somewhat more exasperating analysis of North American religion, which tries to show how evangelical faith has become a version of the subjectivism so characteristic of other forms of American religion, Bloom argues that the quintessential American religion, including everything from the Mormons, Christian Science, Seventh Day Adventism, Jehovah's Witnesses, Pentecostalism, the Southern Baptist Convention, and African American religion—in short, so much of Protestant evangelicalism—to new age religion, is essentially gnostic in character.[68] He calls the typical American faith, liberal *and evangelical,* "gnosticism." North American evangelicals, he claims, do not strive to maintain the faith of the tradition or the authority of the tradition, and especially do not pay any respects to the institutional forms of Christianity. Indeed, they appeal to a highly selective "Jesus" of their individualistic religion and not to the Christ of the creeds at all. "Urging the need for community upon American religionists is a vain enterprise; the experiential encounter with Jesus or God is too overwhelming for memories of community to abide, and the believer returns from the abyss of ecstasy with the 'self' enhanced and 'otherness' devalued."[69]

The "Jesus" who is "standing" at the center of this experience, according to Bloom, is a very solitary and personal American Jesus. He is, furthermore, the resurrected Jesus rather than the crucified Jesus or the Jesus Christ who has ascended to the Father. Indeed, Bloom makes the interesting argument that, given the sectarian ideal of the primitive church in so much American evangelicalism, the Jesus of American evangelical faith is a highly selective Jesus from the New Testament who is continued in the contemporary context. "When they speak, sing, pray about walking with Jesus, they mean neither the man on the road to eventual crucifixion nor the ascended God, but rather the Jesus who walked and lived with his Disciples again for forty day and forty nights [following the resurrection]."[70] Jesus is the resurrected friend, walking and talking to me along the side of the road or "beside the Syrian sea" or "in the garden" in moments of private luminosity with the repentant sinner. "He walks with me, and he talks with me, and he tells me I am his own." What is missing, according to Bloom, is "simply most of historic Christianity," and certainly anything like the Christ of the creeds and of theological orthodoxy.

Though I sometimes think Bloom does not have a very subtle grasp of the complexity of the evangelicalism he is describing, he does, however, seem to be on to at least one characteristic of evangelical christology that

sets it (unconsciously and unintentionally) quite apart from historic christology and marks it as *a very modern form of christology*. The validity, truth,
and efficaciousness of the reality of Jesus Christ depends on being authen-
ticated by the private, autonomous, subjective individual, which is the
essence of modern liberal culture which stands in stark contrast to traditional cultures, the authority of tradition, even postmodern forms of
Christian faith.

On its soteriological side, evangelical christology partakes of some of
the same liberal assumptions that have marked liberal christology since
Schleiermacher. It is the redemption experience of the believer that provides the basis for any talk whatsoever about the Redeemer!
Evangelicalism, to be sure, unlike much liberalism, honors the language
of the orthodox creeds, but its heart strings tug it sharply away from
orthodoxy and tradition to the subjective individual in very important
ways. Deep in its heart, I think, evangelical christology is in danger of losing its creative strategy of mediating historical Christian faith into the
modern context, and of being but one more form of modern, liberal christology. Among most evangelicals, the heart finally prevails with its
unique individuality or even gnostic capacities for self-awareness and
self-fulfillment. It runs the risk of identifying the inner experience of the
self and/or the soul with or in (or as) God (as long as the head keeps
affirming the creeds of the church).

What I am arguing is that evangelicalism is one form (and a creative
modern form) of the Western mystical tradition. What is distinctive about
it is not so much a claim to a direct and immediate experience of God but
its claim of a direct and immediate experience of Jesus as a constant companion by one's side or in one's heart. In this respect evangelicalism is at
least an heir, if not a direct descendent, of pietism, with its emphasis on
the religion of the heart, and especially its emphasis on the new birth and
new life in Christ. The dilemma, however, as I see it, is that in fact its christology as soteriology is rooted too deeply in a distinctive kind of modernity, specifically, an American form of individualism or subjectivism, and
in extreme cases, a form of gnosticism. Obviously, this critique does not
mean evangelicalism is wrong or bad faith. It does, however, question
whether the evangelical claim to be the sole authentic bearer of orthodox
christology as an alternative to modernity in contemporary America will
stand analysis.

Although there is not a distinct(ive) evangelical christology in the sense
that evangelicals offer a christology which differs from the formulations
of one substance, three persons, and one person, two natures, there is nevertheless an implicit danger in its soteriology of subordinating this
creedal christology to more important concerns and claims about the
inner life, or even implicitly denying orthodox christology, by eliminating

it from the vocabulary and purview of the believer in favor of personal experience. Orthodox christology is usually unspoken in evangelical faith, and sometimes it is even ignored because the creeds themselves are "theological speculation" and therefore not really representative of the distinctively inner world of evangelical faith.

There is, nevertheless, a genuinely evangelical type of christology. It presupposes the christology of Nicea and Chalcedon to be the biblical, traditional, and true christology. But the religious core of evangelical faith, and what is creative about it, is the unique way this christology plays itself out soteriologically in its doctrine of the immediate, direct experience of Jesus Christ in the faith of the believer. In this sense, evangelical christology is a distinctive emphasis in answering one of the basic questions in christology: what is the relation of christology to soteriology. Furthermore, evangelicalism is one creative interplay of tradition and modernity. Whether or not it is the only way to accomplish this intrinsic requirement of modern Christian faith is the center of the debate between evangelicals and the various liberal theologians discussed in the next three chapters. Although it is continually in danger of imbibing the worst of modernity from the point of view of one who defends the christology of "the faith of the Christian church," viz., extreme individualism, subjectivism, even gnosticism, it is, nevertheless, one of the creative efforts of Christians in the modern world to come to terms with modernity while intending to be faithful to the tradition. The following chapters explore other efforts at constructing Christian faith in the modern and postmodern context. What makes evangelical christology interesting, authentic, and compelling for many is that it claims that "he walks with me, and he talks with me, and he tells me I am his own." Any Christian shaped by modern consciousness, which is all of us, must come to terms with the interpretations and claims of this distinctive form of christology.

CHAPTER FOUR

Liberal and Postliberal Christologies

In the 1986 movie epic, "The Mission," Father Gabriel, played by Jeremy Irons, and Rodrigo Mendoza, played by Robert De Niro, feature two profound but radically different understandings of Christ. The movie is a beautifully shot historical drama about the fate of an eighteenth-century Jesuit mission among the Guarani Indians in the Brazilian jungle, the Mission of San Carlos. This "mission above the falls" becomes a pawn in the conflict between Spain, Portugal, the Vatican, and the natives, who "prefer the sea and wind not brought any of us to them," a struggle which ended with the Treaty of Madrid in 1750 when Spain ceded seven of its missions to the slave-trading Portuguese. Robert Bolt ("A Man for all Seasons") offers a visually stunning exploration of broad themes such as war versus pacifism, guilt versus redemption, corruption versus innocence, conscience versus the demands of empire, the sword versus the cloth, and politics versus religion. Ultimately Gabriel and Mendoza have to decide whether Christ is identified with institutional religion and the ethic of love (exemplified by Gabriel, the innocent and pacific Jesuit priest who boldly marches into the assault on the village holding high the cross as many of the faithful follow him to their death) or with the sword and the ethic of rebellion and liberation (exemplified by Mendoza, the ex-mercenary and slave-trader who abandons his recent vows and again draws his sword to save the native population from colonial rule, this time against the Europeans who shell the villagers).

Made at the height of the controversy in the Roman Catholic Church over Latin American liberation theology, Gabriel and Mendoza disagree on how to meet the threat to the natives: prayer and passive resistance or anger and armed resistance. Each explores in dramatic ways several questions: who represents Christ (Gabriel or Mendoza), what is the role of a priest (liturgy or revolution), who does Christ identify with (the Church or the natives), and how does Christ work in the struggle between the church, the governments, and the slave-traders (martyrdom through sacrifice or through violence)? Is Christ represented by the priest, his ethic of love, his pacific faithfulness to the cross in the face of gunfire, and the promise of the next life amidst lost innocence and helplessness, or is Christ represented by the ex-slave trader, who resists injustice through armed resistance? At the end of the movie, neither approach is effective, for neither violence nor pacifism prevail, simply the darkness of a very odious period of Western history. Which decision, however, was closer to the Christ each claimed to represent? The ethic of love versus the ethic of liberation, a debate rooted firmly in christology, has been at the core of the divergence between nineteenth- and twentieth-century liberal and liberation theologies. That dispute is embodied in the two main characters of this film.

I. Liberal Christology

In chapter one I discussed modern and postmodern perspectives as they apply to the search for the historical Jesus. In this chapter I expand the meaning of these two terms to the larger context of christology proper; here I use modern and liberal, postmodern and postliberal as nearly synonymous.[1] In theology, the term modern has a narrow and a broad meaning. In the narrower sense, modern theology designates "modernism," a specific school of Roman Catholic theologians toward the end of the nineteenth century which adopted a critical attitude toward traditional Christian dogmas and a positive attitude toward biblical criticism, with stress more on the ethical than the theological dimensions of faith, and a Protestant movement on the Continent and in North America at the end of the nineteenth and early twentieth century with similar commitments. In the looser and more inclusive sense, "modern" and "liberal" are interchangeable terms in the sense that modern culture since the Enlightenment, especially among elites but increasingly within popular culture, has been "liberal" in its assumptions, orientation, agenda, beliefs, and goals. I summarized the liberal perspective in section four of the last chapter. To be sure, there were significant pockets of resistance to modern liberal culture before postmodern criticisms, such as traditionalism (G. K. Chesterton, d. 1936, T. S. Eliot, d. 1965, C. S. Lewis, d. 1963) and fundamentalism (Harold Lindsell, b. 1913, Carl Henry, b. 1913), but liberal values have shaped not only the agenda of self-identified liberals and cultural elites; it has also deeply influenced the assumptions and perspective of persons who identify themselves as conservatives and evangelicals as well, as I discussed in the last chapter. What I explore here are christologies which explicitly adopt the perspective of liberal theology, and some contemporary postliberal christologies which are consciously critical of and an alternative to modern liberal theology.

The sources and language of classical christology go all the way back to the early church and dominated, with minor variations, for something like thirteen centuries, right down to the beginning of the modern period, say 1750. Two key questions since the Enlightenment have been whether the radical discontinuity between the divine and the human assumed in the classical creeds must be sustained, and whether the language of substance or being, which formulates that discontinuity, though used for centuries and enshrined in the ecumenical creeds, is necessary, "if one can find other and more up-to-date expressions in which one can express the problems formally discussed in the language of 'substance' and the like."[2] Liberal theologians have attached less importance to the ontological language of substance transmitted to us in the tradition and have focused more on the present experience of redemption known by the believer through faith in a Christ who has more continuity with us. As a result, functional description and/or metaphysical language of relationship has replaced the classical ontological language of substance or being among liberal theologians since the middle of the eighteenth century.

The key characteristic of liberal christology is that it bases christology on grounds other than the authority and language of tradition, whether that tradition be biblical or creedal. Specifically, it is christology based on an appeal to history (either the historical Jesus or Christian faith as a movement through history) or on human experience (reason, metaphysics, phenomenological description, moral consciousness). Whether it be the rationalistic christology of philosopher Immanuel Kant ([d. 1804], Christ as that moral and spiritual ideal that lodges in every human being), the humanistic christology of the father of liberal Protestant theology, F. D. E. Schleiermacher ([d. 1834], our understanding of what a human being is or can become as the clue to the particular status ascribed to Jesus as the Redeemer), the idealistic christology of the philosopher Georg Hegel ([d. 1831], Christ as the self-emptying of the Absolute into history), the positivist christology of liberal Protestant Albrecht Ritschl ([d. 1889], concentration on historical questions about the life and teachings of Jesus for the ordering of life in this world), or the twentieth-century existentialist christology of Rudolf Bultmann ([d. 1976], kerygmatic claims about the meaning of Jesus Christ for human existence),[3] liberals seek to build christology from below on the assumption of some kind of continuity between the divine and the human. The significance of Jesus for the religious life of the community, known through a social scientific study of either Jesus or the Christian movement, or the significance of Jesus for the inner religious life of the individual or the community, known through philosophical reflection, description of moral life and practice, or description of the religious consciousness of the believer, is the basis for liberal christologies. Jesus is either the founder of a historical movement in history or a shaper of the inner religious life of the believer.

One of the most impressive versions of liberal christology in the twentieth century has been that of Scottish theologian, Donald Baillie (d. 1954). A review of his christology will help set the major contemporary representatives of liberal christology, process christologies, within the larger context. In one sense he participates in the twentieth-century neoorthodox theology of paradox and grace, but he also represents the liberal tradition from Schleiermacher who speaks of incarnation primarily as the *presence of God* or *God's activity* in Jesus Christ instead of divine and human substances or natures conjoined in one person. The ancient understanding was that the world was composed of different kinds of substances or things, and that the relationship between them can be distinguished from the things themselves. The way to attribute uniqueness to Jesus was to claim for him a distinctive kind of substance. Liberals do not hold that substance metaphysics is part and parcel of Christian faith. They think of a functional equivalent of Chalcedon by finding God's unique presence in and through the human life of Jesus in processive and relational terms. "We are not speaking of something that is in principle unique, but of an interaction of the divine and the human which occurs in many different ways and degrees in all human openness to God's presence."[4] God was present to and in Jesus to a distinct degree; what God intended in and through Jesus is unparalleled elsewhere in creation.

Baillie begins with what he takes to be—in very orthodox fashion—the central problem of christology, viz., what does it mean to say that God was incarnate in Jesus Christ? In what sense was Jesus both God and a human being? How could one life be both completely human and completely divine? The key chapter in his classic in christology, *God Was in Christ*, is chapter five. Baillie replaces the language of substances and persons, categories that almost inevitably drive one toward mythology, in the strict sense, of a divine being invading this world from another world "out there," and then returning to that world (an alien on a space ship readily comes to mind), with the language of "the paradox of grace." The language of grace, not the language of substances and persons, provides the model for his entire christology. "A far deeper and greater paradox than those which we have been considering lies at the very heart of the Christian life and vitally affects every part of it. It is what we may call the paradox of Grace. Its essence lies in the conviction which a Christian man

94

possesses, that every good thing in him, every good thing he does, is somehow not wrought by himself but by God. . . . What I wish to suggest is that this paradox of grace points the way more clearly and makes a better approach than anything else in our experience to the mystery of the Incarnation itself; that this paradox in its fragmentary form in our own Christian lives is a reflection of that perfect union of God and man in the Incarnation on which our whole Christian life depends, and may therefore be our best clue to the understanding of it."[5]

Using this model of the Christian experience of grace, then, instead of the language of *ousia* and *personae,* Baillie takes Jesus to be "true God" in the sense that "in the Jesus of the Gospels it is not 'self-consciousness' that strikes us, but God-consciousness. Throughout the story we get the impression of one who, with all His high claims, kept thinking far less of Himself than of the Father. . . . Self-consciousness was swallowed up in His deep and humble and continual consciousness of God."[6] This concept of God-consciousness has been at the center of liberal christologies since Schleiermacher, and we will see below that it moves again to the center of the christology of process christologies.

Baillie's argument, then, is that the fragments of the paradox of grace in our own lives provides us not only with the intuition or insight into christology but also with the very metaphor and model with which to understand the meaning of the incarnation. If it is true of us, "is it not the same *type* of paradox, *taken at the absolute degree,* that covers the whole ground of the life of Christ, of which we say that it was the life of a man and yet also, in a deeper and prior sense, the **very** life of God incarnate?"[7] (italics added).

Baillie's argument is that the difference between Jesus and us is in one sense a matter of degree, but since we are talking about grace and the consciousness of God in Jesus, the matter of degree in him *becomes a matter of kind,* so that we can say of Jesus that because of the perfection of his God-consciousness, he is fully God. Although human choices are always involved in whatever we do, we must remember that in the last analysis such human choice is never prevenient or even co-operative, but wholly dependent on the divine prevenience. We must say that in the perfect life of him who was "always doing the things that are pleasing to God," this divine prevenience was nothing short of incarnation, and he lived as he did because he was God incarnate. Thus the dilemma disappears when we frankly recognize that in the doctrine of the Incarnation there is a paradox which cannot be rationalized but which can in some small measure be understood in the light of the "paradox of grace."[8]

The criticism of Baillie represents the criticism of liberal christology as a type: the issue of continuity versus discontinuity (and absolute uniqueness) in language about incarnation. From the left Baillie is criticized for making Jesus too unique; from the right, he is criticized for not making Jesus unique enough. Thus, John Hick (English-American philosopher of religion, b. 1922) argues that although Baillie wants to make Jesus utterly unique by making the degree of his God-consciousness a difference in kind, he seems not to have noticed "that the idea of the paradox of grace . . . does not by itself entail this. It leaves open the further question of the relationship between the operation of God's grace . . . in Jesus and in other outstanding religious figures."[9] Likewise, evangelical theologian Clark Pinnock considers liberal christology to be inadequate because liberals "see redemptive grace everywhere in the world in principle quite independent of Jesus, though evoked for us by him. God's grace is independent of Jesus in principle. He does not in any way cause that grace to exist. Rather, he is the symbol of it and the sacrament of it. . . . It is a pattern Christology, not a decisive event."[10]

The adequacy of liberal christology, however, is defended by process theologian John Cobb's (b. 1925) different assessment of Baillie's christology. Arguing that at least the Antiochene wing of classical christology might find Baillie's explanation congenial, Cobb says, "In Baillie's account it is clear that God is truly, constitutively present in Jesus. The God who is present has all the characteristics that God everlastingly has. But for true God to be truly present does not mean that every characteristic of God characterizes the one in whom God is present. . . . Chalcedon reaffirmed the Nicene point against Arius that the divine that is truly constitutive of Jesus' person is truly God—not a preexistent divine being distinct from God or separable from God. Baillie affirmed this too."[11] The issue posed by liberal christology is whether language based on metaphors and/or metaphysics of continuity between the divine and the human is adequate for an idea of incarnation which grounds adequately the kind of redemption the church experiences in Jesus Christ.

II. Process Christology

I now consider the "type" of christology which continues the liberal tradition from Schleiermacher through Baillie, process christology. "Process christology" refers to christology interpreted within the framework of process theology, which in turn is based on process philosophy, the metaphysical visions of Alfred North Whitehead and Charles Hartshorne, the two "fountainheads" of process philosophy. I will not recount the metaphysical scheme in detail but will only refer to some process notions as they apply directly to a process christology.[12]

It is important to begin by recognizing that process theologians are playing the orthodox game. That is, they give high regard, if not normative status, to the guidelines of Nicea and Chalcedon when it comes to constructive christology. This means, primarily, that they intend to promote a doctrine of incarnation and to speak of the full divinity and full humanity of Jesus Christ. Thus, John Cobb, the author of one of the two most important process christologies, says he rejects any minimalist christology. "I share Davis' rejection of what he calls minimal Christology. I share his affirmation of incarnation as central to Christian faith. I share his appreciation of Nicea and Chalcedon as basically faithful to the New Testament witness. I want to think christologically in continuity with them."[13] Also, David Griffin, the other major process christologist (along, perhaps, with British-American process theologian, Norman Pittenger) is as direct as Cobb when he says his purpose is to speak "intelligibly of God's special action or presence in Jesus."[14] Delwin Brown, another American process theologian, is most explicit regarding this criterion when he says, "My view affirms the judgements of the successive Christological councils to the effect that the divinity incarnate in Jesus' humanity is full divinity, that the humanity of Jesus in which divinity was incarnate is real humanity, and that this incarnation in Jesus pertained to the whole of Jesus' person and vocation."[15]

Given the high regard process theologians give to the idea of incarnation and to the guidelines of Nicea and Chalcedon, it is important to recognize that they imply (and the legitimacy of their entire project depends upon) my earlier distinction in chapter two between the creeds as "linguistic rule" and the creeds as metaphysical explanation. If this distinction holds, it means there is a significant difference between accepting the criteria of how one is to speak if one is going to speak with orthodox Christians (fully human/fully divine) and accepting the specific metaphysical language and scheme of the third and fourth century church councils (*ousia, personae, hyothteses,* etc.). The vast majority of process theologians accept the former; they reject the latter as normative for an adequate Christian christology in our age.

Hence, process theologians believe they are completely within the guidelines of Nicea and Chalcedon to offer a process christology based on the metaphysics of process philosophy and theology in place of the metaphysics of classical Greek philosophy in giving an account of faith in Jesus Christ. The most distinctive difference is that process christology replaces a metaphysics of substance (divine substance and human substance) with a metaphysics of events and activity, divine as well as human. While doing so, they claim they remain faithful not only to Jesus Christ but also to the creeds of the early church because what is normative in those creeds is the claim that if one is going to speak with the church catholic one must be able to describe how Jesus Christ is God incarnate and how Jesus Christ is both human and divine. These orthodox claims, they maintain, are quite independent of what metaphysical scheme one uses while working within these guidelines.

To put the claim even more bluntly, one is no more "orthodox" in the strict sense of the term by speaking the language of Greek philosophy (substance, person, hypostasis, etc.) than by speaking the language of process-relational metaphysics (events, relationships, etc.). What is finally normative is *that* one is able to speak of incarnation and full humanity and divinity, not *how* one speaks of either one of these. The debate, of course, is whether or not the metaphysics (the "language") one uses is adequate and fully sustains the claim one is making. But the answer to that debate cannot be decided beforehand or by definition simply because a different language is used. It can only be evaluated after the project has been attempted.

Process christologists claim, then, that a process-relational framework does indeed provide one with a metaphysical language and vision by which one can make sense out of the church's claim without being caught in obscurantist metaphysics (philosophies of substances rather than relationships) or sheer mythology (a divine being who invades this world from another, alien world). Since the guidelines are fixed (incarnation, and truly human, truly divine) but the interpretive content is open (are these notions best conceived in terms of divine substance or divine activity and presence?), process theologians believe they are free to offer a new interpretation of Jesus Christ today.

What we see in process christology, then, is a current christology offered from within the strand of the modern theology known as the liberal tradition in theology. This stream of theology began at least with Schleiermacher, whose christology focuses on the activity of God in Jesus and the fullness of the God-consciousness in Jesus instead of a divine substance incarnate in human form. One of the key themes in every type of liberal christology, then, is the continuity between the human and the divine in a mutual inherence. As a consequence, liberal theologians, including process theologians, are not driven to the radical disjunction between immanence and transcendence, and therefore not to thinking of two radically different worlds (in which one must be invaded by the other), two different realms (which are essentially unrelated to each other), two different kinds of substances (which cannot inhere within each other).

Thus, those Christians who have a strong sense of the immanence of God, of some kind of correlation between the human mind or experience or feeling or consciousness and the divine life, of the importance of human experience and reason in thinking about God, and of the "naturalness" of God's activity in the world (in distinction from supernatural, otherworldly, in-breaking, invading activity of God (a la, say, Kierkegaard [nineteenth-century Danish father of existentialism] and Barth), are likely to find themselves attracted to some form of liberal christology, process christology being but one form of this general type. Christians for whom a radical distinction between the divine and the human must be maintained will likely be unsatisfied, if not horrified, by the too-cozy connection between God and the world in the various liberal theologies. There is a long and respectable tradition in the church, from the early Christian Apologists on, representing these liberal themes in Christian theology, and process theology is one of the recent representations of that tradition today.

John Cobb and David Griffin offer a christology in "processive and relational terms," a christology of the unique presence and activity of God in Jesus who is the Christ. Cobb has published most extensively in process christology. In 1975 he wrote a major book on christology, which has become, along with David Griffin's, one of the two most influential christologies written from the point of view of process theology. However, Cobb has also made some significant changes in his christology along the way, taking account of Jewish and Buddhist, as well as postliberal Latin American and feminist critiques, of his earlier effort.

In his first major essay on christology, Cobb identified Christ as a living symbol, not a proper name or common noun.[16] At the same time, Christ is not an entirely fluid symbol. Christ is also tied to Jesus, either as he was or as he was remembered by his followers. In addition, the symbol of Christ is also connected to Christian salvation and to God. Thus, although Christ is defined in part by Jesus, Christ is also a term more broadly connected to God within a perspective that goes beyond Jesus.

Cobb begins by identifying Christ as the Logos. More specifically, Christ is identified as "creative transformation." The term Christ "refers beyond the language and what the language effects to a power or reality that can be distinguished from human language and has reality even when not named."[17] It is the reality of creative transformation which transcends humanity but expresses itself through creatures.[18] "The Logos in its transcendence is timeless and infinite, but in its incarnation or immanence it is always a specific force for just that creative transformation which is possible and optimal in each situation."[19] It is the principle of order and novelty within the divine creativity. Christ, however, does not simply designate the Logos as these principles, but refers to the Logos as incarnate, hence as the process of creative transformation in and of the world.[20] The implication of this understanding of Christ as Logos is that Christ as creative transformation is effectively, if unconsciously, present and felt in all events in the creation. The Logos is truly incarnate in the world; Christ is a reality in the world. Christ, then, is not simply a name for Jesus or for God; Christ as a cosmic principle points to a reality which exists whether we recognize it or not. Christ is visible even where Christ is denied. The Logos designates the universal reality of creative transformation; Christ is the image which names the Logos as incarnate by which Christians orient themselves and commit themselves.

However, Christ also names Jesus. The Logos as the principle of creative transformation is also Christ as Jesus, specifically through his message and his objective efficacy throughout history. "The conclusion is that the encounter with Jesus' words even today is an experience of creative transformation, or otherwise stated, that Jesus' words can be the occasion for the deepening of the incarnation or the fuller realization of Christ."[21] His objective efficacy continues for those who believe in him today. "The real past event of the crucifixion and resurrection of Jesus, involving his total being, has objectively established a sphere of effectiveness or a field of force into which people can enter. To enter the field is to have the efficacy of the salvation event become causally determinative of increasing aspects of one's total life."[22]

Indeed, Cobb moves on to talk about Jesus' person as Christ, saying, "In Jesus there is a distinctive incarnation because his very selfhood was constituted by the Logos."[23] The Logos constituted the selfhood of Jesus in the sense that the Logos would be identical with the center or principle in terms of which the other elements in his experience were ordered. "In Jesus' authentic sayings an existence expresses itself which does not experience this otherness of the divine. Instead, his selfhood seems to be constituted as much by the divine agency within him as by his own personal past. We may think of Jesus' structure of existence in terms of an 'I' that is co-constituted by its inheritance from its personal past and by the initial aims derived from God."[24] Although Christ is present in all things, Jesus Christ is the paradigm of incarnation. "In that case Christ would not simply be present in a person but would be that person. The distinctive structure of Jesus' existence was characterized by personal identity with the immanent Logos. Hence it is a matter of literal truth to affirm the identity of Jesus with Christ. In all things Christ is present. Jesus *was* Christ."[25]

In Cobb's later writings on christology, creative transformation does not exhaust the reality of Christ for Cobb. He reconsiders his identification of Christ with creative transformation because such an identification comes too close to implying a negative, even hostile, judgment about the other religions. Through more serious encounters with Judaism, Buddhism, Latin American liberation theology, and feminism, Cobb has asked whether the structure of christological thought which identifies Christ with creative transformation is adequate. "The question for me, therefore, is whether a Christology of creative transformation, shaped in the context of reflection about culture, can incorporate—and be creatively transformed by—the convincing insights of liberation christology."[26] In his earlier formulations, he tended to identify the incarnation too closely with Christ. And this implied too much a limitation on the transformation of God to the reality of Christ as Logos. "I now propose that we reject the exception of the incarnation from the general unity of the Trinity in its activities *ad extra*. Let us think instead quite straightforwardly that it is God who is incarnate in Jesus and that this God is the Trinity in its total-ity. Then *Christ* names God in God's relation to the World without limita-tion. . . . It is the Triune God who is incarnate in Jesus. . . . *Christ* names the suffering one as much as *Christ* names creative transformation."[27] Similarly, Cobb's encounter with feminist has prompted him to expand Christ as Logos to include Christ as Sophia. "I am proposing a Christology in which Christ names Sophia as she embodies herself in the world and receives the world into herself. To turn to Christ is to turn away from the wisdom of the world to the wisdom of God. Jesus is the incar-nation of Sophia, the divine Wisdom."[28]

The other classic presentation of a process christology has been offered by David Griffin.[29] He, too, like Baillie, uses an analogy to talk about the meaning of incarnation, but in Griffin's case the analogy is not so much the experience of the paradox of grace as it is the experience of the self as such. God's acts are thought of as analogous to human acts. Instead of the paradox of grace, God's presence in Jesus is thought of as God's univer-sal presence in us as grace. Griffin's question, then, is how to speak of the incarnation as God's special action or presence in Jesus. His basic proce-dure is to claim that we can understand Jesus as a special act of God by using the analogy of the mind's relation to the body.

The mind-body analogy comes straight out of his process metaphysics and works something like this: the act of a person in the primary sense is the mind's giving of initial aims to the cells of the brain, which express the mind's purpose for the body. The mind's action in relation to the body is *formally always the same*. The act of a person in the secondary sense, how-ever, her or his bodily actions, entails great diversity. It is in this regard that we may speak of a special act of a person. When it comes to the mat-ter of special acts, then, we may say that some external actions of a person reflect the character and purpose of the person to a greater degree than others. Those external acts which express a person's character to an espe-cially high degree are her or his special acts. They especially express that character and purpose which constitute the person's deepest selfhood. "For a bodily act to be a 'special act' of a person, it must be of a type espe-cially suited to express his deepest selfhood; it must be based on an inten-tion which especially reflects this selfhood; and his body must actualize that intention to a high degree."[30]

Using this analogy to the self and its acts, then, Griffin speaks of "God's special and unique" act. The analogy works like this: God's primary acts are formally always the same, namely, constituting Godself in each moment by responding to the world, receiving its experiences and making decisions for the next stage of creative advance. A special act will not involve acting in a different way structurally and therefore involve saying God interrupted the normal causal relations. God's *special acts* are God's acts in the secondary sense. Although every event in the world is an act of God in the sense that it derives its initial aim from God, an act is a special act when 1) it is especially suited for expressing God's eternal character and purpose, 2) the event is based on particular initial aims from God that especially reflected God's general aim (although God formally acts the same way for all events, the content of that aim for different entities will differ), and 3) it actualizes the initial aim presented by God to a high degree. [31]

God's *supreme act,* on this model, would be an act in which the second and third of these are actualized to an unsurpassable degree in an event in which a new vision of reality was expressed through a person's words and deeds. Griffin, then, wants to speak of *Jesus as God's supreme act* in the sense that: 1) Jesus' message of word and deed is a vision of reality which contains a new view of God's character and purpose. Its newness consisted of the way varying elements of the tradition were weighed, with God's love given priority over justice. 2) Jesus' active ministry can be understood as being rooted in God's aims for him. He received aims that directly reflected God's eternal aim and his correlative character. He not only had special insight; his special activity was based on impulses given him by God. "Jesus' specialness can be understood as rooted first of all in God's aims for him, the content of which was different for Jesus than for all other men. . . . The aims given to Jesus and actualized by him during his active ministry were such that the basic vision of reality contained in his message of word and deed was the supreme expression of God's eternal character and purpose."[32] 3) Jesus' active ministry was rooted not only in God's aims for him but upon his free decision to proclaim God's will.

In summary, then, Griffin concludes:

> The Christian belief that Jesus is God's decisive revelation can be understood to be a real possibility in terms of the following conceptualization. Partly because of the content of the divine aims given to Jesus during his active ministry, and partly because of Jesus' conformance to these aims, the vision of reality expressed through his sayings and actions is the supreme expression of God's character, purpose and mode of agency and is therefore appropriately apprehended as the decisive revelation of the same. The finality of this expression is due to the fact that at least at decisive moments Jesus identified himself with the divine aims for him, so that he provided no hindrance to the expression of the divine Logos other than that which is inherent in human nature as such.[33]

A wide variety of criticisms have been leveled against process christologies: the efforts to present christology in philosophical language is misled; even if one accepts the agenda to state christology in philosophical language, this metaphysical scheme is incompatible with the historic Christian witness; this is one more gnostic christology which depends on human wisdom (this time, the wisdom of philosophical knowledge in place of the discovery of the true self as divine) instead of divine revelation both for the content and form of the christology; the process philosophical scheme does not affirm the substantialist claims of orthodox christology, so is really an alternative christology to the christology of the orthodox church; any christology from below based on a principle of continuity is simply to name as divine whatever we admire in Jesus, which is, in turn, whatever we admire about ourselves.[34]

However, the most typical criticism is rooted in the difficulties in making claims about the "absoluteness" or "ultimacy" or "supremacy" or "singularity" or "uniqueness" of Jesus as God incarnate in process christologies. I raise this particular issue because it goes to the heart of all christologies since the earliest church: do christologies based on continuity between the human and the divine and between Jesus and us make Jesus Christ sufficient for our salvation? All Christians, liberal and evangelical, agree the answer to this question must be yes. The place where they differ is whether or not "sufficiency" depends on "absoluteness" (or "discontinuity" or "singularity" or "total uniqueness") to be adequate for salvation. The critics of process christologies claim that Jesus Christ of process christology is not sufficient for our salvation precisely because he is not "uniquely unique," and so is not divine enough as the incarnation of the divine substance to be our savior. As noted above, Clark Pinnock argues that Jesus Christ from a process perspective is not special enough for our salvation. We need something "singular" for our salvation. Process christology, so the criticism goes, offers Jesus only as an example, a model, an illustration, a pattern of the universal principle of God's incarnation in all things. But salvation requires a being of substance which is an exception to this principle, and which becomes incarnate, and thereby saves us.

Process theologians respond by asking a series of rhetorical questions. What, indeed, is the biblical claim by and about Jesus? How does the New Testament interpret the meaning of the incarnation, in relational or substance categories? Is the process interpretation an alternative interpretation of Nicea and Chalcedon, or is it faithful to and a legitimate reinterpretation of Nicea and Chalcedon? Is the process viewpoint any less intelligible than more traditional christologies? But the most decisive issue is the question of its religious adequacy. What kind of Jesus Christ is necessary for our salvation? To answer that question, one must simultaneously answer a whole range of other theological questions (how is God related to the world? what is the human problem? what would a sufficient answer be?). Decisions about the adequacy of a process, or any other christology, hinges on one's judgments about the religious adequacy of any christology (which has always, I think, been the central question of and about christology) and about a wide range of other theological conclusions that provide the context for any adequate christology. Regardless of what scripture and tradition teach, we will not let Jesus Christ be anything more or anything less than we think we need for our salvation. For many modern Christians, the only kind of Jesus Christ who can save us is the Christ who shares a divine-human relationship analogous to all humanity and who, simultaneously, incarnates the God side of that relationship in such a way that he incarnates supremely, and thereby salvifically, God with us. Christians oriented either to philosophical thought or christology from below or both are likely to find process christologies intelligible, adequate, and compelling alternatives among the many faces of christology.

III. Postliberal Christology

I turn now to a fundamental alternative to the efforts to interpret the incarnation within the assumptions and categories of liberalism. Contemporary postliberal theologians offer a variety of criticisms of liberalism—its hidden political agenda of repression and exploitation, its delusions about the capacity of reason to objectively know the truth, its preoccupation with the autonomous subjective individual, and its assumption that language is based on experience instead of experience constructed by language. But its primary criticism of liberal christology is that it focuses christology toward abstract theory about humanity and divinity instead of the concrete importance of Jesus for the life of praxis. Although most contemporary African American and Latin American christologies presuppose, or eventually reaffirm, a high doctrine of the incarnation, they typically formulate their christologies in relation to a specific soteriological concern, viz., the significance of Jesus for the contemporary oppressed community.

Those theologians who self-consciously identify their theology as postliberal are part of a larger movement within our culture which can be described as postmodern. The term "postmodern" announces the suspicion, and for many the hope and promise, that the late twentieth-century and early twenty-first-century situation in art, architecture, literature, science, philosophy, theology, politics, the media, and general culture and society has changed so much that it deserves to be seen as a new epoch.

The tag declares the conviction that the present intellectual and cultural situation, especially in advanced capitalist and industrialized societies, is discontinuous with modernity and is at the edge of a new stage beyond it.[35]

Postmodernism has provided a trenchant criticism of the social injustices of modernity. It aims to liberate those groups who have been oppressed by the political power structures of modernity. It detects a shift from European and North American political and economic power and social paradigms to new paradigms and new centers of power that are emerging on other continents, as well as within these two. Specifically, with the waning of socialism and the chaos within capitalism, the center of focus in political and economic power is beginning to move inexorably from the First and Second worlds to the Third and Fourth worlds, and from the Northern to the Southern hemispheres, or at least toward more diversity. Women, ethnic minorities, and other groups long ignored by the keepers of the Enlightenment in North America and Europe, have begun to raise their own voices expressing a different experience and perception of the world.

The late twentieth and early twenty-first-century West has been profoundly traumatized by twentieth-century history. The vast scale, speed, and technological efficiency of "man-made mass death" in our century, beginning with World War I and continuing through Soviet concentration camps, the Holocaust, World War II, Hiroshima and Nagasaki, the continuing threat of nuclear and ecological destruction, and the re-emergence of ancient tribal conflicts, has created a new world context. Many have come to see these mass deaths as the outcome of characteristically modern developments in science and technology, political, sexual, social and economic organization, and forms of "progress" that have had devastating global consequences. They signal the end of modernity, for the continuation of modernity appears to threaten the very survival of life on the planet. Although liberation theologies continue much of the liberal social gospel movement, they are genuinely postmodern. Indeed, postmodern means, in part, liberation from modernity. As David Griffin says, "Liberation theology in the United States should take the form of a postmodern theology, a theology aimed at liberating America and other first-world nations from modernity. . . . Liberation from modernity is a precondition for liberation of third-world peoples and life in general."[36]

However, continuities exist between the modern and postmodern agendas. While Jon Sobrino distinguishes between European (progressive) and Latin American (liberation) theologies, which are "two distinct types" of theology,[37] he considers liberation theology to be one of "two distinct phases of the Enlightenment" (Kantian and Marxist). While both liberal and liberation theology share thoroughly modern goals, namely *freedom*, the agenda of freedom differs between liberal and liberation theology. The first phase of the Enlightenment was interested in the liberation of reason from all authority; the freedom of individuals from every form of dogmatism, from all authoritarianism, from historical error, from myth, and from obscure meaning; the second phase is concerned with liberation "from the wretched conditions of the real world." Thus, both modern and postmodern theologians agree that Christianity must be joined to the project of freedom and that the tradition must be reinterpreted. But liberal theologians were interested primarily in understanding and interpreting the consciousness of the modern individual in its freedom from tradition, whereas liberation theologians are more interested in the rupture of the modern consciousness and change in the suffering of those outside the modern context. These two ways of doing theology, then, distinguish between concern for rationality and concern for transformation. In the former, the question for theology is more the truth of revelation at the bar of natural and historical reason and concern for the meaning of faith in a situation in which this truth has become obscured. The latter discerns a new kind of problem, the problem of the meaning of the real situation, the problem of transforming a reality so that it may take on meaning and the lost or threatened meaning of the faith may thereby also be recovered.

Sobrino claims, then, that modern and postmodern thinkers have different approaches to reality. Modern thought approaches reality through mediations of thought and through dialogue; postmodern thought approaches reality not as an object of thought, but as concrete history to be transformed. Each has a different crisis: the lack of existential meaning in the subject (the believer as believer) versus the crisis in reality itself (meaningless wretchedness). "The first perspective leads to an effort to reconcile faith with the meaningless reality within the subject. The second believes a reconciliation to be possible only if an attempt is made to solve the objective crisis. . . . The enemy of theology has been less the atheist than the inhuman."[38]

For liberation christologies, then, the primary question is what Jesus Christ has to be with liberation from the chains of modernity (injustice). When one reads postliberal christologies closely, however, one notices that the shift is more a reorientation of christology to soteriology than it is an outright rejection of Chalcedon. Furthermore, this shift that occurs is not new. I have already discussed the fundamental blurring of the line of distinction between christology proper and soteriology in most modern christologies, including Jesus research, evangelicalism, and liberalism. Indeed, most twentieth-century christology has argued that christology is inseparable from soteriology, and has argued the priority of the latter over the former. The line of distinction between christology and soteriology has collapsed because we have acknowledged there would be no christo-logical question in the first place apart from the saving significance of Jesus Christ. Also the reversal of the priority of soteriology to christology is based on the modern reading of how the New Testament was formed as witness to Jesus, in part on the conviction that the movement in chris-tology is properly from salvation to christology, the latter reflecting the modern preoccupation with method and the conviction that we can only move from epistemology to metaphysics, from knowing to being, from how we know to what we know.

Liberation christologies as postmodern christology continue the sote-riological focus of modern christology, but thoroughly reshape both the soteriological needs and how Jesus Christ answers those needs. In most cases a strong notion of incarnation is finally affirmed, but in none is the christology either begun or identified with incarnation per se. Christology is in some significant sense "from below." It begins with the historical Jesus and with the cultural context in which salvation through him is experienced. One might even say that christology proper is but one aspect of (and usually subsequent to) the original or primary chris-tological question of salvation through Jesus Christ as liberator. The question, "How is Jesus God?" is set within the context of the primary christological question, "Is Jesus the worker of our salvation today, and if so, how?"

Thus, what is new in the various liberation christologies is not so much christology proper; the concepts of incarnation in most cases remain Chalcedonian. Nor is the novelty a shift toward soteriology away from christology proper; that shift is characteristic of all phases of modern the-ology. What is new is the meaning of soteriology. Postliberal liberation christologies differ from the liberal christologies not so much over the meaning of incarnation as in their understanding of what "below" refers to. They continue the liberal strategy of approaching christology from below,[39] but now "below" takes on a radically different focus because the meaning of the redemption wrought by Jesus Christ is reconceived in a postliberal liberative way. In liberation christologies, "below" refers both to Jesus as one of "the low" as well as to "the low" among the wretched of the earth, more to communities of oppression than to the inner subjec-tive world of the self-conscious individual. For liberal christologies Jesus is constitutive of the inner religious life of the believer, while for post-liberal christologies Jesus is constitutive of the liberation from various oppressions of different communities of believers. "Below" takes on a sociological and political instead of a strictly methodological meaning as in the liberal christologies.

IV. Postliberal African American Liberation Christologies

One of the most significant forms of postliberal christology have been the liberation christologies, interpretations of Jesus Christ pursued in relation to liberation themes, including African American, Latin American, Asian, feminist, gay, and others. In each of these priority is given to orthopraxis over orthodoxy. Recognizing that reflection is inevitably shaped by the lens through which one sees the world, postliberal christology is emphatically grounded in the concrete social and personal experience and activity of particular groups of people. Within liberation christologies, the beginning point is the ethical and practical life of the community, especially the poor, the disenfranchised, the exploited, women, and other minority groups.

We have already considered one element of African American christology when we discussed evangelical christology. African American religious experience typically is characterized by many of the same themes I described in the chapter on evangelical christology; indeed, I consider African American forms of Christian faith to be one of the major components of what we mean by evangelicalism in North America. No discussion of evangelical christology in the North America can be adequately described without a consideration of Black evangelical faith.[40]

As I argued in that chapter, one of the major features of evangelical christology is that the christology, orthodox as it might be, is expressed more in the music of evangelical Christians than in an explicit appeal to the creeds. Both African American orthodox doctrine and postliberal liberation themes are carried more in the hymns sung by believers than by creeds recited or theology written. Thus, in trying to define "Black christology," Lewis Charles Harvey describes the way the camp meeting spiritual, the jubilee spiritual, and the church song answer the question which has been asked by Black Christians since 1619: "What does it mean to 'steal away' to Jesus when one had been stolen away from African and enslaved in America?"[41] Harvey proposes the following thesis: "In Black Gospel music, Jesus Christ is regarded as the answer to the question of the meaning of Black existence. The most fundamental statement made about Jesus Christ is that he is Everything. He is Everything because he is Friend, Protector, and Liberator. It is in fulfilling these roles and functions in the lives of Black people that he is regarded as the answer to the question of Black life."[42] Harvey's Black christology, then, shows how in the Gospel music of the Black church, Jesus is represented as the friend who is concerned about people and their troubles, and is a constant companion who is near and can be trusted to carry one's burdens, as a protector who guides away from danger and possible pitfalls, and as a physical and spiritual liberator of the individual Christian.[43]

The person responsible for founding and defining Black Theology, and for elaborating a Black liberationist christology is James Cone, professor of theology at Union Theological Seminary in New York City. The earliest and still one of the clearest statements of a Black christology of liberation are his second and third books.[44] Throughout these books Cone argues that Christ and black experience interpret each other. Thus, Jesus as God's work of liberation present in scripture interprets the content of God's word of promise to Black people, and the Black church's situation of oppression and liberation provides the context for interpreting the biblical meaning of Jesus Christ. Both are sources and norms for an adequate christology, and they define each other in a dialectical way. One does not move from one to the other, but each reshapes the meaning of the other as one works back and forth from these two sources and norms of christology.

In his first book in systematic theology, Cone proposes a christocentric view of theology. "Christian theology begins and ends with Jesus Christ. He is the point of departure for everything to be said about God, humankind, and the world."[45] The meek and mild, gentle Jesus and the exalted Christ of the creeds are irrelevant to the experience of Black people. Like the theologians of the second and third quest of the historical Jesus, Cone roots his christology in the historical Jesus. "We want to know who Jesus was because we believe that that is the only way to assess who he is."[46] Without some continuity between what Jesus actually was and is today, christology becomes little more than the ideological projection of the self-interests of the group offering a christology. Thus, Cone is in search of the actual historical Jesus of the New Testament. That Jesus, however, is significantly different from the Jesus of the three phases of the modern quest of the historical Jesus. Black theology believes that "the historical kernel is the manifestation of Jesus as the Oppressed One whose earthly existence was bound up with the oppressed of the land."[47] To understand the actual historical Jesus is to understand the degree to which he identified with the poor. To see Jesus in any other way is to distort the actual historical Jesus. Through a critical study of the New Testament accounts of his birth, baptism, temptation, ministry, death, and resurrection, we discover that the real Jesus stood unambiguously upon the identification of God with the poor precisely because they are poor. "The finality of Jesus lies in the totality of his existence in complete freedom as the Oppressed One who reveals through his death and resurrection that God is present in all dimensions of human liberation."[48]

The significance of Jesus Christ for us in our time and place, however, is not his identification with the poor as an abstract concept, but with the oppressed in our society. It is the dispossessed in their situation of oppression and liberation who determine the meaning of Jesus. "We know who Jesus was and is when we encounter the brutality of oppression in his community as it seeks to be what it is, in accordance with his resurrection."[49] In the United States, the oppressed are represented by and as Black people, "Black" meaning both its racial or ethnic designation and the oppressed of the land. Cone is thereby led to speak of "The Black Christ." Jesus is not white in any sense of the term, either literally or theologically. "The black community is an oppressed community primarily because of its blackness; hence the christological importance of Jesus must be found in his blackness. If he is not black as we are, then the resurrection has little significance for our times. Indeed, if he cannot be what we are, we cannot be who he is."[50] Worked out soteriologically, Cone's christology means that the black revolution is God's kingdom becoming a reality in America. "It has to do with the quality of one's existence in which a person realizes that persons are more important than property."[51]

In his subsequent book, Cone elaborates more fully the christology he introduced earlier. Here he emphasizes the social context of any christology, arguing that the social existence of the interpreter is always determinative of the answer to the question "Who is Christ?" "It is therefore the people's experience of the freedom of Christ in the context of injustice and oppression that makes them want to know more about him."[52] For Cone, however, throughout each of his books, there is always a dialectic between the context and the scripture. Context is inescapable; christology is always written for a specific context. But one cannot make Christ into simply anything which might serve the interests of one's context. The dialectic must always take into account the actual Jesus of the scriptures. "Who Jesus is for us today is not decided by focusing our attention exclusively on either the social context alone or the Bible alone but by seeing them in dialectical relation. . . . We must say unequivocally that who Jesus Christ is for black people today is found through an encounter with him in the social context of black existence. But as soon as that point is made, the other side of this paradox must be affirmed; otherwise the truth of the black experience is distorted. The Jesus of the black experience is the Jesus of scripture. The dialectic relationship of the black experience and Scripture is the point of departure of Black Theology's Christology."[53] African American christology also appeals to tradition, but the tradition that is appealed to stretches back to Africa and its traditional religions and to the experience of Africans in America.

In this second book on methodology, then, Cone emphasizes that Jesus is not only who he was but also who he is and will be. "While the wasness of Jesus is Christology's point of departure, thereby establishing Christ's inseparable relationship with the historical Jesus, the isness of Jesus relates his past history to his present involvement in our struggle."[54] To say that Jesus is Black derives primarily, then, from Jesus' past identity, his present activity, and his future coming as each is dialectically related to the other. When his past Jewishness is related dialectically to the significance of his present blackness, we know that Jesus is Black because we know of his soteriological significance for the situation of injustice and oppression in which the oppressed are liberated. "If Jesus' presence is real and not docetic, is it not true that Christ must be black in order to remain faithful to the divine promise to bear the suffering of the poor?"[55]

V. Postliberal Latin American Liberation Christologies

I conclude by exploring how the two poles of all liberationist christology, Jesus and social context, are interpreted in a Latin American context. I refer primarily to Jon Sobrino's, Leonardo Boff's, and Jose Miguez-Bonino's christologies.[56] With them I am describing Roman Catholic and Protestant christology within a Latin American setting. The motivations, shape, controversies, criticisms, and contributions of this particular form of liberation christology are marked self-consciously by the Latin American context of oppression. The context is clearly identified. Indeed, the context is built into the method of developing a christology. In most post-Enlightenment christologies in the West, the white, male, North American and North European interests in shaping the pictures of Jesus and the salvation he brings were hidden under the guise of the claim that the context for christology proper should be, can be, and was, neutral or universal. Universal humanity and timeless reflection were the appropriate media in which to understand the objective truth of scripture or the absolute and universal meaning of Jesus Christ. Latin American liberation christology, on the other hand, like Black liberation christology, not only recognizes the delusion of pretending that any christology was universal and timeless, it builds context and perspective into the very center of the hermeneutic of christological construction.

"Social location," then, is a key term in all liberation christologies. If a christologist is a member of the dominant group(s) in a culture, that person is not forced to recognize their social location because they can assume, or at least pretend, that numerical predominance and social power are identical with universal human situation. Latin American christology, however, like Black christology, argues that it intends self-consciously to construct christology from the situation of oppression, injustice, and exploitation. This "actual situation" in Latin American liberation theology is typically interpreted in terms of Marxist analysis, namely, in terms of "class conflict," where class is understood as the basis of all social organization and conflict as the grounds and nature of all social change. But if other conceptual schemes ("scientific categories") appeared which would provide a more accurate or adequate interpretation, the Marxist categories of most Latin American christology would readily be replaced.

Thus, Jose Miguez-Bonino interprets Christianity in Latin America as shaped by the sixteenth-century Spanish conquest and colonization and nineteenth-century Anglo-Saxon modernization and neocolonialism.[57] The former shaped Christianity according to the manner of semifeudalism in Spain, viz., patterns of land ownership and class stratification. (85% of all fertile land is still in the hands of 5-10% of the population.) The church became subordinate to the interests of these landowning families. In the second phase, the age of modernization, intellectuals from North America presented themselves as in opposition to the old order, but these (Protestant) "liberators" from the North tied the culture inevitably to the North Atlantic system, thereby making Latin America more and more dependent on North America and more and more unified around capitalist culture. Latin America was incorporated into the modern world, but as a junior partner, or as a giving, serving partner in the development of the owner's profit. Domination and dependence became the real meaning of the modern liberal project. As a result, repression, oppression, and exploitation become the key terms in understanding the contemporary social situation.

Because of the distinctive situation in Latin America and the role of the church there, these liberation theologians have been more threatening to the status quo in the long run in terms of their ecclesiology than in terms of their Marxism. The real issue, for these theologians, is what Jesus Christ contributes to change in the social system, including the church as well as the larger society. For them, christology has to do primarily with how the biblical tradition in general, and Jesus in particular, provide us with a spirituality that can energize political attempts to alter the basic structure of the ecclesiastical and social system so that the many no longer need to depend on crumbs from the privileged few. Thus, the christologies that are developing out of the Roman Catholic base communities, for example, and the implications of that priest-led-but-grass-roots development for ecclesiology, is much more threatening to the church and society than theologians who use Marxist categories of analysis.

The real issue for Latin American theologians, then, is more christology and ecclesiology than political and economic theory. The question is not whether or not Marxist analysis is true; it is "true" only to the degree that it proves to be a useful tool for social analysis. The more pressing question is does the living eucharistic presence of Christ (Roman Catholic), or the spiritual encounter with Christ in Bible and preaching (evangelical), leave us with the basis for an activist involvement in the political arena? The answer of the base Christian communities in Latin America has been no. The need for salvation in the contemporary context needs an ecclesiology, and therefore a christology, that is based on more than eucharist or evangelical piety as presented in the older Spanish Roman Catholic Church and modern North American and European theology.

The solution in Latin American christology, as in Black christology, is to build a christology which operates by way of a dialectic between the contemporary context and the historical Jesus. This is the reason liberation christology is preoccupied with Jesus. Dissatisfied with the ideological captivity of traditional sacramental or evangelical christology, they find liberation from the oppression of the current context in the historical Jesus and his vision and embodiment of the Reign of God. In some respects, then, the Jesus of liberation christology looks in some respects like nineteenth-century liberal Protestant scholarship, except Jesus now looks more like a peasant revolutionary instead of a bourgeois German burgher. Specifically, liberationists are interested in the life and teachings of the historical Jesus (they are unwilling to identify him with ecclesiastical christology), and so their scholarship tends to present a historical Jesus according to the same methods and canons of the old liberal Protestant Jesus. But there are fundamental differences from classical liberal christologies. Drawing on their dialectical method, their picture of Jesus is not a bourgeois teacher of high moral inspiration, but rather a messenger of liberation from cultural, political, and economic oppression. Like the older liberals who appealed to the teachings, message, and activity of Jesus, they also appeal to scriptural evidence for a portrayal of Jesus' ministry and preaching. But they uncover his real message by conceiving him in relation to the zealots, Palestinian political life, the Pharisees, the synagogue, and apocalyptic expectations instead of the sermon on the mount to uncover the political posture of Jesus as a liberationist. Liberation stands at the very heart of the message given to the church by Jesus.

The appeal to Jesus, however, is not merely to an attractive model created from academic scholarship. As another form of a christology from below (in this case social as well as methodological), they are less interested, at least originally, in an incarnation christology than in the liberating spirit of Jesus as it is alive in the church as Christ's body in the world. This body is summoned to manifest his spirit and practice in the socioeconomic structures of which it is a part. Thus praxis replaces belief, orthopraxis replaces orthodoxy in christology.

The aim, then, is to give Latin American Christians a better understanding of Christ. Such a christology eventually must be ecclesial, historical, and trinitarian. But the meaning of these three criteria is shaped by the context in which they are developed. That has always been the case of christology, but now different people in different contexts are writing christology, and that christology looks different, in significant respects, from the Christ of most Western christologies. Such an effort does not necessarily repudiate church, history, or even dogma. Indeed, most Latin American christologies end in a high christology. But they recognize the contextual nature of all christology, and so begin below with the significance of Jesus for Latin American oppression and liberation. The picture of Jesus, and of Jesus Christ, looks significantly different from the Jesus Christ of the creeds and of much Western liberal christology. One of the most significant faces added to christology in the contemporary discussion is Jesus Christ—Liberator.

CHAPTER FIVE

Feminist Christology

The setting for the 1996 movie, "Breaking the Waves," directed by Danish film-maker Lars von Trier, is a repressed, closed community with deeply-rooted fundamentalist Christian beliefs, located in the north of Scotland in the 1970s. Bess McNeill (Emily Watson), a naive, simple-minded, but deeply spiritual young woman, who loves all the normal human experiences her community frowns upon, meets and falls in love with a Danish oil-rig worker from outside the village, Jan (Stellen Skarsgaard), an unbeliever. According to the elders of the community who rule with an iron fist, life is not for enjoyment; it is for serving God. Sex is not for pleasure; it is for procreation. Outsiders are not welcome; they are consigned to hell. Bess, however, finds herself happier married to Jan than she ever could have imagined. The miracle of mutual sexual expression has transformed her. But when Jan returns to his rig to earn a living, Bess prays to God that he soon return to stay. Jan does return to stay, paralyzed, his neck broken in an accident aboard the oil rig. As Bess and Jan are unable to enjoy a sexual relationship, Jan urges her to take another lover and tell him about the details of the sexual encounter. "They will keep me alive," he insists. Bess believes that God is testing her and Jan's love, much the way God tested Job. This makes her more deter-mined than ever to fulfill Jan's request and sacrifice whatever she can for his good. First, she tries to seduce a friendly doctor, and when that fails, she is reduced to fondling a stranger on a bus, then dressing like a prosti-tute and picking up men at bars. Every time she has a sexual encounter, Jan's condition improves. She comes to believe she can keep her dying husband alive by prostituting herself, sacrificing herself to sexual brutal-ity to save the life of the man she loves.

As Bess becomes more and more deviant in her sexual behavior, she comes even more convinced that her actions are guided by God and are helping Jan to recover. The point seems to be that Bess, with her fierce faith, believes that somehow her sacrifice can redeem her husband's circumstances. And her sacrifice, apparently, does; Jan recovers. "God gives everyone something to be good at. I've always been stupid, but I'm good at this." She believes her willingness to sexually debase herself for Jan is his salvation, so much so, that she is willing to be with men that seasoned prostitutes are afraid of. She doesn't care what others think because inside she knows what she is doing is right. Her best friend, Dodo, the only supporter of the marriage, is enraged as whispers go about the village, asking Bess, "Are you sleeping with other men to feed his sick fantasies? His head's full of scars—he's up to his eyeballs in drugs." It is never quite clear why Jan, an apparently good man, has made this request of the woman he loves—because he is himself cruel and twisted, because he is selfish and desperate, or because he is trying to trick her into having a fuller life.

This disturbing story forces some ideas on the viewer that must be unequivocally accepted or rejected; the viewer needs almost as much blind faith as the heroine to understand the story. One seems to be asked to swallow the story's premise whole: blind faith can bring real good from horrific degradation. On one level, at least, the story strikes any modern, reflective, and moral person as a desperate, sullen, and even sick tale. However, Christians who know the story about Jesus may find this tale to be more complex and ambiguous than our modern sensibilities suggest. Is Bess' behavior insanity or emulation of Jesus' sacrifice? Can reason, medical science, self-respect, and even sanity coexist with the irrational, the spiritual, the miraculous, and redemptive self-giving love? Any modern Christian, alert to feminist or even humanistic concerns, will surely ask, is not Bess the most obtuse person one would ever want to meet? Is not she undergoing self-destructive delusions? If lovemaking is truly spiritual and redemptive, how can Jan find salvation through Bess sexually debasing herself? Is not pure misogyny at the core of the film? Are not she and Jan disasters psychologically and morally, zeroes out of ten on the self-respect and moral consciousness scale?

Yet, Christians who know the story of Jesus and Christian theology may also ask, is Bess not like Jesus, a self-giving instrument of salvation? Does she not possesses a radical (Abrahamic and Kierkegaardian) faith which survives in a society and a community shaped to deny it? How much of this story is insanity, and how much is redemption? The movie raises christological issues in the most dramatic, stark, and unavoidable ways, for the perspective Bess represents has deep theological foundations in the Christian story of salvation. Bess' sufferings parallel those of Jesus—

she is condemned by the holders of the Law, suffers for the sake of the one she loves, and ultimately offers a path to salvation for him. Is not this story a cinematic christological parallel to the story of Jesus? Is Bess a sinner, or is she the very kind of person Jesus himself was, sacrificing himself on the cross for the atonement of the world? "They [Jesus and Bess] entail not a defilement of goodness but an embodiment of goodness. This goodness seems absurd to others. But then the world saw Christ and 'knew him not.'"[1] Is this not a story of redemptive martyrdom? Through the sacrifice of her life as a result of a beating, Jan's life is changed. "Bess embodies absolute love, pure innocence and the paradoxical combination of joy and terror in following God's commands. So is Bess a convincing Christ figure?"[2] Or, must we condemn the perspective of the film as misshapen christology? Or is perhaps christology itself the root of the problem? "This film says that because of a woman's sacrifice (in this instance, her total sexual degradation, even unto death), a man is healed and returned to functional life. Does anyone in this brutally sexist civilization really need that story again?"[3]

This story, then, poses two profound questions for contemporary christology. First, how are we to respond to a story in which a woman defines herself primarily in terms of her relationship to a man (in this case in relation to her husband whom she loves), and the meta-story in which women define themselves and their relation to God primarily through their relationship to another man (in this case the man from Nazareth)? Second, can we defend a theology of redemption in which human wholeness is achieved through the sacrifice of one person for another (in this story, a woman's sacrifice of herself for her husband), and in the meta-story a man whose cross and death is the only basis of redemption of all relationships human and divine? This chapter will deal with the former question; the next chapter will deal with the latter question.

I. Why Christology Is a Decisive Issue in Feminist Theology

The problems arise for feminist theology because of the definitive role that Jesus—the man from Nazareth—plays in historic orthodox as well as modern liberal and postliberal christologies. Both in scripture and the Nicean and Chalcedonian creeds, Jesus himself, who is called the Christ, is unique, definitive, archetypal, and normative both for the Christian understanding of the nature of God and of human beings. In addition, he is decisive for the Christian's relation to God, to the community, to other human beings, and to oneself. He, the man from Nazareth, is the criterion for full or complete humanity. The fully human person is Jesus, the man from Nazareth. This fundamental claim of Christians in their scripture, in their liturgies, and in their creeds has become a major stumbling block for many Christian feminists in their efforts to think through their response to Jesus Christ. "Of all the doctrines of the church christology is the one most used to oppress women."[4] Why is this primary claim by the church such a problem for some feminist Christians?

The problem with christology for some feminists "is that Jesus was a male human being and that thus as a symbol, as the Christ, or as the Second Person of the trinity, it would seem that 'God' becomes in some way 'male.'"[5] The problem is not so much that Jesus was a man, but that this man is considered unique, symbolic of God, even God Himself. "The specific Christological problem lies in the fact of a male savior, the significance of the maleness of Jesus, and the uses and effects of the male Christ symbol for the lives of women."[6] A symbol of divinity and complete humanity which is male seems not to include all of humanity, or at least to give male human beings privilege. "Is it not the case that a religion in which the Godhead is represented as male, or central to which is a male human being, necessarily acts as an ideology which is biased against half of humanity? Is it not the case that such a religion is by its very nature harmful to the cause of human equality?"[7] The maleness of Jesus has become so central to christology and so powerful in reinforcing the patriarchal structures of the church that women are inevitably repressed and oppressed by his maleness. *Essential humanity is identified as maleness when Jesus is made normative for the meaning both of divinity and humanity.* No female consciousness or qualities or experiences are represented in christology with which a feminist can identity. "Christian theology has dignified maleness as the only genuine way of being human, thus making Jesus' embodiment as male as ontological necessity rather than a historical option."[8]

Christology, then, is a key factor in insuring the patriarchy of the religious system as a whole and of the repressiveness of the ecclesiastical system in specific. As the normative human, he establishes the male as normative humanity. Those who have vested interest in preserving the patriarchal system with its male superiority emphasize the maleness of Jesus as the ideal human being, and, indeed, make his maleness an essential component of his humanity and thereby essential for christology. For example, the Second Vatican Council's (1962-1965) statement on the "Decree on the Ministry and Life of Priests" says "Priests are taken from among men and appointed for men in the things which pertain to God, in order to offer gifts and sacrifices for our sins. . . . This was the way that the Lord Jesus, the Son of God, a man sent by the Father to men, dwelt among us and willed to become like His brothers in all things except sin. The holy apostles imitated Him; and blessed Paul, the teacher of the

Gentiles, who was 'set apart for the gospel of God,' declares that he became all things to all men that he might save all."[9] Subsequently, the "Declaration on the Question of the Admission of Women to the Ministerial Priesthood" said: "Because a priest 'truly acts in the place of Christ' there should be a 'natural resemblance' between Christ and His ministers in keeping with the 'sacramental sign' of Holy Orders."[10]

Five years before the "Declaration" of 1976, J. Kilmer Myers, Episcopal Bishop of California, distributed to the public a "Statement on the Proposed Ordination of Women to the 122nd Diocesan Convention, October 1971." His first point in his statement was that a priest is a God symbol whether he likes it or not. The reason is that God is represented in masculine imagery and the male image alone "pertains to the divine initiative in creation." The priest partakes of "Christ's Priesthood which is generative, initiating, giving." The key to his argument, though, was this: "The sexuality of Christ is no accident nor is His masculinity incidental. This was the divine choice. Jesus continued that choice in His selection of men to be His Apostles."[11] The implications of the argument is that maleness and/or male language is essential to the identity of Jesus Christ. Some, such as Mary Daly, suggest that the logic goes even farther. "If God is male, then the male is God."[12]

The presupposition for christology has always been the patriarchal perspective of the scripture and Christian tradition. The biblical framework is patriarchal to the core, not simply in some of the language used. As the context for christology, the Bible assumes God to be a King/monarch who is disobeyed, who requires repentance, and who then offers forgiveness when repentance is offered. The scheme of sin and salvation, set within this framework of power and authority, obedience and disobedience, subordination and repentance is patriarchal not only in language but its construction of the world. Any alternative perspective, such as an earth/fertility/rebirth scheme, is not only ignored in the biblical perspective; it is condemned and repressed as idolatry and subsequently destroyed by the male prophetic tradition. The interpretation of Jesus as God and savior participates in and reinforces this patriarchal structure. The Father/Son relationship, the Messiah who is a king-warrior, the Logos who is the superior in the body/mind dualistic scheme, and the redeemer who liberates us from the earth and our bodies: all of these images and metaphors reinforce an essentially male or patriarchal view of the world. In addition, atonement theories, especially the satisfaction and substitutionary theory of atonement, assume and underwrite a theology of the abuse of the son by the father, and reinforce the worst of the patriarchal scheme of abuse and suffering which is to be endured as redemptive. The patriarchal scheme goes to the very heart of christology. This has caused some feminists to conclude that "through the very nature of

Christology, there can be no Christology which is compatible with feminism."[13]

II. Different Dimensions of the Christological
Problem for Feminists

Not all feminists are as despairing as Mary Daly or Daphne Hampson
about the incompatibility of Christianity and feminism. First, however, it
is important to recognize that there is a continuum of feminists engaged
in christology. I include this survey because of the number of women who
enter my classes believing that unless one is an "extreme" feminist, one
can have no interest in or sympathy with feminist christology. So I begin
by acknowledging there are some women for whom the male Jesus,
including the masculine language about Jesus Christ within the doctrine
of the trinity and christology, is no problem at all. There are, for instance,
to be only somewhat misanthropic, many women who like things the way
they are, not only socially, political, and economically, but also, reli-
giously. They have benefitted, or at least they believe they have, from systems of female-male relations that have been described by feminists as
patriarchal. Ascribing any destructive liabilities to the traditional roles of
men and women as nothing more than a failure to maintain their proper
roles in God's plan, they understand themselves as supported, admired,
and even adored, by women as well as men, as faithful and blessed custodians of these traditional values and virtues. They have successfully
"managed" the system as it is, and they see not only their lives but also a
smooth running social order threatened by any fundamental changes in
worldview and in female-male relations and roles. Any challenge to christology by feminists is a challenge to the properly ordered world of God's
creation.

There are, furthermore, Christian women who are not conscious, or at
least self-conscious, of feminist concerns in the church and theology
because their own past experiences and present circumstances in the
church have not brought these issues to the forefront of their consciousness and aspirations. Their own lives in their home and in their church, at
least as they consciously perceive and interpret them, are not liable to the
abuses, violences, violations, repressions, and distortions that are
described by ideologically oriented and politically active feminists. Of
special significance for christology is the number of Christian women
whose experiences and needs are precisely those described and answered
by traditional christology, viz., they are women for whom sin as guilt
growing out of disobedience and salvation as the forgiveness of the
Father through the substitutionary atonement of his Son Jesus is the core

spiritual issue that a christology must address. This view is particularly characteristic of evangelical women, including both women who have no feminist sensibilities at all, but also many who identify themselves as contemporary Christian feminists, such as Virginia Mallencott, Letha Scanzoni, Nancy Hardesty, and Rebecca Pentz. Any feminist christology, or any christology with feminist themes must, for them, be set within the larger context of the traditional Christian focus on sin and salvation.

Second, there are Christian women for whom the issue of masculine language in christology in general and the maleness of Jesus in particular are interesting theological questions, but are subordinant to other issues of faith and theology. They are not the central or the defining problems of contemporary faith. Jesus Christ as interpreted in scripture and tradition speaks to the central spiritual needs of women today, although the significance of his maleness for christology is something that must be interpreted and negotiated when appropriating the normative tradition because that issue has been raised to consciousness by feminists within the church. One of the three basic "types" of feminist theology described by contemporary womanist Jacquelyn Grant, "biblical feminist christology" represents this point of view.[14] Virginia Mollenkott was an early representative of this kind of feminism, and Rebecca Pentz, another evangelical feminist, represents the same point of view. Scripture and tradition, in their understanding of human need and God's answer in Jesus Christ, are normative, but they are interpreted so as to eliminate, or at least minimize, the sexist and patriarchal liabilities of the tradition. Although they believe Christian faith and feminism are compatible, their appropriation of feminism is measured by the norms of scripture and tradition interpreted through some feminist sensibilities.

Third, there are women for whom "the male issue" in christology is the central theological problem for the church today. Such persons do not claim that all other theological issues are irrelevant or illegitimate, but that our consciousness of the problem is so alive today and the opportunity is so ripe for essential change in the church and in our society that feminist theological concerns must be made the central item on the theological agenda if fundamental reconstruction is to take place. Feminist christology entails a "feminist transformation of traditional symbols, a transformation that tries to take account of the contemporary experience of women and other marginalized groups."[15] This is the view Grant describes as "liberation feminist christology," or "reform christology"[16] and that Kathleen Sands describes as "the moral consciousness of feminist theology" (in contrast to "the mystical and aesthetic voice" of the more "radical" feminists).[17] This view is represented by such theologians as Anne Carr, Patricia Wilson-Kastner, Elizabeth Schussler-Fiorenza, Rosemary Radford Ruether, and Margaret Farley.

For some women within this group the maleness of Jesus and the role of that maleness in patriarchal christology is such a barrier to their own feminist consciousness and religious sensibilities that that issue alone is an all-encompassing question for any reconstruction of christology. Any defensible christology must be reconstructed on some other grounds than the grounds the patriarchal tradition has employed. Insofar as christology is appropriate to female consciousness and identity, the male Jesus as normative for human identity (which as christology leads to idolatry of the male, or, maleolatry) must be repudiated and replaced by a Christ principle, such as gnosis (Elaine Pagels),[18] sophia (Susan Cady),[19] diving deep (Carol Christ),[20] partnership (Letty Russell),[21] or erotics of power (Rita Brock).[22] This is the viewpoint Grant describes as the "rejectionist feminist perspective in christology."[23] Brock speaks of this perspective as "the feminist redemption of Christ,"[24] while Sands refers to it as "mystical and asethetic" feminism or "Goddess feminism."[25] Some have never been Christian feminists but have gone directly to humanism. "I am therefore not Christian not least for the sake of the kind of human relationships which I want to see flourish."[26]

Finally, in distinction from feminist christology, some "African American womanist" theologians have concluded that all of these three forms of feminism are actually White racist forms of christology, at least to the extent that they ignore the christological question as it is shaped outside the context of the White race and the middle class.[27] Feminist christology is as much the problem for womanists as traditional patriarchal christology is. The reason is that feminists have tended to subsume racism under the category of sexism, including even such radical feminists as Mary Daly, and so subsume and so subordinate the importance of race as a form of oppression to gender, as gender in feminism tends to be identified with white forms of oppression and with white forms of liberation. In addition, feminist christology, in its quest for partnership, has substituted coalition and reconciliation as a White woman's ideology in place of womanist liberation. More specifically, feminist christology proposes "fulfillment" as its primary category for feminist christology, and that concern has little connection with a Black woman's concern for "survival." So Black feminism is a contradiction in terms. Womanists such as Grant, then, remain with Jesus as the grounds for a Black female liberationist christology.[28]

III. Varieties of Feminist Christology

Many feminist and womanist theologians are unwilling to accept the indictments of christology as accurate or adequate or exhaustive, or to accept these dilemmas as insurmountable even if they are descriptively accurate. Christian feminists believe the doctrine of Christ is not intrinsically male-centered and that Christ can be shown through new interpretations to support the full humanity of women in their identity as feminists and womanists. There are a number of proffered transformations of the symbol of Jesus Christ which understand the life, death, and resurrection of Jesus of Nazareth, the Christ event, to be liberating and empowering instead of repressing. Many find in Jesus Christ not only the symbol of patriarchy and repression but also of subversion and transformation. How is this possible? Are Christian feminists simply unenlightened, laboring under an invisible burden of false-consciousness? I will examine a variety of transformative responses which "[do] not assert male-superiority as a constitutive Christological principle."[29]

First, although no feminist denies that Jesus was a male, some women have found a positive resource in affirming the maleness of Jesus as significant for christology. They understand Jesus as a reliable male in his day and the most reliable and affirming male in their lives as women. As some of the more conservative "biblical feminists" have argued, "Jesus was a feminist." He was a feminist in the sense that he was a supporter of women and lived within the presence of women. Women were as much a part of reign of God as were men. Beyond the fact that women were among his followers, he was a power for the liberation of women in his day. He was not only a faithful friend and companion, but he preached and lived contrary to the social conventions and expectations of the female-male relationships of his day; his own relationship to women empowered them. He judged patriarchy, he was iconoclastic, he was anti-hierarchical, he was a model breaker. Anne Carr refers to the "liberating stories about Jesus' relationships with women, his daring reversals of patriarchal family, religious, and social orders in relation to the kingdom, the involvement of women in his ministry. . . . Contemporary women find transformative truth in the witness of the New Testament to Jesus remarkable freedom and openness to women."[30]

Furthermore, Jesus' maleness is important because in the first century only a male could model the rule of God as servant because only males had the power and the role expectations for the exercise of the kind of power that can be sacrificed in a redemptive way. Since servanthood was the model for the reign of God, no one would have noticed a woman behaving in such a way since that was the role expected of her. Thus, the maleness of Jesus has christological significance. "The maleness of Jesus is of essential importance for the Incarnation. In order to bring a new word to the world the Messiah had to be a male. Servanthood was indigenous to the role of women in that culture; but a man speaking of being a servant in a radical way? That was new! . . . To the extent that only a man (male) could make this radical agape message clear in a male dominated, patriarchal society—yes, the maleness of Jesus is essential for our understanding of the Incarnation."[31]

The incarnation as male also emphasizes the bodiliness of any meaningful idea of incarnation. It is important to emphasize Jesus as a male in order to repudiate any idea of the incarnation as "anhypostasia" (the idea of an abstract human being which can exist apart from a concrete human [male or female] body). The problem with christologies which define humanity apart from sexual identity is that they do not deal with concrete humanity, which is male or female. "To speak of Christ or women and men abstractly as human beings is to create the illusion that people are sexually neutral and that their bodies do not matter. . . . that sexual difference is ignored or glossed over. . . . The Church Fathers in spite of their grounding in neo-Platonic philosophy, realized that in order to affirm the reality of the incarnation of God in the flesh, it was necessary to stress the sex of Jesus."[32] In such a view, however, the gender of Jesus is significant because it emphasizes the *particularity* of the incarnation, not because it claims that redemption can come only through a male.

Second, some feminists and womanists limit any oppressive use of Jesus to those characteristics of the story about Jesus reflective of the cultural context of the first century. Those features of the story do not belong to Jesus himself. Any anti-female characteristics of the story about him which are not liberating for women are identified with the sexually oppressive elements of the context of the first-century story teller, such as the efforts of the Gospel writers to play down or reframe the role of women among his followers and at the resurrection. These sexist biases are not essential to the gospel story. They exist as conditioned elements in which the transcendent gospel of Jesus is framed. The culturally grounded sexist elements of the record stand under the judgment of Jesus, or the earliest Jesus movement, or the gospel about Jesus Christ. The actual role of women in the ministry of Jesus and in the earliest church, along with Paul's preaching that in Christ there is no male or female, is the "real" or the "persisting" gospel which judges the cultural context of ourselves and even of the scriptures themselves.

Third, most feminists of the "revolutionary" type resolve the problem of the maleness of Jesus by making a significant, if not thoroughgoing, distinction between Jesus and Christ. Jesus is the man from Nazareth from first century Palestine, while Christ is the eternal and universal Logos or Sophia or Eros of God, the principal of salvation, which has transcendent significance past, present, and future, beyond its embodiment in a first century male. This gives the maleness of Jesus no christological significance. Jesus becomes important insofar as he embodies as a human being the Christ principal, or the Logos, or the Sophia, or the Eros of God, not insofar as he was a male kind of human being. This solution minimizes or even eliminates the maleness of Jesus as christologically significant.

One variation of this strategy is the womanist effort to build a liberationist christology in the basis of a dialectic between Jesus of the first century and an African American woman's experience of Jesus today. Grant rejects the usual distinction between Jesus and Christ as a distinction growing out of White feminist's agenda. Nevertheless, in the end she retains something of this distinction. The Black women's experience of Jesus, not a divine principle of creative transformation, or wisdom, or logos, or eros, but Jesus of history is the content of the experience. Her Jesus was a Jew and therefore was Black. Jesus' humanity is important, and it is in his humanity that he is our savior. But, "I would argue, as suggested by both Lee and Sojourner, that the significance of Christ is not his maleness, but his humanity. The most significant events of Jesus Christ were the life and ministry, the crucifixion, and the resurrection. The significance of these events, in one sense, is that in them the absolute becomes concrete. God becomes concrete not only in the man Jesus, for he was crucified, but in the lives of those who will accept the challenges of the risen Savior the Christ."[33] Thus Grant does resort to a concept of Christ, which she calls "the Christ mandate,"[34] even though her Christ is more tied to the significance of the historical Jesus for the life of Black women than it is to a divine force or power or principle, as in much feminist christology. Jesus is the reality of Jesus as the Christ in the life of Black women, where "there is no difference made between the persons of the trinity, Jesus, God, or the Holy Spirit."[35]

Fourth, most feminists and womanists distinguish between the maleness of Jesus and the humanity of Jesus. "The classical doctrine of the Incarnation speaks of the divinity and humanity of Jesus, not his maleness. The focus is on the fully human as a soteriological issue—God's redemption accomplished in a fully human history."[36] There is a long history in the tradition for this distinction, tracing back to the christological controversy discussed in chapter two. The distinction was at the heart of the "anhypostasia" doctrine referred to above, the teaching that Jesus became Man, not a (hu)man. Jesus was both *aner* (male) and *anthropos* ([hu]mankind). It is as anthropos, as humanity or even as flesh that Jesus is significant, not that he became this particular male person as the means for salvation. Although this idea is not identical to the contemporary idea of androgynous humanity, there is some affinity insofar as "human" is not identified either with male or female but with an "essence" which incorporates both. The difference, of course, is that the idea of an androgynous human being includes both male and female characteristics, whereas in this ancient teaching, Jesus is neither male nor female, but is a sort of abstract human being.

It is decisive to note that *the church councils fought for the humanity of Jesus, not the maleness of Jesus*. No one argued that it is Jesus' maleness that is the medium of salvation. Maleness is no more intrinsically capable of incarnating God in human form than is femaleness, although one or the other is essential to any meaningful idea of human incarnation. The key to the ancient confessions of faith is that God as Sophia or Logos became flesh or human, not that God became male. Maleness (or femaleness) is accidental, not essential, to identity as "human." Stated otherwise and positively, both maleness and femaleness are capable of being fully human and incarnating the divine. In the case of Jesus, the full human being was a male, but his maleness is accidental or incidental to what it meant for him to be a full or perfect or complete human being and God incarnate. No creed has ever affirmed the maleness of Jesus for the notion of the incarnation or the notion of complete humanity.

Some feminists have come to see Jesus as androgynous. He is not thought of as male (or female) but as "perfect humanity," true personhood, and therefore as both male and female in terms of his salvific significance. The term is from botany; it means having staminate (pollen) and pistillate (seed) flowers in the same inflorescence. The analogy is that Jesus is both male and female. Presumably this claim refers not to a biological evaluation of Jesus' gender (being a hermaphrodite) but to the range of human qualities that constitute the very center or identity of who he was both in himself and as the incarnation of God. This language of androgyny has been particularly important among feminists who are attracted to some form of gnosticism or to some forms of the mystical tradition as the most appropriate framework in which to talk about Jesus' humanity as well as his divinity.

Fifth, a more revolutionary feminist solution is to limit the role of Jesus in one's faith. It is *what is incarnate* or embodied or present in Jesus that is important, not Jesus himself. That is, the idea or principle or power of Christ present in him is decisive and salvific in christology, although that idea can be present in any or all humans, not only in Jesus. The more one substitutes the term Christ for the name Jesus, the more decisive the Christ idea or principle becomes in christology, and the more subordinate is the place of Jesus, and especially Jesus as a male. Feminists who go this route remind us that the idea or principle of Christ existed long before and far beyond its exemplification or incarnation in Jesus (indeed, eternally and universally in trinitarian doctrine and in process theology). There are many historical and contemporary exemplars of the Christ principle, not just one, neither Jesus of Nazareth nor any other model. He is not the only one to identify as Christ or Sophia or Logos of God, although one may give him a relative importance in coming to understand and even achieve genuine humanity. This effectively limits the christological role of Jesus to teacher or model or example instead of (sole) redeemer, and leaves open the possibility of speaking of the incarnation of God beyond the person of Jesus, such as incarnation in other persons or every person.

When applying the "Christ idea" or "Christ principle" to soteriology, feminists of this type do not talk about Christ in terms of redemption, which depends on the larger patriarchal framework of scripture and tradition. Rather, they talk about salvation in the light of other images and metaphors present in the tradition and in contemporary women's experience. Images such as creativity, eros, wholeness, fulfillment, new humanity, generation, liberation, and a whole host of alternative images supplement, or even replace the traditional language of redemption in soteriology and christology.

The more thoroughgoing form of this strategy has been the renewal of gnostic christologies among some feminists today.[37] They appeal to the non-canonical gnostic writings discovered at Nag Hammadi, and particularly to the Gospel of Thomas instead of the New Testament Gospels. An entirely different picture of Jesus emerges in the Gospel of Thomas. Jesus was a preacher of the kingdom of God, not as an event expected to happen in history, not as a place, but as a condition of self-discovery of one's own divinity or Christness or Christhood. Gnostics appealed to insight (gnosis), an intuitive type of knowledge, which communicates wisdom or spiritual enlightenment to the believer. The resurrection is not rising bodily from the dead but a moment of enlightenment; the virgin birth is a spiritual birth; God is both masculine and feminine; Jesus is not looked to as source of truth but as the occasion for discovery of one's own truth.

In gnostic christology the kingdom of God symbolizes a state of transformed consciousness. "One enters that 'kingdom' when one comes to know oneself. The secret of gnosis is that when one comes to know oneself, at the deepest level, simultaneously one comes to know God as the source of one's being."[38] Who was Jesus in the Gospel of Thomas? Unlike Mark, where Jesus is a unique human, the Messiah, God's appointed king, Thomas' Jesus does not regard himself as the only begotten son of God but as a teacher to his disciples, saying, when you come to know yourselves and to discover the divine within you, then you will recognize that you are the sons of the living Father. *You do not become a Christian but a Christ yourself.* When you read the Gospel of Thomas, you discover that you are the twin brother or sister of Christ; when you recognize the divine within yourself, then you come to see, as Thomas does, that you and Jesus are, so to speak, identical twins. Jesus, therefore, directs the disciple toward his or her own way to discover the divine within oneself. Instead of following him or imitating him, they are to find their own way. "The 'living Jesus' of the Gospel of Thomas points one not toward the church, but toward oneself—toward a solitary, radically individualistic process of spiritual exploration."[39] Such a Jesus serves to undercut the church hierarchy, the creeds, and the canon. He points the way toward one's own solitary, interior search for the truth of one's own divine nature.

Sixth, the most extreme position I will examine is called "the feminist redemption of Christ."[40] Feminist christology, argues Rita Brock, should liberate Christ from the unholy trinity, father-son-holy ghost, that has cradled Christ in its patriarchal arms. Speaking of Christ as the principle of erotic power, "the power of our primal interrelatedness," she attempts to save Christ from captivity to Jesus and to patriarchy. Her christology is not centered in Jesus, but in relationships and community as the whole-making, healing center of Christianity. She moves beyond Jesus as the Christ. Christ is identified as the Christa/Community of erotic power of interconnectedness, the revelatory and redemptive witness of God/dess's work as wholeness of community in history. Jesus neither reveals nor embodies this principle or power of Christa/Community, but himself is brought into being through it and participates in the recreation of it. "If feminism can be reconciled with Christianity, such reconciliation is not possible because Jesus, as the heroic figure, reveals a nonpatriarchal vision of community in which women may participate. The reconciliation is possible because of the work of women and because feminist insights about erotic power intersect with the Christian confession that divine reality and redemptive power are love in its fullness. Using feminist experience and analyses of male dominance and a feminist hermeneutic of erotic power on the biblical texts, it is possible to catch glimpses, within androcentric texts, of the important presence and influence of erotic power within the Christa/Community. Erotic power in the texts sustains and cocreates the whole and compassionate being."[41] Christology, then, relocates Christ in the healing community of which Jesus is but one historical part. The Christa/Community of erotic power is the connectedness among members of the community who live with "heart," the human self and our capacity for intimacy.

IV. Sophia Controversy

I turn now to one form of feminist reconstruction of christology as a case study. Some feminists have tried to reconstruct christology along the lines of a "Sophia christology."

Sophia, the personification of Wisdom, was one of the powerful images in Judaism and early Christianity. She figured prominently in the development of the scriptures, both Old and New Testaments, and in the early church's formation of christology. Sophia continued to be an important image for Eastern Christians—the Emperor Constantine dedicated the principal church in his new capital to Christ as the Holy Wisdom (Hagia Sophia) of God, and the Emperor Justinian rebuilt this great church as a model for all Byzantine Christianity. Until recently, however, Western Christians have not shared this interest in Sophia. Most Protestants are unaware of Sophia, either in scripture or tradition, and Roman Catholics regarded her as an image of Mary (until Vatican II the biblical texts were read on Marian feasts). Thus, when feminist biblical scholars and theologians began to turn to Sophia in the '70s and '80s as a name and image of God and/or for Christ, it came as a big surprise to Western Christians and appeared to be some new heretical development. Sophia appeared to some to be a pagan goddess who was worshiped by so-called Christians in place of the trinitarian God.

Sophia became an explicit point of christological controversy as a result of the publicity throughout the church about a meeting held in November 1993 in Minneapolis. A "Re-Imagining Conference" was sponsored by various ecclesiastical groups as part of a World Council of Churches effort to participate in the United Nations Decade in Solidarity with Women. The conference featured some of the "big names" in contemporary feminist and womanist theology, such as Rita Brock, Beverly Harrison, Delores Williams, and Ada Maria Isasi-Diaz. Critics of the conference, almost none of whom were at the conference, charged the planners and participants with affirming paganism, lesbianism, and other "deviations" from traditional Christian theology, especially with their repudiation of traditional christology and redemption theory. The controversy has been particularly virulent in the United Methodist Church and the Presbyterian Church USA. Indeed, reaction to the controversy prompted the resignation of Mary Ann Lundy, associate director of church-wide planning for the General Assembly Council of the Presbyterian Church USA. Reaction to "The Re-Imagining Conference," then, provides a recent example of the polarization over christology within the mainline Protestant churches in the United States.

"The Sophia controversy" is a controversy which, magnet-like, attracts most of the frustrations and controversies within the contemporary mainline Protestant denominations.[42] Who teaches doctrine in the name of the church? Who determines the theological answers to hard questions, and how?[43] Who can sponsor what conferences in the name of the church? Who can develop and sponsor what liturgies for the church in Christian worship?[44] Is there such a thing as heresy in christology today? When, if ever, can it be said that members of Christian churches worship a god other than the God of Abraham, Sarah, Rachel, and Jacob, the God known in and through Jesus Christ? If answers to these questions can be discerned, what is to be done about those who believe and teach outside the guidelines determined by answers to these questions? Finally, when, if ever, can it be said that groups within Christian churches on either side manifest an uncharitable disposition, and distort, ridicule, and arrogantly judge the faith of other believers? If it can be so discerned, what is to be done by the church?[45] These are but examples of the wide range of questions "the sophia controversy" gathered like a strip of Velcro in the mainline Protestant churches. The controversy was about political power, economic power, and inclusion and exclusion, as much as it was a contemporary version of the christological controversy discussed in chapter two. It was, also, however, a virulent debate about christological doctrine.

Sophia plays a significant role in scripture, Old and New Testaments. This is news to most Protestants, who functionally omit her from their Bibles. *Sophia* is the Septuagint and the New Testament translation of the Hebrew *hochma*, both of which are grammatically feminine. The Hebrew wisdom tradition, in its later cosmopolitan phase, extended this grammatical construction to a personified female.[46] In the Old Testament the female image of Sophia appears as "a secondary persona of God, mediating the work and will of God to creation."[47] Although behind the image of Wisdom, at least some have suggested, lies a goddess who was traditionally characterized as Wisdom, in Hebrew thought "she has become a dependent attribute or expression of the transcendent male God rather than an autonomous, female manifestation of the divine."[48]

Proverbs, the key book for Sophia imagery, describes Wisdom as an "offspring" of God, brought forth from God before the beginning of the earth, cooperating with God in the creation of the world, rejoicing and delighting in the work of creation.[49] In chapters 1-9, Wisdom is frequently personified in female form and praised in exalted terms (1:20-23; 3:15, 18; 8:1-6, 19). Yet Wisdom, as noted above, is not a separate divine being, but rather a personification of one of Yahweh's attributes. In the creation narrative of Proverbs 8:22-31, Sophia's cosmic stature is revealed (8:30, 32), where she is either a master architect or darling child of God, who plays throughout the world she helps to create and delights in human beings. "The Bishops' Statement on Wisdom," published by the Council of Bishops of the United Methodist Church in response to the controversy stimulated by the Minneapolis conference, summarizes the current scholarship on Wisdom by saying, "As the passages stand in their literary context, Woman Wisdom is best considered to be a personification of an attribute of God and not a goddess or a being with separate existence from God . . . . Wisdom may have been modeled on Egyptian and Canaanite goddesses, but Woman Wisdom as a goddess is non-existent in biblical literature. She is portrayed as a sprightly figure, distinctly unsexual when it comes to her relationship with God at creation. She most definitely is not the wife or consort of God. Nor is she a competitor or substitute for God. Woman Wisdom was never an object of cultic reverence."[50] Catherine Keller comments that "it does not take much subtlety to note what was also clear to the earliest Christians: she anticipates the interpretation of Christ as precreation Logos."[51]

In the Synoptics, especially Matthew, Jesus teaches more in the form of the wisdom tradition than the prophetic tradition. Specifically, Jesus is Wisdom personified in the Gospel of Matthew and is Wisdom's prophet in the Gospel of Luke.[52] In the Gospel of John, the Hebrew concept of Wisdom helped shape John's concept of Christ as the Logos. Jesus as the Christ is identified and described in language similar to Israelite Wisdom.[53] Like Wisdom, the Word was with God from the beginning (John 1:1-2, Proverbs 8:22-23, Wisdom 6:22, Sirach 24:9). Both manifest God's glory (John 1:14, Wisdom 7:25) and bestow light and life (John 1:9, 45; Wisdom 7:26; Proverbs 3:18). Like Wisdom, the Word descended from heaven to bestow God's truth (John 1:14, 17-18; Sirach 24:8-11; Baruch 3:37; Wisdom 9:9-10) but was not generally received (John 1:11, Proverbs 1:24-27, 1 Enoch 42). Sophia, the Wisdom of God expressing God's immanence, the presence of God in creation, revelation, and redemption, was identified with the Logos and taken over to explain the divine identity of Jesus.[54] "Theologically, Logos plays the same cosmological roles as Sophia as ground of creation, revealer of the mind of God, and reconciler of humanity to God. The use of the male word Logos, when identified with the maleness of the historical Jesus, obscures the actual fluidity of the gender symbolism by appearing to reify as male a 'Son of God' who is, in turn, the image of the Father."[55]

Jesus Christ as the Wisdom of God is found in Romans 11:33, Ephesians 3:10, and Hebrews 1:3 (which seems influenced by Wisdom 7:25-26). Paul explicitly calls Jesus Christ "the wisdom of God" (1 Corinthians 1:24, 30). Wisdom imagery also lies behind the christological hymns, such as Colossians 1:15-17.[56] This text, along with Hebrews 1:2-3, and John 1:1-18 are the three most extensive New Testament affirmations of Christ's deity. While passages in Hebrews 1-2 and elsewhere also echo the Wisdom tradition, the term Logos, which is used by the Jewish philosopher Philo, is usually preferred to Sophia.[57] The roots of the Logos concept in the Wisdom tradition, however, are still evident, as in 1 Corinthians 1:23-24, and in the primary christological hymns of the New Testament. The Sophia image, then, hardly forms some peripheral, unorthodox element in Scripture.[58] As the Bishop's statement claims, "Wisdom clearly becomes Christocentric in the New Testament."[59]

In a matter of time, however, the church followed the pattern of Philo, giving predominance to Logos, grammatically masculine, as the key term. "Philo of Alexandria used Sophia and Logos interchangeably as symbols of the working of God in the world, but Philo also insisted on the male

Logos as superior to the female Sophia and thus prepared the way for the substitution of Logos for Sophia."[60] Nevertheless, the early church theologians refused to abandon Sophia to the Gnostics. They followed the lead of Philo and identified Sophia with the Logos, and thus, in light of the Fourth Gospel, with the divine in Jesus Christ.

Numerous orthodox Jewish and early Christian texts, then, have identified Sophia either as an 'hypostasis' or an attribute of God. She represents a biblical vision of the Wisdom or Word by which God creates, guides, and redeems. "This Sophia, not a goddess but simply a biblical female metaphor for the Holy, is what a few pastors and theologians have presumed to explore. She has offered a luminous—if rather modest—point of connection between traditional biblical language and the feminist evolution of faith. She does not replace but rather refreshes traditional talk of God and Christ."[61] However one exegetes specific verses referring to Sophia, the basic point is clear: the central New Testament passages which affirm Christ's deity draw on language about the Wisdom/Sophia as well as the Word/Logos of God. "Feminists find the latter view most convincing within the monotheistic setting: we have to do with a feminine personification of God's own Wisdom."[62]

Feminist biblical scholars and theologians, then, have shown how deeply rooted the christology of the New Testament is in the wisdom tradition of scripture. In doing so, they have provided biblical grounds for including feminine imagery at the heart of christology, thereby not only critiquing sexist christologies, but also increasing the depth and breadth of meanings of Christ today. What is important for catholic Christians who are upset by this development as a new heresy to recognize is that most feminists distinguish Sophia christology from a Sophialogy.[63] In the latter, Sophia is a goddess (an alternative Goddess to the male God) of whom Jesus is her prophet. Sophia christologies, on the other hand, speak clearly of the one God. Sophia is in some cases another a name for the one true God, an alternative to Yahweh or Trinity as divine names. For most, however, she is an aspect of God, a personification of an activity of God, a mode of the divine being and economy expressed in feminine imagery. Most Sophia christology works within the traditional Christian faith, identifying Sophia (or thinking of her as analogous to) the second person of the Trinity, the "one" who became incarnate in Jesus. This kind of christology employs the image of Sophia, with its female characteristics and implications, instead of the Logos, with its male characteristics and implications, as a basis for broadening and reconstructing christology. But there is only one God, the God who is truly God as much as the God who is spoken of in male language is said to be truly God.

There are, to be sure, critics of the use of Sophia imagery in christology who want to shatter sexist christology and to include female imagery at the core of the meaning of Jesus Christ today. Can Christians speak of Christ as the Sophia of God? Can Christians pray to Christ as Sophia? The problem, apparently, is this: critics claim that although sophia imagery might be present in the scripture and applied in tradition to Jesus Christ, it is used by feminists to designate a non-Christian deity, and this is what Christian feminists who employ Sophia language about God and Christ are advocating when they talk about a Sophia christology. I read the claim that there was an ancient Near Eastern Goddess named Sophia, and that "neo-pagan feminists" are reappropriating that use of the term and are thereby replacing the triune God with this alternative Goddess named Sophia, clearly an idolatry and a heresy as fundamental to trinitarian Christianity as one could possibly imagine. Thus, Bishop Earl Hunt says, "No comparable heresy has appeared in the church in the last fifteen centuries. . . . This is material which must be eradicated from Christian thinking now." Thus, the critics' unabashed claim is that sophia christology is a heresy.

I have yet to find one footnote among these charges to a source naming, referring to, or describing a Goddess named Sophia. Professor Larry Wellborn, my colleague, who has researched my question, claims there is no evidence that there existed in ancient times a goddess religion which worshiped a goddess named Sophia (though there were many goddesses in ancient cultures). Sophia, who is an alternative goddess of a "pagan" religion now being adopted by Christian feminists, seems to exist only in the imagination of critics and not in history. As Catherine Keller says, "The heresy hunters themselves have created the goddess Sophia. She is their projection, their obsession."[64]

Nevertheless, facts have little to do with this debate. Some people believe there was such a Goddess who was an alternative to God, and believe that the replacement of the trinitarian Christian God with this Goddess as object of worship and theology is the agenda of sophia christology. What matters here is that people believe that certain feminists are advocating a replacement of Christian trinitarian theism with a neo-pagan feminist Goddess named Sophia, not what evidence there is or is not about such a goddess or about such a feminist agenda. To be sure, there are some thoughtful and subtle critics. Thomas Oden has tried to keep some kind of balance within his criticism of sophia christologies. He is critical of those feminists who use only those wisdom passages that seem to reify Wisdom into a deity distinguishable from the Triune God as their language for the divine. It is the reification of wisdom that creates the problem for him, for reification treats the idea of Wisdom as a personal deity differentiated from the holy Trinity (sophiology). However, he argues, as long as the wisdom tradition is interpreted as an "anticipation" of the Word of divine wisdom in creation which becomes in due time incarnate in Jesus, the use of the idea of sophia in christology is acceptable, indeed, it stands in a long line of orthodox exegesis. "Ancient ecumenical Christianity has welcomed measured nonidolatrous attempts to view sophia as a type of Christ, a view familiar to the history of orthodox exegesis."[65] However, when sophia is reified "as a goddess," Oden argues, "no one would ever expect faithful women to sit by compliantly. It is only when a docetic-gnostic view of wisdom is bootlegged into the liturgy in order to try to validate radical feminist political objectives that the integrity of the Eucharist is called into question. The boundary has been crossed when the idea of *hochma/sophia* is reified into a goddess who speaks 'feminese'."[66]

V. The Contribution of a Sophia Christology

There are, I must grant, proposals to use Sophia language in liturgy and theology as an alternative to the (male) God of classical Christianity. Equally problematic are feminists who employ the name in a systematically ambiguous way so as to avoid or even deflect the question of whether Sophia is an alternative or a complementary image to apply to God. This ambiguity contributes to the openness and richness of the discussion; it also contributes, I suspect, intentionally or unintentionally, to the routine name-calling on both sides of the argument because the usage remains so undefined as to be open to many interpretations.[67] However, there are many feminists who explicitly use the term Sophia within a traditional christology, who maintain that we can enrich the meaning of traditional christology by making Sophia an important or even central category in christological thinking. Two important advocates of Sophia christologies today are Elizabeth Johnson[68] and Susan Cady.[69] Neither of these theologians seeks to establish Sophia as a Goddess, or any sort of divine feminine being superseding or replacing the biblical God or Christ. Sophia christology, it is clear, is a strand of biblical thinking about Jesus Christ. Orthodox christology drew on Sophia images and themes. The tradition, however, ignored or repressed this resource of the tradition. Contemporary Sophia christologies are enriching christology by recovering female dimensions of the meaning of the incarnation of God in Jesus Christ. Orthodox christology needs Sophia christology to elaborate the full reality of the incarnation.

Sophia christology has been defended by evangelical feminists, such as Rebecca Pentz, who argues that following Jesus does not require relinquishment of feminist principles, and that an orthodox christology does not contradict feminism.[70] She defends Sophia christology by distinguishing between Sophia christology and Sophialogy. Indeed, she argues that

Sophia is the mother of incarnational christology. In the New Testament Lady Wisdom is identified with Christ.[71] In the Prologue to the Gospel of John, Sophia christology is implicit in the hymn. Adela Yarbro Collins says, "Most of the things said about the Logos in the Prologue (of the fourth Gospel) are things typically said about Wisdom, personified as a woman or goddess in the Jewish wisdom tradition. . . . If one can say that the Logos was God, then one can say that Sophia was God. The Gospel may not have intended to do so, but the prologue and the portrayal of Christ as Sophia imply . . . a feminine dimension of divine reality."[72]

Sophia christologies, Pentz argues, "are clearly biblical." It is possible consistently to say that Sophia describes one aspect of God's activity in the world. Sophia is nothing more or less than God's wisdom personified, in which case she would be divine and not simply a creature, but at the same time not a distinct goddess. Her divinity and her incarnation in Jesus are affirmed. "A Sophia Christology would only be inherently heretical if Sophia always or usually was conceived as a subordinate creature. All we need for an orthodox Christology is a substantial strain in the wisdom literature affirming wisdom's divinity (and her incarnation in a human)."[73] Given this assumption, a Sophia christology falls within the range of what has traditionally been called orthodoxy. Indeed, Pentz goes so far as to argue that orthodoxy needs a Sophia Christology. By seeing that Jesus is the incarnate Sophia of God, we see that the maleness of Jesus does not necessarily block her femaleness. Jesus incarnated feminine as well as masculine representations of the divine. Furthermore, "A Sophia Christology does make it clear once and for all that if we are to be on the side of God's wisdom, we must oppose all oppression. A Sophia Christology assures us that God has entered the battle against oppression and evil by enfleshing her wisdom in Jesus. Jesus is Lady Sophia incarnate."[74]

It seems to me there are biblical and theological reasons a Sophia christology is necessary in any effort to reconstruct christology in the context of our contemporary quest for liberation, a criterion implicit in drawing my conclusions at the end of each chapter. I agree with the critics of the use of Sophia language that worship for Christians can be addressed only to the one, triune God. Worship of any other god or goddess is not Christian worship (1 Corinthians 8:5-6). The question is whether Sophia christology is subject to such criticism. I think the foregoing discussion shows clearly it is not. The review, I think, shows the biblical and theological necessity of this language and imagery in any adequate christology. But such a conclusion is frustrating for the extreme left and right in this controversy, and essentially boring to most people, because the real issue is not as much doctrinal as it is methodological, that is, basic issues of power, authority, and legitimacy in christological construction.

Christology is always a political as well as a theological enterprise. Anyone who denies or ignores the social context of christology does not understand the grounds, character, and consequences of any theology. Theology always reflects the distribution of power in its construction of reality. At the same time, christology is not merely political ideology. It is also grounded in and reflects religious and theological realities. So there are theological as well as social and political matters at stake in "the sophia controversy." Therefore, I want to argue that our experience of the Christian God, who is the triune God, is quite diverse,[75] and the language which is appropriately used as image, metaphor, symbol, analogy, and doctrine for this God is (and should be) as rich and diverse as our experience of God in the tradition and individually. Here Elizabeth Johnson provides a brilliant exploration in contemporary constructive christology.[76] The Christian God is known and praised through a wide range of creatures and activities, and Sophia is one good candidate along with Logos (and a whole range of other images, metaphors, and analogies) to describe the full reality of Jesus Christ. Christian worship and Christian theology historically have employed many adjectives and names to God, and feminist christology has been one of the most important voices in our understanding of the full reality of Jesus Christ in our context today.

In the midst of this controversy and some of the many movements today to enrich christology, I offer a suggestion which can move this christological debate beyond name-calling. Since Sophia is presently unknown or unused by most Western Christians, especially Protestants, this name, and the imagery associated with it, would best be used in conjunction with other imagery clearly and more familiarly referring to God and to Christ. The problem is most likely to arise when that name or term is invoked exclusively, thereby allowing some Christians to infer that a different deity is being addressed or identified by the image. I would make the same point about the use of Logos as the exclusive identification of Jesus Christ. If "'Re-Imagining" enthusiasts would connect Sophia more clearly with traditional Christian teachings, or at least acknowledge the legitimacy of requests that this be done; and if "Re-Imagining" critics would acknowledge the inevitability of some ambiguity when new horizons of imagery are explored in liturgy and theology, then much of the furor over scripture's Sophia imagery as applied to contemporary christological discussion would subside.[77] There are moments when I am convinced that if the word "wisdom" had been used in the public discussion of a feminist christology, and the word "sophia" had been left to scholars' academic journals, the public furor would have been much less. But the decision about whether or not to use the term "sophia" in liturgy and theology reveals how inseparable are the political and theological issues in christology.

The larger issue of Sophia christology, when candidly acknowledged, is the legitimacy of the influence of contemporary feminist experience and imagery in the church's teaching about Jesus Christ. To what extent does christology depend solely on the formulations of the tradition, and to what extent does it depend on the authority and content of feminist experience and concerns? This issue is evident in a review by David Bauer of Nancy Carter's *Jesus in the Gospel of Matthew: Who Do You Say that I Am?*, a study guide produced for the General Board of Global Ministries of the United Methodist Church. Although he affirms the work insofar as it appeals to the authority of New Testament scholars Raymond Brown and Jack Kingsbury, he rejects the work as a whole as "fundamentally flawed" because the authors "ultimately refuse to accept the point of view of Matthew regarding the nature of revelation."[78] Instead of acknowledging the authority of the reviewer's understanding of Matthew's christology, the authors of this book, Bauer claims, opt for "classic nineteenth-century liberalism and even certain post-modern 'New Age' theology." The text is used simply as an occasion for the authors to embark on their own self-reflection and their belief that God has revealed himself through their stories as much as through the historical work of Jesus Christ. Their experience-oriented theology invites us to replace Matthew's (or Bauer's) christology with those more relevant and acceptable to us.[79] Bauer clearly rejects the authority of women's experience and agenda in christological construction.

A second issue posed by the Sophia debate is the oldest one in Christian theology. How can Christians sustain monotheism while making claims about sophia (and logos) as divine? The Sophia controversy revisits the ancient debate about polytheism and idolatry and whether trinitarianism theism, through a logos or Sophia christology, can avoid polytheism. I discussed this issue in chapter two as the core of the christological controversy. That issue is still alive in any creative effort to reconstruct christology. In reviewing Susan Cady's *Wisdom's Feast,* Randy Petersen says, "Cady speaks much more clearly to the oneness of God. She's not interested in presenting Sophia as some sort of separate goddess or sub-god." He continues: "If Sophia is a separate deity, then Sophia worship is idolatry and a radical departure from traditional Christianity. But if Sophia is another name for the one true God, then it might be possible to celebrate Sophia within traditional orthodoxy."[80] So as has always been the case, the core of the debate is not christology in isolation, but the most fundamental problems of Christian faith, viz., how to talk about one God (monotheism), and how to talk about that one God with enough complexity and distinction so as to refer to a dynamic and social meaning of God (trinity), without reducing the meaning of God to a plurality of gods. For Christians, christology proper has always been about that problem above all others, and the contemporary Sophia controversy, insofar as it is about theology, is the issue in the church today which engages the religious interests of Christians in somewhat the same way that the controversy between Arius and Athanasius engaged the public interest and debate in the fourth century.

Quite apart from the typical "she said . . . he said" level of this debate, the questions of theological substance remain to be debated within the church today. Honest, civil, and charitable conversation and debate will not appeal to those who would banish imagination from theological thought or who think tradition is fixed and settled or who reject out of hand all revisions of ancient doctrine. Nor will it appeal to those who regard tradition as so corrupt that it must be entirely re-imagined or so bankrupt that continuity with it is not to be prized. For those of us who stand between these two extremes, the controversy over Sophia christology may recapitulate some of the same passions, positions, and agendas of the earlier christological development, and show that christology is always about more than theological speculation, but goes to the heart of what Christians understand the purpose of faith to be. I believe the emergence of Sophia christologies is one of the most important developments in expanding the meaning of Jesus Christ (or recovering the gospel of the earliest church) in our search for the liberation of women and men from an exclusive, and so oppressive, theology.

CHAPTER SIX

Christology and the Atonement: Is Atonement Theology Sacralization of Abuse?

I. The Scandal of the Cross

"In the summer of 1963 I worked at a company in Atlanta called the Rural Express Company. One of my best friends worked with me, Harold McClinton, a star football player who went on to play for about twelve or thirteen years in the NFL as a middle linebacker for the Washington Redskins. That summer we made the telephone books for the southeast area of the United States. Our job was to place forms on a table that was probably as wide as a regular folding table used for banquets. Close by, within twenty or thirty feet of where we were working, was a water fountain. It was a brand new, cold, water fountain, but we could not drink from it because it was for whites only. Our water fountain was about five or six hundred feet away from the working area in the warehouse where they stored the paper. It was an old green water fountain and the water was always lukewarm.

"One day Mac and I decided we were going to drink from that water fountain, whatever it cost us. I drank first, then Mac, and we walked back to our work stations together. All day long we waited for something to happen. By late afternoon we had come to the conclusion that nothing was going to happen. About 4:00 the machine broke down and we knew that they probably wouldn't get it fixed in time for us to do much more work. So we were resting on the pallet, talking about our victory for the day and what a great stride we had made for freedom. Then up came an older gentlemen who was about 62 years old and had worked for the company for 25 or 30 years. He asked us, 'Boys, did you all drink from that water fountain today?' We said, 'Yeah, we drank from that water fountain.' And he said to us, 'The boss told me that if you all drink from that water fountain again, they're going to fire me.' He went on to tell us that he was three years away from retirement, and the company's retirement plan was structured so that if you got fired before you got to retirement age, you didn't get any retirement benefits. He had a daughter in college he was supporting and a family to take care of. We came to the conclusion that he was telling us not to drink from the water fountain anymore, so we gave him a hard time.

"That night Mac and I felt real bad that we had talked about that man so bad that day. So we made up our minds that the next day we would apologize and tell him that we wouldn't drink from the water fountain. That old man got tears in his eyes and he said, 'You don't have to do that. What I wanted you to understand was that everybody has to pay a price. The two of you are young and you can afford to pay the price, but I'm old.' He continued, 'If you want to drink from that water fountain, you can drink from it. But I want you to understand that the way this system operates is that it always takes the weakest one. You need to be aware of the price that the weakest will have to pay. And then if it still seems right, you've got to do what you've got to do. But never do anything like that without being sure you understand who's got to pay the price and what the price is they've got to pay.' After we weighed the cost, we decided it was not worth the price for that man to have to pay."[1]

The cross has been an embarrassment for Christians from the beginning. How can we reconstruct a disastrous Friday as "Good Friday"? Without a doubt the persecution of the late first century church heightened and shaped the passion narratives of the Gospels. However, unless one adopts the extreme view that the church created the passion narratives out of whole cloth, as Mark's fictional martyrology,[2] or are merely prophecy historicized,[3] the early church proclaimed the crucified prophet as the messiah. The notion of a crucified messiah, however, made no sense in the Jewish world, since the true messiah would establish the kingdom of God, whether that kingdom be the re-established Davidic monarchy or a new eschatological reign of God. A crucified messiah was a blatant contradiction in terms, as unthinkable as a "square circle." Atonement theories—metaphors elaborated to explain how the suffering and death of Jesus could redeem the sins of the world—abound in the history of theology in persistent efforts to turn this scandal into a gospel. The problem today, however, is that atonement theories themselves have become as scandalous as the cross. Bess's behavior in "Breaking the Waves" described at the beginning of the last chapter, and this incident at the water fountain seem not only unjust, but episodes of personal or social pathology. Bess's and the "older gentleman's" interpretations of the cross seem to make them victims; the cross seems to have become an ideology of victimization. The purpose of this chapter is to summarize atonement theories, to critique them in the light of an ideology critique, and to reconstruct them in the light of the concept of incarnation outlined in the first two chapters.

II. Atonement Theories: Six Different Interpretations of the Cross

From their New Testament texts to the present day, Christians have made the cross indispensable to the economy of salvation. "Atonement, understood as the reconciling, redeeming, liberating activity of God in Christ, is essential to Christianity."[4] Our need for reconciliation presupposes that a rift of some kind exists between God's love and justice on the one hand, and our sinful condition on the other. The most fundamental claim of soteriology is that the cross reconciles God and estranged creatures.[5] Atonement theology is a theory about how reconciliation is accomplished by Jesus through his cross and resurrection.

How has the church interpreted the cross as decisive for the reconciling work of Christ? One key New Testament metaphor is the cross as the *sacrifice* of Jesus for our sins. His death as a sacrifice leads to the forgiveness of sins and the justified status of sinful humans before God. The primary framework for this interpretation is the belief in ancient Israel and other ancient cultures that the shedding of blood could remit sins and re-establish at-one-ment between God and the people of the covenant. Sacrifice is one of the most ancient religious practices in the attempt to reduce the alienation between humans and their gods or God. Jon Levenson, a contemporary Jewish biblical scholar, traces the biblical practice back to child sacrifice, which was never wholly overcome in the Hebrew, Jewish, and Christian religions even though the prophetic tradition condemned it as idolatrous and the church spiritualized it in atonement theories. Evidence of the existence of child-sacrifice persists in Exodus 22:28, as well as the stories of Abraham, Jepthah, and Mesha, and in the New Testament with the life-giving death of the only begotten and beloved son at the hands of the father (John 3:16). In ancient Judaism, a point came where the sacrificer could substitute (not replace) an animal, usually a sheep, for the child. However, "the impulse to sacrifice the first-born son never died in ancient Israel but was only transformed"[6] into other forms, such as the paschal lamb, Levitical service, monetary ransom, and Naziritehood, but primarily through narratives in which the firstborn or beloved son undergoes a symbolic death and restoration to life.[7]

Frances Young, professor of theology at Birmingham University in England, summarizes the richness of this metaphor of sacrifice throughout the scripture.[8] She considers animal sacrifice in place of guilty humans in order to placate the angry God, or Jesus as the perfect sacrifice who was our substitute to appease God's anger, to be too narrow a representation of biblical sacrifice. Even if it was rooted in child and animal sacrifice, it was gradually spiritualized through different kinds of sacrifices and different understandings of what sacrifices accomplish. There were, for example, communion-sacrifices, where worshipers share a feast with the god and offer praise and thanksgiving; there were gift-sacrifices, which were bribes or offerings of praise and thanksgiving; there were sin-offerings, which were propitiatory (to placate the anger of the offended deity), aversion-sacrifices (offered to ward off evil), or expiatory (a God-given means of wiping away sin and removing pollution.[9] She concludes that the church thoroughly spiritualized these various sacrifices through firstfruit offerings, offerings of worship, and offerings of self; through fellowship meals and eucharist; and through baptism, spiritual progress, and martyrdom.[10] All of these were used in the New Testament to interpret the sacrifice of Christ, although initially as expiatory sacrifice which dealt with sin once and for all.[11] Timothy Gorringe similarly argues that the idea of sacrifice in the Old Testament is such a complex of ideas that we simply cannot speak of one biblical theology of sacrifice.[12]

While there are other metaphors for reconciliation in the New Testament and other interpretations of the cross in subsequent Christian history, this particular New Testament language of the cross as sacrifice has dominated Western Christian liturgy and theology. The problem for Christian theology today is whether this interpretation of the cross is an answer to or an exacerbation of the problem of sin and suffering. The New Testament metaphor of sacrifice and the atonement theories that have grown from it have come under criticism today as archaic, bizarre, offensive to human sensibilities, immoral, an ideology of repression, and even a sacralization of abuse. Are these criticisms appropriate, and if they are, is there another interpretation of the cross which understands it as decisive for our understanding of sin and redemption in a better way?

Every atonement theory depends on two things. First, it depends on assumptions about the nature of the human problem, whether that be finitude, death, epistemic distance from God, pride, disobedience, rebellion, guilt, bondage, oppression, injustice, ignorance, unfulfilled potential, lack of awareness of our true self, or meaninglessness. Second, it depends on a model built from a metaphor of how the cross functions to reconcile us with God by overcoming the human problem. In this discussion it is important to recognize that, unlike the dogma of incarnation described in chapter two, "no council has fixed an atonement dogma."[13] However, by employing the metaphor of sacrifice along with other biblical ones of ransom, redemption, propitiation, expiation, purchase, reconciliation, and vicarious suffering, the church has provided at least six different atonement theories which give an account of how the cross of Christ is our salvation.

1. Jesus as a teacher of the true higher knowledge. Elaine, a 30-year-old high school English teacher, has been a member of First UM Church all her life. But during Lent and Easter seasons, talk about the cross has always bothered her. She could never understand what the death and resurrection of Jesus two thousand years ago have to do with her life today. Recently, however, while reading the Gospels she discovered that Jesus was primarily a teacher about a higher wisdom; he brought the true knowledge of God and of ourselves. Through his life and death, he taught us to discover that in the deepest recesses of ourselves, our souls, we already know God, indeed, we are a part of God. "The Kingdom of God is within you," Jesus said, and Elaine has discovered that by taking hints from Jesus about the God in us, she has discovered that Jesus, her teacher, prods her to discover the "divine" within herself. Jesus did not come to die on the cross. He came to teach that God is already in us if we only will dive into the deepest recesses of ourselves and discover our own worth, our own sacredness, our own divinity, our own Godness. His birth is a symbol of the birth of the spirit of Christ within us. Easter is a symbol of the resurrection of a higher nature within us. We can discover our own "christness" when we let Jesus, the teacher of true knowledge, serve as a midwife for our own self-discovery, which is our death to ignorance and our birth to our enlightenment about our true selves, our immortality, our complete divinity.

In the early church, the Apologists and especially the Gnostics, saw Jesus as the revealer of the true knowledge of God and ourselves.[14] They diverge in the sense that the Apologists understood Jesus as a mediator of this true knowledge, while the Gnostics consider him an incidental occasion for our own discovery of ourselves as a Christ. Common to this model, however, is the understanding of Jesus as a teacher of the way to salvation. His teachings and his life make him the premier mediator or occasion for this knowledge. The axis on which this model turns is this: Jesus shows us the way, but salvation does not occur until we discover it within ourselves. Since the fundamental human problem is ignorance of our true selves, salvation is accomplished through the achievement of true knowledge. We need a celestial teacher who answers the great questions of philosophy, who teaches us perfect knowledge about the divine law, who provides an example of how we can imitate the pattern set by the Logos in Jesus, who prompts our mystical intuition into the transcendental realities and truths of God and our inner selves. The story of the cross is significant for Elaine in the sense that it is an allegory for the deeper spiritual death to ignorance, which we must undergo in our pursuit of true spiritual knowledge. This theory of atonement is characteristic of ancient Gnosticism as well as its contemporary new age variants, where atonement consists of enlightenment about one's true self and the cosmos.[15]

2. Jesus as a moral example and influence. Clarice, a 45-year-old African American bank vice president with an MBA, has been a member of Mt. Moriah AME Church all her life. She has heard her preacher often say that just as Jesus suffered on the cross for us, we are called to emulate his suffering for the sake of others. Her experience is that this is what African Americans, and especially African American women, have been forced to do for four hundred years in America. Rereading the story of Jesus, however, led her to a new understanding of the cross. From Clarice's new point of view, the cross is our primary example of historical evil trying to defeat good. His redemption has nothing to do with surrogacy or substitution. Rather, she noted the influence of Jesus for moral good on those around him. The Gospel stories show that the spirit of God in Jesus came to give humans life—to show salvation through his perfect vision of setting right the relations between body, mind, and spirit. Jesus, in persevering to the cross, fully re-presents God's own love and forgiveness of us; he provides us with an inspiring moral example to follow. When we follow him, empowered by his example, love and reconciliation occur between God and us and each other. The inspiration of his ideal and example provides power for us to emulate him. Reconciliation comes as a result of our efforts to follow Jesus' example.

This theory has affinities with the first one, but it focuses more on the power of the influence of Jesus' moral example. It assumes that human beings need the motivation to engage in the love which characterizes God and is re-presented by Jesus, especially his self-giving love on the cross. His example reminds us of God's love and forgiveness and inspires emulation. Usually identified with Peter Abelard in the twelfth century, this theory rejects a radical doctrine of original sin, as found in Augustine and the Protestant Reformers. We need simply to know what is good (God's love and forgiveness), and to resolve to do the good, which is aroused by the example of Jesus' life and death on the cross in love (grace). The moral influence theory sees the atoning significance in Jesus' death in his capacity to provide us with an inspiring, even compelling, example to follow. Jesus, in persevering to and through the cross, fully embodies God's love and forgiveness. Once we have followed him, empowered by his example, love between God and us is restored and reconciliation occurs. The reasonableness of the ideal he exhibits provides the motivation and power to emulate it. Reconciliation, then, comes as a result of our effort to follow Jesus' example, an effort that is aided by the grace of the compelling power of that example he provides by going to the cross. Atonement is more than a mere moral example; it is Jesus' influence which reconciles us to the loving and forgiving God by our responding to that love and emulating it. The moral power inherent in his example draws us to the love of God and neighbor.

3. *Jesus as the final scapegoat.* Terry is a 50-year-old engineer at Wright Patterson Air Force Base, five years away from retirement. He has been a competitive person all his life, even to the point of blaming anyone else whenever plans do not go the way they were designed to go. His parents and family love him, but he needs to justify himself by finding a scapegoat on whom to put the blame in moments of disappointment and threat. Many of his colleagues in the research department react the same way, but he longs for the day when neither he nor his colleagues need to justify themselves by finding someone else to blame when faced with moments of threat. Terry has come to see Jesus' death as a revelation of the violence that results from our self-justification, a sign of the bankruptcy of our methods of scapegoating. Jesus in his teachings ("do not repay evil for evil") and his death ("he turned his face toward Jerusalem") reveals the consequences and failure of all schemes of self-justification. The gracious gift of divine justification instead of self-justification became visible and attractive. The apparently endless vicious circle of sin-expiation-forgiveness, which does not change in any fundamental way the situation of human beings, is overcome through our acceptance by God in place of self-justification. Through the cross we can declare, "No more scapegoats."

This interpretation of the cross has been developed into a full-blown theory by Rene Girard as part of his meta-theory of the origins and maintenance of culture and religion.[16] He offers a theory about why we are so prone to rivalry and conflict which often leads to violence. Aware of a lack within ourselves, we look to others to teach us what to value and who to be.[17] The self is a set of mimetic relationships. Our imitation of the other evokes desire; mimesis leads to rivalry. "All human communication tends towards a relationship of mutual violence, where accusation follows accusation and attack is countered by attack."[18] We are prone to conflict because the model we imitate can become our rival if we desire the object he or she is imagined to have, or other imitators of the same model compete with us for the same object. "Mimesis leading to violence is the central energy of the social system."[19] Humans, however, discovered release from the violence through unconscious convergence on a single victim, through which the energy is dissipated and a relative peace is restored.[20] The first scapegoating was experienced as so effective that the whole chain of events became a mechanism repeated in ritual.[21] The scapegoating mechanism is ritualized in religion through sacrifice, so that religion is the basis and maintenance of culture. Myths arise to declare scapegoating a divine necessity. Sacrifice and rituals of scapegoating represent, therefore, in camouflaged form, the disorder resulting in the expulsion of the victim, and the order stemming from the newly found relief from conflict and violence. Sacrifice, therefore, is sacralized violence; religion is organized violence in the service of social tranquility. Even when cultures no longer practice sacrifice directly, they continue to target individuals or groups as scapegoats so that the latent violence can be contained through a social mechanism.

The Hebrew and Christian scriptures, however, can be read as an unveiling of the scapegoating mechanism, thereby putting an end to it.[22] Although the New Testament passion was like all other events of victimization going back to the foundation of the world, it was also different.[23] It is, first of all, a revelation of the bankruptcy of scapegoating mechanism, an exposure of the scapegoating mechanism as contrary to the will of God. The suffering and death of the Son become "inevitable because of the inability of the world to receive God or his Son, not because God's justice demands violence or the Son relishes the prospect of a horrible execution."[24] Furthermore, Girard also offers a nonsacrificial interpretation of the death of Christ—"God without sacred violence, God without scapegoating"[25]—by making a distinction between sacrifice as murder and sacrifice as renunciation.[26] The passion can be seen as "the willingness to give oneself to others and to commit oneself to God, not for sadomachistic purposes (i.e., to inflict injury on others or oneself, ostensibly for the sake of faith), but out of love and faithfulness to the other."[27] A variation of this claim is "that Christ's death can validly be called a sacrifice, one which purifies the negative link between violence and religion and reconstitutes the positive meaning of sacrifice as transformation."[28] Whereas a bad model makes our mimesis rivalrous, a good model will provide a mimesis of love. Jesus' death reveals something about us and about God. It reveals our radical incapacity to understand our own violence, even when it is displayed in the most explicit fashion. "To say that Jesus dies, not as a sacrifice, but in order that there may be no more sacrifices, is to recognize in him the Word of God. . . . Where violence remains master, Jesus must die. Rather than become the slave to violence, as our own word necessarily does, the Word of God says no to violence."[29] We cannot any longer project our human violence onto God. Jesus' death and resurrection put an end to the closed communities founded on scapegoating.

4. Jesus as a victorious conqueror. Frederick, too, has listened all his life to hymns and sermons about the cross as sacrifice. He came from an upper-middle class family, has the terminal degree in chemistry, is employed in research by a major Indianapolis drug company, has a fourteen room house and a "Leave it to Beaver" family. He is the epitome of "success." But Frederick is a desperate man. He worries constantly about his job security, his status, his health, and some days, even about his sanity. He is a slave to a life of quiet desperation. During Lent it began to dawn on him that "the power of the cross and resurrection" is not so much the claim Jesus paid to God the price of death, but that Jesus triumphed over all of the powers of death that enslave us, not only physical death, but the threats he endures every day, like his job security, his credit card debts, his family stability, and his free-floating anxieties. As a United Methodist, he sings Wesley's hymn about Jesus "setting the prisoner free"; he sings how Jesus' death and resurrection "breaks the powers" of fear and bondage. Jesus "sacrificed" all of those things dear to him, including life itself, to the reign of God, and brought "eternal life," new life, authentic life out of his death on the cross. Frederick knows our fundamental problem to be enslavement to the powers of sin, death, and despair. Christ battled these powers, defeated them, and his victory accrues to us who participate in him. His cross and resurrection liberate us from political, social, economic, and existential oppression. Liberation occurs both through the example and influence of Jesus (as with Delores), through his resistance to the powers of violence and destruction (as with Terry), and through his triumph over the powers of death in its many forms through his resurrection to new life.

Widely known as Christus Victor, this theory was advocated by such theologians as Origin, Irenaeus, Gregory of Nyssa, and Augustine. The model suggests our rescue by Christ from bondage. Christ was able to defeat the powers of darkness and ransom or free us. Though the dominance of this theory receded throughout the Middle Ages, it was recovered by Luther at the beginning of the Reformation, where it receded again until the recent past when it was revived in the 1930s by Gustav Aulen, who designated it "the classic theory" of atonement.[30] In this theory, the fundamental problem of the human condition is enslavement or bondage. We are enslaved to the powers of sin, death, and the devil. God in Christ battles these powers, defeats them, and the consequences of that victory accrue to us. God alone accomplishes the victory in Christ. This model, in demythologized forms, has been appropriated by contemporary liberation theologians, where they interpret the significance of the cross relative to our liberation from political, social, and economic oppression instead of from the guilt of sin and the threat of death (although sin and death are still threats, but now the emphasis is on their threats within a social context). The warrior imagery, the militaristic and triumphalist imagery, as well as an implicit cosmic dualism, which lie behind the ancient version of this model have become problematic today, as the imagery itself runs the risk of contributing to oppression by the concept of power which underlies the model. In contemporary process and liberation interpretations, these risks are overcome by thinking of Jesus as the liberator from demonic social powers and for liberation and life instead of Jesus as the victor over evil cosmic forces. Among contemporary advocates of this theory, "Christ the victor" and the moral influence model tend to converge, for liberation takes place both through the example and influence of the historical Jesus and through his resistance and defeat of the powers of death and destruction through his cross and resurrection.

5. Jesus as our satisfaction of God's justice. Jack, 28, was raised in a Roman Catholic home in the Midwest. As a child he followed his parents' moral and religious teachings. Family life was neat and orderly. Acquaintances respected Jack's upright life, and his parents were held in high honor in the community and the church for the exceptional job they had done in raising him and his two younger sisters. However, after college Jack became involved with his college roommate in a Ponzi scheme which bilked scores of people out of tens of thousands of dollars. No one understood why Jack did this, including Jack himself, but when he was arrested, tried, and convicted, he and his family were dishonored in the community and in the church. Jack's problem was how he could "redeem" himself, financially, legally, but most important, spiritually. How could he reestablish the orderly, moral, respectable world he had lived in before his inexplicable error? Jack returned to the church, and he heard the preacher say that what Jesus did on the cross was to reestablish our relationship with God after we had dishonored God. Honor and harmony can be restored only through an act of punishment whereby an offering that is greater that the act of disobedience is rendered up to restore God's justice and honor. That is what Jesus did on his cross for us with God.

The atonement theory that has dominated the West, especially the liturgy and theology of the medieval church, assumes that the basic human problem is *disorder which dishonors God.* The order of divine justice that governs the world has been disturbed by sin, and the honor of the governor of the world has been besmirched by this disorder. Consequently, God had to reestablish the divine honor. The requirements of the moral order are satisfied because justice is fulfilled, honor is restored, and atonement is accomplished. The great representative of this theory remains Anselm of Canterbury (1033-1109) in his book, *Cur Deus Homo?* Why did God become incarnate? For Anselm, God's purpose in creating humanity was rooted in God's infinite love. From the beginning

God intended our perfect happiness. But happiness requires total and voluntary harmony between God's will and ours. Since we disobeyed and fractured the cosmic harmony, that disharmony can be restored either by punishment and the denial of our happiness, or by an act of satisfaction whereby an offering that is greater than the act of disobedience is rendered up to restore God's justice and honor.

Unconditional forgiveness is not an option, since such an act would introduce even further irregularity into God's universe and the world would be even more unjust and dishonorable. On the other hand, no human can offer adequate satisfaction because each human is already obligated to total obedience. If a human offered himself or herself in order to pay the price to restore honor, there would be no extra moral or spiritual capital available to render just satisfaction. Therefore, something drastic had to be done. God was capable of making such an offering for the sins of the world. However, incarnation was necessary if this plan was to work, for the satisfaction had to be made by a human, so we know *cur deus homo*, why the God-human. The incarnate Son offered his sinless life to die on the cross as punishment to restore the honor of God. Because that death was unwarranted, since he was also God as well as human, and so cannot but go unrewarded, and because the Son needed nothing for himself, the reward accrues to the advantage of those for whom the Son dies. Justice and order have been restored to the God-human relationship and righteousness can now reign.

6. *Jesus as our penal substitute.* Elaine was raised in the Presbyterian Church on St. Simons Island, Georgia. Now a 43-year-old recruiting officer for the Navy stationed in Newport Beach, she is still an active member of her church, singing in the choir and teaching a high school age Sunday School class. A "typical" Presbyterian, she has made her share of misjudgments, mistakes, even deliberate disobedience of biblical laws, but she has never committed any "big" sins. From her earliest years, however, Elaine has sung about how sinful, how unworthy, how much of a "worm" she is in the eyes of God. She has felt a burdensome distance between herself and God, partly because of God's holiness, but partly because of the immense debt she owes to God because of her sin. She is not quite sure how much of her guilt is due to her misdeeds, and how much she can blame on the original sin of Adam and Eve, but she feels herself to be debt-ridden. There is no way she can repay it, but it is due to God if God's justice is to be upheld. So Elaine has an overwhelming sense of how much Jesus gave up to pay the debt she owes to God. His death was necessary to satisfy divine justice (instead of honor, as in Jack's view), so Christ's death became the punishment for her sin. He became the victim of the wrath of God in her place. Now she can live with confidence

and gratitude that she is accepted by God because of the price Jesus paid on the cross for her guilt.

The penal substitute theory, represented most notably by the Reformer John Calvin, is in large part a further development of Anselm's theory of satisfaction. The difference between Anselm and Calvin is that whereas the restoration of order is central for Anselm, Calvin is more concerned with the vindication of the law, which stems from the righteousness which is God's own being.[31] Anselm's Christ pays our debts; Calvin's Christ bears our punishment. The difference is compensation for personal injury (Anselm) versus punishment for a violation of the law (Calvin). A God of righteousness cannot endure iniquity. A debt is owed to God because of our disobedience; iniquity must be punished. Christ the mediator steps in as our substitute and takes the pain and the penalties of sin unto himself. Christ's death is our payment, our punishment, for our sin, because he serves as our "substitute."

The fulfillment of the divine law can be accomplished only when the offender and offense have been punished. Christ simultaneously fulfills the law and suffers the punishment for our sin; that is, he becomes the victim of the wrath of God in our place. Although he fulfilled the law and so deserved no punishment, he still suffered the punishment that the law ordinarily pronounces against transgressors: God's wrath. He suffers God's condemnation for us; he receives the punishment for our capital offenses, and by doing so he satisfies the law as our substitute and frees us from God's wrath. Christ assumes the just penalty, and in exchange, bestows upon us his justice and his resurrected life. God transfers Christ's righteousness to us—it is called "imputed righteousness" in Reformation theology. The import of all of this is the exchange which takes place between Christ and us. The righteousness and justice of Christ is transferred to us, in what is sometimes called the "wonderful exchange." This interpretation of the cross remains the primary framework of evangelical Protestantism. Indeed, fundamentalists still consider "the substitutionary theory of the atonement" to be the required theory which must be believed by every true Christian.

III. Criticisms of Satisfaction and Substitutionary Atonement Theories

Every atonement theory rests upon a distinctive understanding of the human problem, and on a certain cluster of images, metaphors, and social models by which to interpret the restoration and fulfillment of the divine-human relationship.[32] Each theory has its strengths and weaknesses. However, the latter two of these theories in particular—the dominant ones reflected in the liturgies and piety of Western Christianity—have come under serious moral and social criticism today. These criticisms are so thoroughgoing and compelling that atonement theology itself seems to be in jeopardy. At issue, primarily, is the language of Jesus as sacrificial surrogate and the use of his death on the cross to legitimate gender, familial, ecclesiastical, and societal structures that create and sustain such qualities as nonassertiveness, passivity, and diminishment of the self.[33] We have been forced to ask, "What is the connection between atonement theory and forms of oppression, injustice, and even violence?" that dominate our moral and social awareness today.

Liberal and Evangelical Critiques

Although it is possible to find some truth in each of the major atonement theories, some are more adequate to interpret the biblical God of justice and mercy who redeems than others. Some have such liabilities that we would be better served to demote them. For instance, any gnostic interpretation of the cross is a direct challenge to any doctrine of the incarnation. But the substitutionary theory of atonement is equally a challenge to the triune God of scripture. Although some of Paul's passages seem to support such an interpretation of Christ's work, this theory should be challenged because the primary biblical story does not support it and "because of the affront which it offers to reason and conscience."[34] Liberal theologians have consistently been the most vigorous critics of this particular atonement theory. The reasons are primarily that it stands in conflict with the biblical view of God's love and mercy and a moral vision of justice. Substitutionary atonement is an affront because it proposes a repugnant, "sub-Christian" view of God when measured by scripture. "God's justice . . . is hardly maintained by the immoral judgement of an innocent victim instead of the guilty sinner, and it is hardly good Trinitarian theology to envisage a loving Son set over against a wrathful Father as mediator on our behalf."[35] In liberal theologies, distributive theories of justice, focused on the deterrence of the offender or at least the offense, that is, focused on the reformation of the offender, have replaced ancient theories of retributive justice, justice which exacts an appropriate penalty and punishment of the offender both for the needs of the victim of injustice (recompense) and the needs of the community (protection and health).[36] In modern liberal culture, distributive justice is a morally superior form of justice; it is more humane, and it is more effective. Although there may be deep psychological and sociological roots for revenge and punishment in human culture, a moral theory of justice, and especially justice based on love, envisions justice as fair, focused on the offender, proportional, and restorative. Desire for revenge and punishment result in an endless cycle of violence and should be expunged from a humane and progressive society. The depth of this struggle to assess the role of revenge and punishment in justice continues to be explored in our society in such powerful contemporary movies as "Sleeping with the Enemy," "A Time to Kill," "The Chamber," and "Dead Man Walking."[37]

Although Protestant evangelicalism has been one of the strongest advocates of substitutionary atonement, some contemporary evangelicals along with liberals have been critical of it. Clark Pinnock makes the cross central to the work of Jesus Christ, particularly as an atoning sacrifice. However, as an evangelical Christian, he has some problems with the language of "substitutionary atonement." The evangelical focus on the cross as penal substitute is "too crude." Jesus is made to appease the Father to make him willing and able to be merciful to sinners, making it sound like God has to be persuaded or placated to love sinners through the death of an innocent victim. Evangelicals need to think through what the effect on God was of the work of Christ on the cross. Did God hate sinners before the cross but was persuaded to love sinners after the cross? Did the cross actually change God AD 32? "Surely it would be better to say that God is love, everywhere and always, and that what we needed from Christ was a decisive presentation of it in history. . . . Jesus' death then should not be seen as the cause of God's love but the final and irreversible expression of what God has always been like and has always been doing in history, which had until the time of the Cross been inadequately seen."[38]

Womanist and Feminist Critiques

Some of the most insightful critiques of traditional atonement theories have been offered in a growing body of literature written by womanist and feminist theologians. Their moral and theological critiques are less focused on liberal theories of justice and divine love and more on the social context and consequences of atonement theories. Womanist theologian Delores Williams begins her discussion of the cross as atonement with the African American females' "historic experience of surrogacy."[39] Because Jesus died on the cross in place of humans, he represents "the ultimate surrogate figure." "Surrogacy, attached to this divine personage, thus takes on an aura of the sacred. It is therefore fitting and proper for black women to ask whether the image of a surrogate-God has salvific power for black women or whether this image supports and reinforces the exploitation that has accompanied their experience with surrogacy. If black women accept this idea of redemption, can they not also passively accept the exploitation that surrogacy brings?"[40] What is required, according to Williams, is to free the redemptive work of Christ from surrogacy and to free the cross from the sacralization of surrogacy it has attained in much atonement theory.

From her point of view, the cross does not represent the surrogacy of the Son at the will of the Father for the salvation of all, but rather represents "historical evil trying to defeat good." The image of Jesus on the cross is the image of human sin in its most desecrated form. The cross itself has little to do with the redemption that Jesus brings us. It is, for Williams, more the occasion or the context for the redemption work of Christ, not the cause or content of redemption. Redemption of humans can have nothing to do with any kind of surrogate or substitute role Jesus was to have played in a bloody act that gained victory over sin and evil, lest it reinforce the role of the victim and of the surrogate figure. "Jesus did not come to redeem humans by showing them God's 'love' manifested in the death of God's innocent child on a cross erected by cruel, imperialistic, patriarchal power. Rather, the spirit of God in Jesus came to show humans *life*—to show redemption through a perfect ministerial vision of righting relations between body (individual and community) and mind (of humans and traditions) and spirit."[41]

Criticism of classical atonement theory is also one of the central agendas of feminist christology. The primary point feminist critics offer is that by making the cross the central element in atonement, and by celebrating the suffering and death on the cross as the feature of the cross that makes it atonement for our sins, the cross functions to justify and reinforce the suffering and acceptance of abuse by all Christians, and especially by women. Atonement theory has been the primary force in shaping Christian women's acceptance of abuse. "Divine child abuse" is paraded as salvific, as the child who suffers the abuse without raising a voice is lauded as the hope of the world. Internalization of this theology traps women in an almost unbreakable cycle of abuse by accepting suffering and surrogacy as redemptive. As Rosemary Ruether puts it, Christian women are in a "double bind": they deserve suffering for guilt and they receive the promise of becoming a Christlike agent of redemption for one's victimizers through innocent suffering.[42]

Among most feminists, including some evangelical feminists, morality is not defined primarily in relation to theories of distributive justice, but rather primarily in relation to understandings of power, to social systems and their symbols and structures, which systematically undergird patterns of exploitation and oppression. Some evangelical feminists acknowledge their deep ambivalence toward atonement theory. "It is morally abhorrent to claim that God the Father demanded the self-sacrifice of his only Son to balance the scales of justice. A god who punishes through pain, despair, and violent death is not a god of love but a sadist and despot."[43] Thus she argues that her "criticism of a sacrificial interpretation of the death of Jesus is colored by its historical effects upon women." It is "a recipe for depression and self-hatred."[44] Jesus on the cross encourages oppressed people to accept their suffering under their taskmasters as somehow redemptive, while at the same time it is supposed to give them some kind of comfort. However, "In my opinion, in the discussion about the ideological and oppressive abuse of the doctrine of the atonement we have to distinguish clearly between descriptive and prescriptive theology. If suffering people choose to identify with Jesus on the cross and find there comfort, strength, and inspiration to live, then the role of the theologian is to reflect upon these experiences of redemption. But when theologians, missionaries, and preachers blame on a subjugated people or an inferioirized sex the sins that led to the death of Christ and demand penitential self-denial, the result is not redemptive."[45]

Many feminists, however, have not been receptive to any interpretation of the cross as redemptive. It is intrinsically, by the very model of power and relationships which underwrites its efficacy, a sacralization of abuse. For some, in all three predominant forms of atonement doctrine—ransom, substitution, and moral—the death of Jesus is required by God to make salvation effective. Even the Christus Victor and the moral models are founded on the belief that an innocent suffering victim, and only an innocent suffering victim, has the power to confront us with our guilt and move us in a new direction.[46] The cross of Jesus remains a necessary part of God's plan that will end in triumph; therefore, the cross is still the will of God. In the satisfaction and substitution theories, where this criticism is most immediately appropriate, God is presented as a tyrant who demands punishment which must be satisfied by an innocent victim. Suffering, therefore, is sanctioned as the experience which frees others from guilt, or frees God to forgive, or re-presents God's love. "And when parents have an image of a God righteously demanding the total obedience of 'his' son—even obedience to death—what will prevent the parent from engaging in divinely sanctioned child abuse? The image of God the father demanding and carrying out the suffering and death of his own son has sustained a culture of abuse and led to the abandonment of victims of abuse and oppression."[47]

One of the most forthright critics refers to all atonement theories as "the abuse of the Son of God." The patriarchal father-god fosters dependence of the child and is punitive. Within the framework of original sin, "the punishment of one perfect child has to occur before the father can forgive the rest of his children and love them. In more benign atonement forms, the father does not punish the son. Instead the father allows the son to suffer the consequences of the evil created by his wayward creation. Hence the father stands by in passive anguish as his most beloved son is killed, because the father refuses to interfere with human freedom."[48] Trinitarian formulations of atonement which try to absolve the father of punitive action by arguing that the consequences for human sin are taken into the divine existence still teaches that suffering (human) is taken away by suffering (divine), and so the sin-punishment-escape scheme is still securely maintained intact. "Hence the experience of grace is lodged, I believe, not so much in a clear sense of personal worth gained from an awareness of interdependence and the unconditional nature of love, but in a sense of relief from escaping punishment for one's failings."[49]

IV. Current Proponents of the Substitution Theory

Is it possible to affirm the predominant atonement theory in the West in the light of these criticisms? Some have attempted to do so, essentially by arguing that the use of atonement theory as an ideology of abuse depends upon a misunderstanding of the logic of the atonement theory and a misuse of its social implications. I will examine the effort of Robert Letham, senior lecturer in Christian Doctrine at the London Bible College, to redeem the hardest case, the substitutionary theory.[50] He acknowledges that ideas of retributive justice and penal substitution are problematic for liberal Christians. However, he believes that substitutionary atonement is essential to Christian faith, and that a nonlibellous defense of it is possible.

The key to his defense is his claim that God's justice requires the punishment of sin and the sinner. Even though the whole concept of retributive justice is unacceptable in liberal culture, punishment for sin is, nevertheless, absolutely necessary. Having decreed salvation (which God was under no compulsion to do), there was no other way compatible with God's nature by which we could be saved. Because of the justice of God (God will give everyone their due), and because of the nature of sin (as an assault on God and so a contradiction of God's holiness), God must punish sin. If sin were to go unpunished, it would be at the expense of God's holiness. Punishment, therefore, is at the heart of of atonement. However, Christ on the cross endured our punishment in our place; a penalty was inflicted on him by God who prescribes the penalty and exacts it. Although this was undeserved because he was the sinless Son of God, he was made sin for our sake, subject to the full brunt of the divine curse that hung over sin. Lethem believes that the three major objections to this particular theory are unfounded if the model is understood in its proper meaning.

1. It has been regarded as inherently unjust that an innocent party should suffer and the guilty go free. However, in the opinion of Letham two things must be considered. First, the guilty do not go free in this theory. Their guilt is fully recognized and they are punished with the full sanction of God's law. The key issue is that they receive this penalty in Christ; he is our representative and our substitute. "We his people do indeed receive our just desserts for our misdemeanors inasmuch as Christ, having united himself to us in his incarnation, fully discharges the debt we owe."[51] This is the same line of argument that Irenaeus and Athanasius made for the incarnation (see chapter two), except now the logic is applied to the problem of sin as guilt (hence the penal theory and forgiveness) instead of the problem of sin as liability to mortality (and hence the theory of being made immortal like God).

   2. *The penal theory has been regarded as advocating a sadistic God.* What kind of God can delight in, or at least require, an innocent one to suffer on the cross, especially his own "dearly beloved son"? Is this not a picture of a God who is little better, if, indeed, not a good deal worse, than a sadist, desiring to inflict crushing punishment on a guiltless victim? This criticism, however, is misled, Letham thinks, when we ask exactly who it was who had such accursed grief inflicted on him. It was Jesus Christ, who was consubstantial with the Father from all eternity, who suffered and died in our place. Thus it was God himself who endured the penalty as our substitute. "Was this a suffering inflicted from without upon a grudging, resentful, and unwilling victim? Not at all." Rather than presenting a cruel and distorted picture of God, what penal substitution shows us is that God's love for us is such that God himself was prepared to pay the ultimate price that love can pay. "When we remember the unity of the Son with the Father in the trinity of the Godhead, the scene is transformed."[52]

   3. *The third objection has to do with God's law in relation to divine justice.* There is a general distaste among liberal Christians for thinking of God and salvation in legal instead of personalistic categories. Such hostility to God's law, however, is in strange contrast to Scripture itself. "It may be helpful for us to see the penal substitutionary death of Christ in the context of God's loving provision for the deliverance of those who otherwise were without hope."[53] The atonement as penal substitute stems from the love of God, and since God's love is just love, and his justice is loving justice, the cross is a demonstration par excellence of that love in a way that is commensurate with his justice. There is so much evidence that a sense of order is a key component in human social and psychological wholeness that it is an easy move to the metaphysical and theological ideas of wholeness in the universe and in God. The power of the retributive theory of justice and satisfaction and substitutionary theories of atonement surely lie in this perception. So deep is the sense of human good addressed in this theory that "we have to recognize something which is inescapable in both penal theory and the theology of redemption."[54]

V. A Reinterpretation of the Cross as Atonement

Letham presents, in my opinion, the strongest case that can be made to defend the classical theory of atonement. The core of his defense is the claim that because it is the incarnate God who pays the price, the theory is not subject to the charges of divine child abuse and sacralization of abuse. It is God who suffers redemptively, not a victim upon whom God decrees suffering as redemptive. However, I think it is not possible to redeem the satisfaction and substitutionary theories of atonement even in this way. The internal logic of the theory remains intact. Redemption is possible only when a scapegoat is put to death as punishment. One must ask why the (self)punishment of God by God—some kind of divine masochism—is any more redemptive than the sadistic suffering of the divine child. Suffering as punishment is redemptive. But the deeper reason I find Letham's defense unacceptable, nuanced though it be so as to reject the most horrendous implications of traditional atonement theory, is that it ignores the deepest Christian insight into the divine power to redeem, viz., God incarnate in Christ through the power of the Spirit. Letham's defense presumes the non-trinitarian view of divine power which undergirds the classical theory and so continues to underwrite, willy nilly, a sacralization of suffering, surrogacy, and abuse, in principle if not in practice.[55] On that basis alone, I accept the criticisms of the classical interpretation of the death of Jesus on the cross as atonement for sin and evil. The problems, in my view, are decisive. Traditional atonement theories are part of the problem of suffering and evil, to be resisted and transformed, instead of the answer to the problem. Even though sophisticated caveats seem to reduce the charge of sacralized abuse, they nevertheless maintain the scheme of abusive punishment as the only grounds for redemption. *Abusive punishment is structurally at the core of what defines and constitutes redemption.*

At the same time, I maintain that the cross is central to any Christian understanding of redemption. There can be no christology which stands anywhere within the bounds of "catholic" Christianity which does not interpret the cross as decisive for our understanding of God and of redemption from sin, suffering, and evil. The cross is not only a historical fact; it is theologically central, even constitutive, of what we know about the work of God for our redemption. The cross itself has redemptive possibilities and redemptive dimensions which are distinguishable and even separable from the abusive features of traditional atonement theory. It can be reinterpreted as redemptive in ways which avoid, even reject, the liabilities of the classical models. It can be reframed for a world where justice is needed without getting caught as a theological justification for the spiral of violence.

1. Jesus' death on the cross unmasks our fundamental human condition. The cross is unqualified evidence that the world stands in need of redemption. As unbridled violence against the innocent one, the cross lays completly bare the dark chasms of the human heart, the truth about our bent toward violence, our unconscious projection of our own aggressions on someone else, and the mechanism of scapegoating we employ, especially in our religion, to vitiate our proneness to violence.[56] That unmasking shows how deceptive the pretense of violent power is in our world. In the most violent act possible directed toward the most innocent human imaginable, the deceit and the failure of violent power is unveiled. The one who taught us to love one another, even the enemy, calls the hand of abusive power and reveals in his death the mechanism of violence and the deceit which motivates it. Jesus' death uncovers the deep-seated tensions present in our established ways of containing our uncontrolled rage by projecting it onto the innocent victim, and therefore he unmasks as delusionary the familiar forms of harmony through controlled violence.

The cross of Jesus Christ is part of the revelatory word that redeems. It exposes and denies the retributivist theory of justice. Rather than the endorsement of one final punishment, it announces its end of such punishment. The problem is that Christians have been unable fully to distinguish between the end of sacrificing from the idea that Christ is the final sacrifice. The death of Jesus is the *end* of sacrifice, not the *final* sacrifice. God raised Jesus from the dead, not to reward him as the final sacrifice in a scheme of blood vengeance, but to end sacrifice by vindicating his nonviolent, pure, unbounded love, and his revelation of the truth about God's relation to us as the basis of our relationships with each other, which can be based on love, mercy, and grace instead of sacralized violence. "When we realize the extent to which all punishment involves revenge, the maintenance of power, and scapegoating, we realize that only the mercy of God, as expressed in Christ's absolute self-giving, is supreme."[57] The cross "breaks the power of reigning sin" by the depth of its power to show us ourselves in our estranged relation through collective delusion from the one whose name is Love. As the author of the letter to the Hebrews puts it, "by erasing the sins of all with his own blood, Jesus put an end to ritual sacrifices in which it was always the blood of another that was shed."[58] Jesus' cross does not make the final reaffirmation of violence as redemptive, thereby sacralizing it as the final propitiation of God's vengeance and justice. His death puts an end to the need to project our violence onto anyone anymore, including God.

None of this suggests that Jesus' death on the cross does not have redemptive possibilities in its power to unmask evil. Christine Smith has been particularly helpful here. For her, no cross, including the cross of Jesus, is ever in itself changed into a moment of glory, not even by the resurrection. She "will never understand or embrace language that suggests that Jesus' death on a cross, or any death on a cross, breaks the power of sin, transforms human conditions, or shatters evil."[59] Nevertheless, there are transforming possibilities surrounding the cross. Certain approaches to it might contain redemptive possibilities. When human beings understand that they are choosing the cross out of freedom and faithfulness, they often are given a clear understanding that the very love and life they embrace and model in their own sacrifice participates in the transformation of the world where crosses prevail.[60] The cross and death can be accepted as an expression of solidarity with those who have been crucified throughout history. Taking up a cross may be the ultimate act of solidarity.[61] Furthermore, the cross and death may be the locus and the moment of the defeat of evil. The very moment and act of embracing the consequences of solidarity with suffering may become the moment and act of resurrection as victory over death and the cross,[62] like cinematic Christ-figures Sister Helen Prejean in "Dead Man Walking," R. R. McMurphy in "One Flew Over the Cuckoo's Nest," Luke Jackson in "Cool Hand Luke," and Percy Talbot in "Spitfire Grill."

As Rosemary Ruether puts it, redemption "did not come about through or because of the cross, but as a refusal to accept the message of the cross, an insistence that life will win over death in the end."[63] Or, as Smith puts it, "If atonement means that human beings are not solely bound by the sinfulness of their own condition; if it means that in the face of Jesus' ministry, life, and death, human beings have seen new possibilities for their lives and their ministries in the world—then we can believe that Jesus' death on the cross was redemptive. If atonement means that human beings are saved from a fatalistic power of evil in their lives by embracing and being convicted by the power of God we see incarnate in Jesus the Christ, then we can believe that the repercussions of Jesus' death on the cross had redemptive dimensions. If the radical love that Jesus lived and died for is so compelling that human persons seek to find at-one-ment with God, with the human family, and with the earth, then we can believe the impact of Jesus' death on the cross had purpose, meaning, and power."[64]

2. When Calvin was asked in his 1541 Geneva Catechism why the creed moves immediately from Jesus' birth to his death, passing over the whole history of his life, he answered, "Because nothing is said [in the creed] but what pertains properly to the substance of our redemption."[65] Karl Barth, the great twentieth century neocalvinist, says, "I take the liberty of saying that here Calvin is wrong. How can anyone say that the rest of Jesus' life is not substantially for our redemption? . . . I should think that there is involved in the *whole* of Jesus' life the thing that takes its beginning in the article, 'He suffered.'"[66] One of the striking features of the new Presbyterian "Brief Statement of Faith" (1983) is that it is the first creed to include (in ten lines, 8-18) the redemptive significance of Jesus' whole life of preaching, teaching, blessing, healing, binding, eating, forgiving, and calling.[67]

The cross does not stand alone as our redemption. Jesus' death itself does not redeems us, nor is his death to be glorified as God's means of redeeming or our way to overcome sin and evil. It is Jesus' death on the cross as a moment *within the scope of the entire life and work of Jesus Christ* as God's work for our redemption that is the subject of atonement theory. It is the whole life of Jesus Christ which is constitutive of our redemption in him and his church. John Macquarrie says, "When one speaks of 'reconciliation,' or still more of 'atonement,' in Christian theology, there is still a tendency to think almost exclusively of Christ's death. . . . Our attention will indeed be focused on the death of the cross, but only because this is the finish and culmination of Christ's work. It has its significance only in the context of Christ's life as its climax and summation."[68] Jesus Christ's cross fits within the context of his nativity, baptism, temptations, transfiguration, passion, resurrection, ascension, and promised return—not his death alone. As C. J. Den Heyer puts it: "Soteriologically speaking, nothing is created on Golgotha which was not there before. The taking away of the sins of the world already begins directly on the incarnation of the Word. It is not necessary here to wait for the death of Christ on the cross."[69] Indeed, ultimately, as Schubert Ogden argues, the constitutive cause of our salvation is the love of God which is represented in Jesus Christ. "The only cause of salvation . . . is the primordial and everlasting love of God which is the sole primal source and sole final end of anything that is so much as possible."[70]

For womanist theologian Delores Williams, Jesus does not conquer sin on the cross. He conquered sin through his life. Specifically, he conquered sin by resistance to it. Jesus did not come to redeem humanity by showing God's love manifested in the death of God's innocent child on a cross. Rather the Spirit of God in Jesus Christ came to show humans life, to show redemption through a perfect vision of right relations with God, creation, neighbor, and self. God's gift through Jesus was to invite his followers to participate in this vision of righting relationships. "Redemption had to do with God, through the ministerial vision, giving humankind new vision to see the resources for positive, abundant relational life. Redemption had to do with God, through ministerial vision, giving humankind the ethical thought and practice upon which to build a positive, productive quality of life."[71] It is not Jesus' death which redeems us but his life. For Williams, then, the resurrection represents the life of "the ministerial vision" gaining victory over the evil attempt to kill it.

Feminist theologian Julie Hopkins makes a similar argument. The cross is a tragedy within the redemptive work of Christ; it is not the means of redemption. "Jesus never proclaimed the necessity of suffering. His ministry was life-affirming; he sought to eradicate pain and social distress and preach Good News to the poor and heavy-hearted. That he could not finally avoid suffering and an early death is a tragedy and a prophetic exposure of the nihilistic tendencies of those who idolize power."[72] The central meaning of the cross is that God is present and in loving solidarity with those who suffer at the hands of violence. "I maintain that it is possible to believe that God was in Jesus reconciling believers to Godself upon the cross without claiming [that] Jesus was uniquely divine or that a blood price was paid."[73] The death of Jesus was not "necessary" in order to accomplish a particular purpose, but rather was the inevitable result of a specific cause to which he gave his life. As Elsa Tamez, Costa Rican liberation theologian, puts it, even though that death was not necessary to effect redemption, it turned out to be inevitable in the actual course of events, just as the resurrection was necessary in order to conquer, but was not inevitable if God had not become incarnate as the God of life.[74]

The redemptive power of sacrifice as the identification with the suffering of the poor is apparent in a telephone interview of El Salvadoran Archbishop Oscar Romero just two weeks prior to his murder. "As a shepherd, I am obliged by divine mandate to give my life for those I love—for all Salvadorans, even for those who may be going to kill me. If the threats are carried out, from this moment I offer my blood to God for the redemption and for the resurrection of El Salvador. . . . Martyrdom is a grace of God that I do not believe I deserve. But if God accepts the sacrifice of my life, let my blood be a seed of freedom and the sign that hope will soon be a reality. Let my death, if it is accepted by God, be for my people's liberation and as a witness of hope in the future."[75]

3. The cross is an essential moment in God's self-revelation to the world. A theology of atonement is above all a claim about who God is and how God engages our sin and suffering. The cross is not a moment of transaction within the Godhead between the Father and the Son which enables the Father to forgive us. Nor is it only the culmination of Jesus' life and ministry in a violent, inevitable, and tragic death which reveals how sinful our world is. Its deepest meaning is found when we see the self-giving compassion of Jesus as the incarnate self-giving compassion of God. Although it seems to me that there is a certain logic to the doctrine of penal substitution, I think it is crucial to note that the only way its defenders can save it from a sacralization of abuse, a celebration of suffering, and a deification of death is to set it in the context of the dogma of the incarnation. Apart from what the cross reveals to us about the nature of God and the divine economy, it seems to me that this theory has such insurmountable liabilities that it must be repudiated.

The cross tells us something about the identity, the very being, of God. The crucified Jesus is also "the crucified God." Because Christians speak of Jesus Christ as the incarnation of God, the claim is that the self-giving of Christ "is continuous with the self-giving of God, and the whole work of atonement is God's."[76] Jesus' death is more than simply a heroic act; it is, also, the self-identification of God with and for the world in all its frailty, vulnerability, suffering, and death. The cross shows that reestablishment of love and trust costs God vulnerability to suffering and death.[77] This is the non-oppressive meaning of the cross as sacrifice: God's self-giving identification with the world. As Emmanuel, God suffers our worst in Jesus Christ. Here is the truth of objective theories of the atonement. Subjective atonement theories which assume that God loves and forgives with no cost, and that all we have to do is to see God's unfailing and unconditional love, are inadequate.[78] God endures even death on the cross to identify with the world. It is also God incarnate who undergoes suffering and death. I would even go so far as to say it is the incarnation, not the cross, which redeems the world from its sin, suffering, tragedy, and evil. "Rather than viewing the cross as some arbitrary design on God's part, we must see it as the outcome of God's primordial option: the incarnation. The cross is the outcome of an incarnation situated in a world of sin that is revealed to be a power working against the God of Jesus."[79] It is God incarnate who is "sacrificed" on the cross through the power of identification, resistance, confoundment, and transformation of sin and suffering.

The cross, then, is redemptive because it is essential to the incarnation—the redemptive "pure, unbounded love" of God in Christ as compassionate and transformative power. To be sure, the cross is not the exhaustive meaning of the incarnation. God as Logos is incarnate in the whole creation throughout time and space, and, for Christians, decisively and normatively in the whole life of Jesus Christ. "The Christ event cannot be the cause of salvation because its only cause, and the cause of this event itself, is the boundless love of God of which this event is the decisive representation."[80] But the cross, as the near side of the resurrection, shows us how far God goes—even to "empty" Godself or to "sacrifice" Godself—to identify completely with the world and through the power of the cross and resurrection to redeem, or re-create, or liberate, or sanctify us. The excessively Protestant reading of Paul's atonement theology, which certainly includes some notions of sacrifice and expiation, is misshapen. "The heart of Paul's atonement theology is not expiation but participation. It is a theology of transfer—from one lordship to another. By sharing in Christ's death one dies to the power of sin, with the result that one belongs to God. . . . Salvation, for Paul, works by being incorporated into Christ, rather than by expiation. . . . The real bite of Paul's theology, then, is not in juristic but in participatory categories."[81]

The cross, moreover, tells us not only about the identity of God but also about the character of God, especially the nature of divine power. What happens on the cross as the absorption and end of violence is a redefinition of power.[82] The power of God on the cross is God's repudiation of violent power as the means of redemption. God does not seek a quid pro quo or an eye for an eye. God's boundless love is distinct in every respect from the mechanisms of violence and the vicious circles of mutual destructiveness. The cross as revelation of the character of God shows that ideas of vengeance, retaliation, satisfaction, and payment must be eliminated from our teaching about the character and power of God. The cross reveals more God's renunciation of accounting for our sins than a mechanism of violent punishment. When such truth appears, the powerful are toppled from their thrones, the oppressed are elevated. As contemporary womanist theologian JoAnn Marie Terrell puts it, "the cross is not taken up apart from what the rest of the story affirms; namely, that Jesus was God incarnate, who lived, struggled and died in suffering solidarity with society's victims."[83] It is through the compassion of the cross that the God of pure nonviolence and love liberates us from our entanglement with evil. The suffering God delivers us from our desires, passions, and perverse thinking which enslaves us to violence and destruction.

The cross is the near side of our atonement, but the resurrection as the far side of the cross is the full revelation of the love and mercy of the incarnate God. The God who raised Jesus from dead despised the death of Jesus on the cross. But as the incarnate God, God brought resurrection life out of Jesus' death on the cross. The cross means nothing but one more human tragedy apart from the power of resurrection. God turns human wrongdoing around, and uses it against itself. The compassionate and transformative power that makes for life is liberated from the violent and retributive power that makes for death. The God of Jesus Christ through the cross and resurrection stands opposed to violence—especially sacralized violence. God's boundless love and forgiveness negate every mechanism of violence and vicious circle of mutual destructiveness. God's power in the cross and resurrection is the power of transformation—new life. Ideas of vengeance, retaliation, satisfaction, and payment must be eliminated from Christian teaching about redemption.

To summarize a reconstructed theology of atonement bluntly, we are redeemed by the incarnation, not by the cross. It is through the power of the God who is incarnate in the life, preachings, teachings, healings, passion, death, resurrection, and promised consummation of Jesus Christ we are redeemed. Grace, grace, all is grace. No one had to pay any price to anyone—Jesus to God, God to the devil, God to Godself. Rather, the God of compassion and loving kindness redeems us through the divine power which undergoes our suffering caused by our sin and raises to new life those who participate in the power of his cross and resurrection, a power which is powerful enough to promise the end of evil and the completion of the creation in communion with God.

CHAPTER SEVEN

Jesus, Judaism, and Christianity

What was the relation of Jesus to the Judaism of his day? I begin with such an elementary question because I must confess I am appalled by the number of students who come to into my classes assuming Jesus lived above his social context untouched by it or stood in direct opposition to the leaders of first century Judaism and even Judaism itself. Beyond this historical question, we must ask what is the relationship between Judaism and Christianity today? Although this is an even more complex question than the first one, I am equally distressed by the number of Christians who accept the Marcionite division of the Bible between the Old Testament God of wrath and the New Testament God of love, and who write off Judaism through a "supersessionist" approach to it, sometimes expressed as a blatant anti-Semitism, usually as a more subtle anti-Judaism, which molds their interpretation of the Bible and their theology. The deeper issue which underlies both of these two questions is the theological problem of whether Christianity in general, and christology is particular, are inherently anti-Judaic. Convinced that christology is inherently anti-Judaic, Rosemary Ruether says, "The understanding of christology is, I believe, at the heart of the problem. Theologically, anti-Judaism developed as the left hand of christology. Anti-Judaism was the negative side of the Christian affirmation that Jesus was the Christ."[1]

Post-Holocaust Christian theology, at least since the mid-1960s, has had to come to terms self-consciously and explicitly with these questions. What can post-Holocaust christology do with the New Testament teaching that "the Jews" killed Jesus, that God has rejected God's people in favor of another? How can Christians reconstruct christology in light of the fact that Christians have persecuted Jews and carried out anti-Judaic pogroms in the name of Christ throughout its history, as we saw this culminate in the 1940s Holocaust?[2] Aware of the fact that this nearly two-thousand-year history of conflict ended in the genocide of six million Jews, some Christian theologians have argued that christology must be reconstructed in the light of this historical reality. Even if Christians cannot be blamed as the direct cause of the Holocaust, their teachings and practices were neither accidental nor incidental to its occurence. Christians can no longer escape the questions about whether, how, and to what degree their christology contributed to this massive evil by laying the groundwork and fueling the fires of anti-Judaism (and anti-Semitism).

In attempting to engage such questions, it is useful to consider both historical and contemporary phenomena: the teachings, death, and resurrection of Jesus in the context of first century Judaism, and the relation of Judaism and Christianity in the twenty-first century. A great deal of recent biblical and theological scholarship by both Jews and Christians highlights Jesus as a first century Jew. With the enormous increase in our knowledge about Second Temple Judaism (the 600-year period from the rebuilding of the First Temple [520 BCE] following the Babylonian Exile [586 BCE], to the destruction of the Second Temple by Rome in the course of Jewish revolt [66-73 CE]), new information has appeared for a reconsideration of Jesus in his social context and the relationship between the early church and Judaism throughout the first century. I will review some of that scholarship as it reconstructs the relationship between Jesus and rabbinic Judaism, and then "the passion" of Jesus, specifically, the crucifixion, within the context of first century Judaism. Subsequently, I will consider the significance of the resurrection of Jesus for Christians and the theological quandary about the relationship between Judaism and Christianity today.

I. Jesus and the Pharisees

Jesus was a Jew. This statement seems patently obvious, but it comes as a shock, and a dilemma, to many Christians. They have been taught through their New Testament and through sermons that Jesus existed as a heavenly outsider within Judaism, or as a morally peerless insider against Judaism, so that he himself can be understood historically and theologically apart from the Hebrew and Jewish covenant, which was, at best, a prophecy and a mere preparation for him. However, studies in the historical Jesus increasingly have shown the extent to which the context and content of Jesus' ministry and the beliefs of the earliest church make sense only within first century Judaism. Therefore, in order to understand Christianity in general and christology in specific, it is essential to grasp both within their Jewish context and origins. Christianity derives from

Judaism through the person of Jesus, who was by birth, practice, and loyalty a Jew. Regardless of what was new or distinctive about him, Judaism lies at the heart of his life, teaching, and mission.

Even among scholars, however, the significance of the Judaism of Jesus has not been obvious, nor has it been, until recently, central to their reconstructions of him as a historical figure. When twentieth-century New Testament scholars, particularly the form critics of Bultmann (d. 1976) and the post-Bultmannian school, tried to reconstruct "the historical Jesus," they invoked as one of their guiding principles in reconstructing our knowledge about the man from Nazareth in distinction from the church's interpretation of the historic Jesus "the criterion of dissimilarity." As Norman Perrin (d. 1976) formulates it, "Thus we reach the fundamental criterion for authenticity upon which all reconstructions of the teaching of Jesus must be built, which we propose to call the 'criterion of dissimilarity.' . . . [T]he earliest form of a saying we can reach may be regarded as authentic if it can be shown to be dissimilar to characteristic emphases both of ancient Judaism and of the early Church, and this will particularly be the case where Christian tradition oriented towards Judaism can be shown to have modified the saying away from its original emphasis."[3] Anything in the New Testament texts which Jesus and Judaism, and most especially Pharisaic Judaism, shared in common is ruled out by this methodological principle as inauthentic Jesus material. Consequently, Jesus was seldom depicted by form critics as an authentic Jew; if anything, the authentic Jesus was identified as one who denied his Jewishness and the basic teachings and practices of first century Judaism in favor of a thoroughly new teaching about and mediation of God to his followers.

The problem with this approach to the historical Jesus is that it was based not only on the theological assumptions of many biblical scholars, namely, their Protestant theological interpretations of Judaism along the gospel versus law continuum, but also on their lack of knowledge of Second Temple Judaism, which has now been reversed in the last few decades. Specifically, the problem with the principle of dissimilarity is that our recent knowledge of Second Temple Judaism shows how Jewish Jesus was in his own views and practices.[4] James Sanders claims "that Jesus had himself observed these and the other parts of the Mosaic law, and that he had never recommended transgression as a general practice. . . . Jesus was not locked in mortal combat with upholders of the law as a matter of principle. Everyone, including Jesus and his followers, believed that God gave the law to Moses and that he had inspired the other scriptures as well. If Jesus disagreed with other interpreters over details, the disputes were no more substantial than were disputes between the Jewish parties and even within each party."[5]

Increasingly it has become clear that virtually every view attributed to Jesus in the Gospels is also attributed in the Talmud to one or another Pharisaic teacher. It is apparent that the teaching of Jesus is nearly identical to the teaching of his contemporary Pharisees and rabbis. Jesus' way of life and set of beliefs was thoroughly Jewish. "'Religion' in Judaism was not only festivals and sacrifices, as it was in most of the Greco-Roman world, but rather encompassed all of life."[6] Specifically, Jesus shared all of the common beliefs that defined Judaism: monotheism; Israel's divine election and the law; and reparations for transgression of the law through repentance, punishment, and forgiveness. He also shared the main practices which marked observant Jews: the worship and service of God, including worshiping God at the Temple in Jerusalem; circumcision of infant sons; not working on the Sabbath, the seventh day of the week; avoidance of certain foods as being impure; and purification before entering the Temple.[7] Although there were apparently some minor disagreements between Jesus and the Pharisees, such as some purity practices and healing on the Sabbath, "the level of disagreement and argument falls well inside the parameters of debate that were accepted in Jesus' time."[8] As Oxford Professor of Jewish Studies Geza Vermes says, "the one apparent doctrinal conflict between Jesus and Judaism [over unclean food] is due to a deliberate twist given to a probably genuine saying of Jesus by the redactor of the Greek Mark. . . . As far as basic Jewish beliefs are concerned, the only serious clash reported in the Gospels between Jesus and the established authority finds him opposing the Sadducees in their denial of the resurrection of the dead."[9] In Jesus' day and age, such conflicts would never lead to execution.

Who were the Pharisees? The Pharisees were the founders of the Judaism we still identify today as Judaism. They were a group of especially observant and influential Jews, particularly in Palestine, from the second century BCE to the first century CE. We know very little about them, and what we do know, we know from the New Testament, Josephus, and rabbinic literature. Our picture of them depends primarily on which of these three accounts we take to be most reliable. What seems most likely is that they 1) constituted a new scholarly class; 2) formulated the Oral Torah or unwritten law not formulated in the Hebrew Bible; 3) taught in a new way ("You have heard it said, but I say"); and 4) developed a new institution, the synagogue, which rivaled the temple and priesthood. In addition to advocating the idea of the resurrection, they transformed the idea of serving God for a reward, dropped the sharp distinction between those who were good and those who were evil, stressed the idea that the elect were justified by grace and that God's power is necessary for ethical living, and internalized the Torah in the heart of each individual.

Josephus considered them prominent in public life and the group, about six thousand in the first century, most influential with the people, although he himself considered the priests the authoritative interpreters of the two-fold oral and written law. They were popular in part because of their emphasis that God cared about each person. In rabbinic literature following the destruction of the Temple in 70 CE, the Pharisees continued to be characterized as concerned with ritual purity, food tithes, and Sabbath observance. "In seeking to spread a renewed fidelity to the biblical law, they were inevitably promoting social and political change and thus functioned as a social movement that aroused opposition."[10]

There were many ideas Jesus and the Pharisees shared in common. Indeed, if Jesus was close to any of the groups in Palestine in the first century, he was closest to the Pharisees.[11] The Gospels, however, at face value give a very different picture of the Pharisees: they are typically described as hypocrites, blind guides, blind fools, blind men, whitewashed tombs, serpents, and a brood of vipers. Jesus is presented as a sharp, constant critic of "the Pharisees," not only as individuals but also as a group. The problem is that the New Testament picture of the hostile relation between Jesus and the Pharisees reflects, in the light of a historical-critical approach to the texts, and, in the light of our knowledge of Second Temple Judaism, a distorted if not propagandistic view of the Jesus and the Pharisees.

Is it possible to account for this apparent contradiction between the received texts and recent historical reconstruction, and in the process show that Jesus should not be read as a repudiator of Pharisaic Judaism? The answer to this is yes, for there is a significant divergence between the New Testament picture of the Pharisees and current evidence for an alternative view of the Pharisees. How and why does the New Testament present a distorted view of Jesus and the Pharisees?

First, the controversy between Jesus and the Pharisees must not be over-interpreted. The Pharisees were highly self-critical among themselves; the criticisms found in the Gospels do not exceed Pharisaic criticism of themselves from their own literature. Of the New Testament picture of Jesus as a constant, carping critic of the Pharisees, Gerald Sloyan says, "The gospel language against the Pharisees is so strong that Christianity is in the position of having set Jesus the Jewish teacher against all his contemporaries who claimed learning in the law. The opposition is unfortunate. The verdict of the gospels on the scribes and the Pharisees, like that of Jewish sources, more closely approximates the general verdict that can be leveled against all humanity: There are all sorts."[12] Furthermore, the New Testament picture of Pharisees as a group of ritual purists keeping themselves separated from the unclean is overdone. The masses were solidly behind them in their call to a way of holiness. Their mission was to lead Israel in the way of holiness, for the people and not just the priesthood were to be holy. The movement flourished for 300 years and Jesus lived at the mid-point of that period in Israel's history.

Second, the church of the late first century wrote the Gospels, and they wrote the gospels with a myriad of agenda in mind, including an intent to make Judaism look as unfavorable as they could make it look. Prior to 70 CE there were many Judaisms, and one of those forms of Judaism was a sect within Judaism known as "Christian." Following 70 CE Pharisaic Judaism as we know it today triumphed within Judaism as the legitimate successor of Israel's faith; the Christian Church emerged as an alternative claimant to be the legitimate heir. The young church was involved in a life and death conflict over succession with the Pharisees, who were the leaders of synagogue Judaism after the fall of the Temple in 70 CE, about who were the legitimate inheritors of Israel's promise. This clash near the end of the first century over legitimacy was retrojected back into the New Testament, including the Gospels' portraits of the life and death of Jesus.

Just how much actual conflict there was between Jesus and the Pharisees is hard to say. In the Gospels, Jesus expresses marked parallels with Pharisaic interpretation of the Law as it is contained in the Talmud. He was Jewish; he, too, was engaged in a free-wheeling interpretation of Oral Torah. Most of the content and style of his teaching (some have argued all) is Jewish and even rabbinic. There clearly is conflict between Jesus and some Pharisees, which in itself is a typical Pharisaic style. Sloyan summarizes in a breezy fashion what many have concluded about this matter: "Jesus . . . had no difficulty whatever with the genuine article, the sage who sought holiness in the observance of the law. He was an opponent of the counterfeit types recorded in the Talmud. . . . Recent years have witnessed attempts to rehabilitate the Pharisees, even to glorify them. Unfortunately we do not have enough evidence from the period to do either of these things safely. We are on firmer ground in supposing that the gospel rhetoric against them describes only some, as is the case in any age with doctors, lawyers, or the clergy."[13]

II. The Crucifixion of Jesus

Who killed Jesus? In some New Testament texts and in common Christian belief, "the Jews" killed Jesus. Furthermore, they are forever to be held responsible for his death. All the passion narratives concur that the Roman governor Pilate judged Jesus to be innocent and that his death was due to the insistence of "the Jews." Since "the Jews" of first century Palestine killed Jesus, all Jews are henceforth to be known as "Christ killers." This scourge applies to contemporary Jews as well as all Jews in first century Palestine and the Diaspora. Therefore, Jews continue to be the scapegoats for his death.

I will examine here two questions about the crucifixion of Jesus. How historically accurate is the charge that "the Jews" killed Jesus? And how theologically responsible is it for Christians to blame "the Jews" for Jesus' death?

The charge of Jewish responsibility and culpability—sometimes blatant and crude, sometimes subtle and sophisticated—continues to be made among Christian theologians today. Some scholars, who have become especially sensitive to this persisting charge, have shown how even contemporary theologians, such as Karl Barth, Jurgen Moltmann, and Jon Sobrino, continue to declare Jewish responsibility for Jesus' death.[14] This may seem like a strange accusation, since these theologians stand as major opponents of the the work of other "theologians under Hitler" (such as Gerhard Kittel, Paul Althaus, and Emmanuel Hirsch), who fed, if they did not spread, the flames of anti-semitism throughout the period of the Third Reich.[15] In the work of all of these theologians, whether orthodox, neo-orthodox, liberal, or liberationist, the terms Pharisaism, legalism, works-righteousness, and "the Law" continue to be derogatory terms, connected with the essential meaning of sin and death, in contrast to the gospel of grace, which is connected with the life of God. The negative traits of "the Law" are the central characteristics of "the Jews," which led them to kill Jesus. (As an aside, I might point out right here that whatever Jesus did for us Gentile Christians, he did not redeem us from "the curse of the Law," for we Gentiles were never under "the Law" to begin with!)

I begin, then, with the historical question. Did "the Jews" kill Jesus?[16] The answer is that probably some Jews, most notably some chief priests among the rulers of the temple who gladly would do away with a troublesome wandering preacher, collaborated in a secondary role in the crucifixion of Jesus. There is, however, no evidence that the Pharisees brought any charges against Jesus before one of their courts, a *beth din*, or that any Pharisees participated in his death. Rather, Jesus was brought to trial before a sanhedrin, a council of high priests, which was a political, not a religious, body, as it was presided over by high priest Caiaphas, a Sadducee who had been appointed by the procurator.[17] This body had interest in Jesus' teachings only insofar as they had political ramifications and only insofar as they might be interpreted as a challenge to Roman authority. John Dominic Crossan, major leader within the "Jesus Seminar," takes "as historical that Jesus was executed by some conjunction of Jewish and Roman authority. That places the focus, in terms of personalities, on Joseph Ciaphas and Pontius Pilate."[18] The Roman authorities and Ciaphas worked well together, as evidenced by the latter's unusually long tenure of eight years under Gratus, Pilate's predecessor, and ten years under Pilate.[19] Whatever one concludes about the proper answer to the question, "the Jews" did not kill Jesus.

"The mob," stirred up by the high priests, if indeed such a group ever existed, may have been made up of about two percent of all the inhabitants and pilgrims staying in Jerusalem at the time, considerably less than 1/1000 of all Jews then living at the time.[20] At the time of Jesus' ministry in Palestine, eighty percent of "the Jews" lived in the Diaspora. Paul van Buren makes the point that "the vast majority of the Jewish people who were the contemporaries of Jesus could not possibly even have heard of him, since they lived dispersed around the Mediterranean in all parts of the Roman Empire.[21] If there were Jews involved, and there surely were a few at least in secondary roles, these have come to be identified by the later Gospel writers as "the Jews," and they have come to be identified throughout Christian history as "all Jews," who are guilty of killing Jesus and therefore "Christ killers."

In fact, the evidence concerning the Jews as enemies of Jesus is all to the contrary. Many Jews were sympathetic to him. As Pinchas Lapide, a Jewish New Testament scholar, shows, twenty-six passages in Matthew, twenty-eight in Mark, and thirty-five in Luke attest to the fact that large numbers of the Jewish people in Galilee, as well as in Judea, Jerusalem, and many other places, were impressed by Jesus, gladly listened to him for days on end, hung on him, became his followers, accompanied him on his journeys, and repeatedly welcomed him with respect and affection. Lapide says, "I know of no other figure in Jewish antiquity whose popularity and public acclaim has been attested so often and so convincingly."[22] The majority of the people of Israel who were able to come into contact with Jesus apparently gave him a warm, and often enthusiastic, reception.

Historically speaking, then, who was immediately and directly responsible for the crucifixion of Jesus? In terms of historical reconstruction of the immediate cause of the crucifixion of Jesus, Crossan's "best historical reconstruction concludes that what led immediately to Jesus' arrest and execution in Jerusalem at Passover was that act of symbolic destruction, in deed and word, against the Temple. That sacred edifice represented in one central place all that his vision and program had fought against among the peasantry of Lower Galilee. In Jerusalem, quite possibly for the first and only time, he acted according to that program."[23] His symbolic act was perceived as an immediate threat of violence by some Jewish authorities, who quickly implicated some Roman authorities. The immediate cause of his death was not his controversy with "the Jews" in general or "the Pharisees" in specific. What is clear is that "when the crunch actually came, the Pharisees had nothing whatever to do with his death."[24] It was in fact Rome, an occupying power out of sympathy with all Jewish aspirations, that put Jesus of Nazareth to death.

If one must put the blame on someone for historical reasons, Pilate was the one who had Jesus crucified.[25] Crucifixion was a Roman, not a Jewish, penalty. It was Roman troops, the Roman law, a Roman procurator, a Roman execution, a Roman scourging, and a Roman cross that killed Jesus. The Sanhedrin could carry out capital punishment only by stoning, burning, decapitation, and strangulation. "It was not a Jewish religious indictment, but on a secular accusation that he was condemned by the emperor's delegate to die shamefully on the Roman cross."[26]

Pilate receives different estimates from different people, usually depending on the agenda of the assessor and with whom he is being compared. Pilate was, in fact, not an innocent one in whom one could find no fault. Crossan describes him as "neither a saint nor a monster," but he seemed to lack concern for Jewish religious sensibilities and was capable of rather brutal methods of crowd control.[27] He was a procurator thoroughly disliked by the people because of his cruelty and greed. Vermes describes him as "the second-rate and notoriously cruel Roman civil servant,"[28] and Crossan as "an ordinary second-class governor."[29] Under him, the country was in constant turmoil. His cold-bloodedness became so great that Rome relieved him of his responsibilities in 36 CE. Clark Williamson, following Philo, describes him as "unbending and recklessly hard," and his rule was characterized by "corruption, violence, robberies, ill-treatment of people, grievances, continuous executions without trial, endless and intolerable cruelties."[30]

Whoever killed Jesus, "the Jews" did not kill him, any more than "the Romans" killed him, thereby making all Italians then and now Christ killers. If one must establish "responsibility" and "blame" for the death of Jesus, one can only place the blame on the political system of the Roman Empire and, to one degree or another, the various bureaucrats who inhabited and implemented that system. It was in fact Rome that put Jesus of Nazareth to death. But the point is that it is neither historically accurate nor theologically meaningful to say "the Jews" killed Jesus. Christians have claimed that for centuries, beginning with the books of their canon, especially the Gospels of Matthew and John, and many continue to claim it today.

Yet the Gospels blame the Jews and depict Pilate as poised, judicial, and innocent. All four Gospels are reluctant to state plainly that the sentence of death was pronounced by the governor of Judea. Why do the Gospels exonerate Pilate, and, at least in part, represent "the Jews" as responsible for Jesus' death? The answer is that the Gospels are not only a proclamation of a new gospel. They are, also, simultaneously, an apologetic and even a polemical literature directed against the synagogue and Judaism. They were written at the end of the first century when the church and the synagogue were attempting to establish their own distinct identity and to separate from each other. The record and rationale for this separation are reflected in the contemporary literature of both Jews and Christians. The Gospels, written after the destruction of the Temple in 70 CE, provide the record and rationale for this separation for Christians. Likewise, one finds a record of the separation in Jewish texts, where a curse against "the Nazarenes," written somewhere around 85 CE and inserted into the "Eighteen Benedictions," was intended to serve as an exclusion of Jewish members of the Jesus-movement from formal synagogue worship.[31] By this date, then, the break was completed and the negative views of each other were established.

The formation of the Christian canon both reflects this situation at the end of the first century and was itself a major contribution to this decisive break with Judaism as it turned away from the synagogue and set its face toward Rome. Luke wanted to demonstrate to Theophilus that the development of Christianity under Domitian should not be seen as a threat to the Empire, so Pilate repeatedly states that Jesus is guilty of no crime. The Jewish leaders and the crowd are responsible for his crucifixion, he claims. Since the Jews and not the Roman procurator, Pilate, crucified him, Christianity should be the subject of benign neglect by the Empire. In exhonorating Pilate, the church made "a daring act of public relations faith in the destiny of Christianity not within Judaism but with the Roman Empire."[32] In fact, since Christianity is "the true Judaism," it should be granted the status of legitimacy in the Empire.

The redactors of the Gospels, however, faced a problem in their relationship with the Empire. Since Jesus was crucified via a Roman means of punishment, and since the superscription over the cross reflected a political charge, it was crystal clear he died at the hands of Roman authorities as a presumed threat to Rome. He was perceived to be a political criminal (specifically, to be liable for treason), on the basis of the charges of subverting the nation, opposing payment of taxes to Caesar, and calling himself the Messiah, a king. Sloyan says, "That is a clear expression of three seditious offenses. On the basis of any one of them, a Roman prefect could have passed a death sentence with dispatch and not have needed to report the incident to Rome. Failing other evidence, that charge will describe why Jesus died as much as anything we know."[33] However, the church wanted to show that Jesus, and therefore Christianity, were not politically subversive to the Empire, so Pilate had to be depicted as (relatively) innocent of the death of Jesus. Increasingly "the Jews" became the scapegoats of his death.[34]

The contemporary Christian can recognize that this propaganda ploy to establish the Christian case was relatively innocent and harmless at the end of the first century. "Those first Christians were relatively powerless Jews, and compared to them the Jewish authorities represented serious and threatening power. As long as Christians were the marginalized and disenfranchised ones, such passion fiction about Jewish responsibility and Roman innocence did nobody much harm. But, once the Roman Empire became Christian, that fiction turned lethal. . . . It is no longer possible in retrospect to think of that passion fiction as relatively benign propaganda. . . . Its repetition has now become the longest lie, and, for our own integrity, we Christians must at last name it such."[35] The idea and language of first century Jewish responsibility have consequences for which Christians are morally responsible today. Christians need to watch their language. To say "the Jews" killed Jesus and are "Christ-killers" only feeds the flames of the Holocaust and continues Hitler's work. Such rhetoric is the epitome of moral rubbish, indeed, outrage, and Christians ought to stop it.

If Christians need to assess responsibility and blame for the death of the messiah, they should seek the best historical answer to that question they can establish. There is little doubt about what the answer to that question is. However, the question is also a theological one. What and who killed Jesus? For a theological answer to the question, they must return to the center of their theological insight into the death of God's prophet. He was killed because of and through the power of human violence and sinfulness. That condition, responsibility, and guilt is a reality in which we all participate and share. The theological answer is best expressed in Robert Petrich's Choral Variations on "Ah, Holy Jesus": "Who was the guilty? Who brought this upon thee/Alas, my treason, Jesus, hath undone thee./Twas I, Lord Jesus, I it was denied thee:/I crucified thee." Pilate, Ciaphas, the Roman authorities, the Pharisees, the Jews, and the Romans participated then no more or no less that we all now participate in the structures of violence and death which killed the Jewish prophet from Nazareth.

What was the meaning of his death for Jews and Christians? Whatever Jesus' death means for Jews beyond the tragic death of one of their own Jewish prophets at the hands of a foreign occupation, it does not and cannot mean for Jews that it was part of the evidence that Jesus was the Messiah that the Jews have awaited. Indeed, his death is decisive counterevidence to such a claim. The reason for the Jewish refusal to interpret Jesus' death as having any messianic significance is not the hardheartedness of Jews or any lack of perceptiveness or any abandonment of the messianic promise. Indeed, the opposite is the case. The reason for their refusal to acknowledge Jesus as the Messiah is their decision to remain faithful to the promises of God as they are conveyed in the Hebrew Bible as they await the Messiah.

In the view of Pinchas Lapide, an Orthodox Jew and a New Testament scholar, Jesus was not and did not claim to be or did not promise to become "the promised deliverer of the Jews" (the Jewish meaning of Messiah). Whatever caused his suffering and death, and whatever they mean to Jews, they do not mean he was the Messiah because they cannot mean he was the Messiah. "If the intimate circle of the Twelve were not capable of grasping the secret of the 'suffering Messiah' despite repeated instructions from Jesus himself, and if their lack of understanding could outlive even Golgotha, then how can one possibly expect such an understanding from the broad masses of the people of Israel at the time, particularly since to them the idea of a suffering Messiah would have seemed an absurd contradiction?"[36] Furthermore, the Jew believes that when the Messiah comes, the whole world will be different. Shalom, the Kingdom of God, the rule and reign of God will be an accomplished fact in the world. But if one simply looks out the window, one can know that the reign of God has not been established in the world through Jesus. Indeed, the only way that Christians can claim that the Kingdom of God has been established by the Messiah is to redefine what they mean by Messiah and to claim that the Kingdom of God has been established proleptically. I will discuss this below in section four.

III. The Resurrection of Jesus

What does the resurrection mean for Jews? Whatever the controversy was between the church and the synagogue, it was not over of the claim that someone could be resurrected from the dead by God. Nor was it necessarily a controversy over whether Jesus was resurrected by God. Resurrection was a Jewish idea, specifically a Pharisaic belief. Ironically, it was the Pharisees' tenacious belief in resurrection which made credible the early church's testimony that Jesus had been raised from the dead. "Resurrection was not an impossibility; it was the chief cornerstone of the Pharisaic faith. The Pharisees could deny that Jesus had been resurrected, but they could not mock the belief in resurrection."[37] The only thing unusual for Jews about the early Jewish-Christian believers' Easter faith was the claim that the resurrection had taken place in the case of Jesus alone without inaugurating a total transformation of the world as a time and place of shalom or restoration of Jewish sovereignty in their own land. The resurrection of the body and the general resurrection of the dead at the end of time are first-century Jewish tenets. Although isolated instances of the resurrection of the dead can be found in Old Testament and rabbinic sources, "it was not until the early rabbinic period that the doctrine of the general resurrection of the dead became a central feature of Jewish theology."[38] Indeed, one can say that "as long as the church was made up of Jews who believed that Jesus would come to redeem Israel from foreign domination and inaugurate the new age of the sovereignty of the God of Israel, even that a decisive step toward that day had been made with his death and resurrection, other Jews might be skeptical, but there was no reason for conflict."[39] During the earliest years of the church there was no conflict over this point. Many Jews who were Christians remained Jews, until finally the more disputed issue of faithfulness to Torah was raised to the crisis point among Jews following Paul's victory in his dispute about Gentiles in the church. Belief in the resurrection of Jesus was not the primary controversy between the early Christians and Jews.

Nor, does it seem, is this the crucial issue between Christians and Jews today. At least in the opinion of some Jews, such as Lapide, "a distinguished Orthodox Jewish scholar," the resurrection of Jesus is logically consistent with ancient and contemporary Jewish beliefs. Furthermore, Lapide believes that in fact Jesus was resurrected by God for a divine purpose, specifically, to bring about the formation of a community which would carry the central message of Judaism to the world. Basing his belief in his critical examination of the documentary evidence of the New Testament, in ways that sound very much like recent defenders of the resurrection of Jesus today, he accepts the historical facticity of Jesus' resurrection. The resurrection was the foundation upon which the church could carry the faith in the God of Israel to the whole world. The issue between Christians and Jews, then and now, therefore, is not over the resurrection of Jesus, he claims, but over a quite different issue.

Contemporary Christians and Jews surely find Lapide's views to be an anomaly, if not idiosyncratic and disconcerting. Most Jews have, on the one hand, steadfastly refused to accept the Christian claim that God raised Jesus from the dead, and so Dan Cohn-Sherbok speaks of Lapide as "a unique exception, and his views have been almost entirely ignored."[40] On the other hand, Christians have traditionally taken the resurrection to be a distinctively Christian belief and the unique proof of their claims about the messianic status of Jesus. So when a contemporary Jew claims to believe in the resurrection of Jesus but not in the messianic status of Jesus, both Christians and Jews must take note and ask just what the resurrection is supposed to prove and how it is supposed to prove it.

Whether Lapide speaks for himself only, or for a few Jews, I cannot make any judgment. I assume Cohn-Sherbok's observation is correct; few Jews ascribe credibility to the claim of the earliest Christians. But I do not think that empirical observation settles the primarily theological question that is at stake here. Nor does Cohn-Sherbok. He says quite directly, "this is not the end of the matter," either for Jews or Christians, for Jews can be asked to answer why they take the alternative approach, and, even more decisively, Christians must answer what is the grounds for their christological confessions about the meaning of the resurrection of Jesus if a non-believer can also affirm the "fact" of Jesus' resurrection insofar as anyone can affirm it as a "fact." In making his concession to Christians, therefore, Lapide opens one, if not the most, controversial problem of contemporary christology for any Christian. If the resurrection as a historical fact is not the basis, or at least is not the proof, of the messianic claims about Jesus, since clearly some Jews (and some other non-Christians) concede the facticity of the resurrection, then what is the basis for any christological claims to begin with? That is the systematic and constructive problem the Christian is left with, regardless of how representative Lapide is or is not of contemporary Judaism. Unless Lapide is written off by both Jews and Christians as "not a real Jew," his basic challenge is not to his contemporary Jewish faith. His challenge is to Christians who think the resurrection of Jesus is the proof or confirmation of their christological beliefs.

In terms of the details of Lapide's argument, he claims he has an intense devotion as a Jew to Jesus. He accepts Jesus as a central player in God's plan and in whose name a worldwide church was founded. He sees no reason to eject a person such as the Rabbi from Nazareth from Judaism simply because some Christian picture does not suit him as a Jew. Jesus was utterly true to the Torah, as is he (Lapide), and perhaps even more so. So he accepts Jesus as a faithful Jew. Furthermore, belief in the resurrection as a fact about Jesus is possible for him as a Jew without making any christological claims based on that fact or without denying his faithfulness of Judaism.

However, Lapide pushes the issue between Christians and Jews to a deeper level than quibbling about the facticity of the resurrection. He introduces a different claim that moves the center of the christological issue beyond a difference over the resurrection. In principle, Jews and Christians can walk together through Good Friday, he says, and can even come together on belief in the resurrection of Jesus, at least in the Jewish understanding of the resurrection of the dead. That is, they can walk and talk together, agreeing and quibbling, until Easter Monday morning. Then the real, decisive issue between Jews and Christians emerges. Although he can accept the resurrection as a fact, he cannot accept the subsequent Christian claim that Jesus was the messiah, that the resurrection proves Jesus was the messiah, or any of the other high christological claims made by his followers, Jewish or Gentile. Specifically, he cannot accept the claim that Jesus brought to completion through his passion and resurrection the Kingdom of God which Jews have longed for. Only the completion of the messianic kingdom can establish messiahship, not claims about resurrection, regardless of whether those claims are interpreted as historical fact, or as existential self-understanding, or whatever other ways Christians may want to interpret the meaning of the resurrection. What separates Jews and Christians is not the 33 years for which Jews have every reason to be as proud of Jesus as have Christians, nor even his death *and resurrection,* but rather two incompatible *interpretations* of the death and resurrection story, regardless of what "the facts" are about the resurrection as bodily resuscitation or transformation, spiritual appearance, existential meaning or self-understanding, ecclesiastical proclamation, liturgical recitation, or any other description of it. For Christians the resurrection, however interpreted, entails his messianic identity, and that becomes the grounds for their high christological claims. But Jews are still looking faithfully for the Messiah to establish the kingdom of God following the death *and* resurrection of Jesus.

Lapide, therefore, is not a Christian because the resurrection of Jesus does not prove his messiahship. *There is no intrinsic or necessary relationship between resurrection and messiahship.* Jesus belongs to the *praeparatio messianica*—the patriarchs and prophets who pioneer the full salvation of the future Kingdom of God. "For Jewish scholars, the testimony of the resurrection was no proof of the messiahship of Jesus because for them the concept of resurrection is not connected with the messianic expectation of salvation. At the time of Jesus, Judaism was expecting the resurrection of various figures: of Enoch, of Moses, of Elijah, of Jeremiah . . . but not the resurrection of the Messiah. . . . Through the resurrection of Jesus, an access to faith in the one, until then unknown, God of Israel was opened to Gentiles. On the other hand, in Judaism the faith in God did not need to receive new foundations and reasons; it was unquestioned. . . . For Israel, God was on earth already before Christ. I therefore accept neither the messiahship of Jesus for the people of Israel nor of the Pauline interpretation of the resurrection of Jesus."[41]

Lapide is not alone. Even Cohn-Sherbok, who is offended by Lapide's stance, acknowledges the logical possibility of the resurrection and claims there is nothing logically inconsistent with the claim within traditional Jewish faith. But, he asks, is the specific belief in the resurrection of Jesus of Nazareth a plausible belief for Jews? His answer to his question is no, it is not plausible, and he gives two quite different reasons for his decisive answer. His answers are theological. In rabbinic literature there are a dozen or so signs of the messiah age, and in the light of these signs, "Jews refuse to accept Jesus as their Messiah and Savior because he did not fulfil these messianic expectations."[42] Although this is the basic theological reason for the Jewish refusal, this is not his sole reason. But the primary reason is clear. Jesus was not resurrected because Jesus could not have been resurrected because the messiah has not yet arrived. Jews wait for his coming to redeem the world. "Only at that time will the dead be resurrected to enter into a new life."[43] Jesus died and remained dead, and his corpse rotted in the ground.

While Lapide and Cohn-Sherbok as Jews concede the resurrection, either as a fact or as a logical possibility (though not having been proved to Enlightenment skeptics in Cohn-Sherbok's case), neither believes it convincingly proves or could prove the messiahship of Jesus. How do Christians derive theological meaning from the resurrection, then, when others who concede it do not find any such meaning? The reality of the resurrection, in whatever form it is understood, is or can be affirmed by both. If so, the resurrection can hardly be considered to be "proof" that Jesus was the Messiah, since Jews are certainly as reasonable, perceptive, and moral in their beliefs as Christians.

My thesis is that Christians can connect the resurrection and messiahship of Jesus only through a strategy of reconception of messiahship. For the Jew, when the Messiah in fact arrives, the world will be utterly changed in a dramatic way. The kingdom of God will be here; shalom will reign throughout the whole creation. Until then, the Jew waits for the kingdom in promise and anticipation. The most Christians can claim is that the resurrection is the "first fruits" evidence of a fuller reality that waits yet to arrive in the near or distant future of "last things." They believe they see something the Jew does not see. But when reflective they must admit that what they see is the "first fruits," a sign of the coming reign, a promise of its fulfillment, a hope of things yet to come. When all is said and done, there is not as much difference between them as appears at first blush. Actually, they are talking about a different interpretation of the same reality. Christians have, by a sleight of hand, shifted the grounds of the intermural or interfamilal debate about how to interpret the resurrection by redefining the central category of messiaship.

IV. Christians as Semantic Revisionists

According to the messianic promises of Judaism, which Jesus is proclaimed by Christians to have fulfilled, the true Messiah must bring about of the kingdom of God in fact as well as promise. "Judaism looked to the messianic coming as a public, world-historical event which unequivocally overthrew the forces of evil in the world and established the reign of God."[44] But if this is the meaning of the term "Messiah," the Christian must admit that the facts of history do not at all support the claim that the crucified and risen Jesus Christ completed the reign of God. If one looks out any window of any building in any part of the world, no Christian can claim that Jesus is indeed the Messiah, the savior, who has in fact brought the completed kingdom of God to earth, the place of shalom, the time of peace and justice. Insofar as violence, greed, and suffering continue to reign in our world, Christians cannot simply proclaim that the messianic age was realized in the death-resurrection of Christ. Indeed, the only possible way that Christians can claim that Jesus was and is the messiah is to radically redefine what Messiah means. And that is precisely what Christians did and continue to do through their interpretation of the death and resurrection of Jesus as a proleptic promise of messianic fulfillment which will be accomplished in the eschaton. "When this event failed to materialize, Christianity pushed it off into an indefinite future, i.e., the Second Coming, and reinterpreted Jesus' messianic role in inward and personal ways that had little resemblance to what the Jewish tradition meant by the coming of the Messiah."[45] If one begins and ends the discussion about the messianic age within the scope of the Jewish meaning of messianism, then Christians can only agree with Jews that Jesus was not and is not the messiah. However, if one reinterprets the meaning of messianic hope as an eschatological promise for the future confirmed by the death and resurrection of Jesus, as a prolepsis, as a pledge guaranteed by the resurrection interpreted as the first evidence of the anticipated completion of the messianic rule of God, then Christians offer a re-interpretation of messianic hope. But they can offer a possible meaningful alternative only through the strategy of reconception of the messianic promise.

Acknowledgment of the difference between these two divergent messianic viewpoints has enormous consequences for christology. It means that Christians cannot redefine messiahship on strictly christological grounds (the person and work of Christ, the doctrines of incarnation and atonement), but can interpret and confirm their christological claims only on eschatological grounds. Only as prolepsis, only as inauguration, only as initial fulfillment of a messiahship which will be completed some time in the indefinite future can Christians claim that Jesus is the Messiah of Jewish expectation. Jews continue to wait and anticipate; Christians continue to proclaim and anticipate. Jews, by so doing, continue to remind Christians that eschatology is essential to their christology, that the doctrines of incarnation and atonement cannot carry the weight of christology apart from eschatology. Christology cannot pull off its claims about Jesus' messiahship apart from their eschatology. To put it bluntly, Jesus is not yet the Messiah or the Christ for Christians except as "first fruits" evidence, even confirmation, of the new age to come, which means he is Messiah in the Jewish meaning of the term by promise, by anticipation, by faith. Daniel Migliori recognizes this fact when he says, "All these present experiences of the coming of the Lord are fragmentary and provisional. God's justice and peace are not yet realized throughout the creation. The world is not yet redeemed; God's work of salvation is still unfinished. Sin and suffering, alienation and death still mar the creation and are still present in the lives of believers. The final act of the drama of redemption has not been played out."[46]

To proclaim that Jesus is the Messiah is not to claim an accomplished fact, but to claim that the kingdom of God has been inaugurated, that there are signs of its appearance in history, that it is a task yet to be completed, and that the resurrection stands as the first fruits and the promise of the messianic age yet to come to its fulfillment. But Jesus Christ, even within the Christian vocabulary, is not and cannot be the Messiah according to the Jewish idea of messiahship. The only way he can be Messiah for Christians is to redefine of the idea of messiahship and proclaim that Jesus meets that new definition. Specifically, he meets the messianic expectation as sign, inaugurator, as "first fruits," and as promise, but not as fulfillment; that remains even for Christians a hope and a promise. Jesus cannot be the Messiah without this redefinition. The resurrection alone, without seeing it as an eschatological promise of hope and fulfillment, is empty of messianic significance. Christians can make and sustain their argument that the resurrection of Jesus Christ is proof of his messiahship only when they introduce eschatological terms such as now/then, inaugurated/completed, realized/future. Christians see the resurrection of Jesus as proleptic, as a promise, to be completed in the eschaton. But it is no more the completion of the reign of God for Christians than it is for Jews.

Stated positively, the resurrection for Christians is a promise of the messianic age. It is an inauguration of the messianic age, it is the first fruits of the age to come. But it neither proves nor completes the messianic age in the way Jews think of that age to come. So the argument between Jews and Christians over the Messiah is, in an important respect, a semantic argument. Christians can win that argument only semantically, viz., by redefinition, for both Christians and Jews agree on the "facts" of history, viz., the reality of sin, suffering, and evil in the present age. No Christian, surely, can walk the streets, enter their own house, or even examine themselves closely, and say the Messiah has come, unless the Christian redefines messiahship to meet both the empirical facts of history and to create a new set of expectations to jibe with those facts. That issue remains at the core of the difference between the faiths of these two inheritors of the Abrahamic promise and the Mosaic covenant. This difference is stated with bluntness by Jewish Holocaust theologian, Richard Rubenstein. "The Gospel ends beyond tragedy, on a note of hope. Resurrection is the final word. I wish it were so. But I believe my Pharisaic progenitors were essentially correct two thousand years ago when they sadly concluded that the promise of radical novelty in the human condition was a pathetic, though altogether understandable, illusion, that the old world goes on today as it did yesterday and it will tomorrow. Against my deepest yearnings, I am compelled to end with their tragic acceptance rather than the eschatological hope that still pervades my Christian brother after the death of God."[47] The Christian has no grounds on which to prove Rubenstein is wrong, has no grounds on which to prove the Messiah will return to complete the messiahship. They simply live with the faith that the life, death, and resurrection of Jesus is adequate confirming evidence that God will complete the messianic reign. But there simply are no grounds on which to prove which form of anticipation is the most authentic way to be faithful.

V. Faithfulness to God Through Torah and Through Christ

If the primary controversy between the church and the synagogue is not over the passion or the resurrection of Jesus, then, what is the core difference between these two forms of faith? *The Jewish rejection was not of Jesus or even necessarily of Easter, but of Christianity.* At stake is not the Jewish rejection of Jesus himself but the Jewish rejection of the Christianity which arose following his life, teachings, death, and resurrection. Most fundamentally, Jews disagree and depart from Christians over fidelity to the Torah. Jews remained faithful to the Torah as God's gift, while Christians shifted their ultimate loyalty to Christ as God's pledge. Judaism would not become Jewish Christianity; it would become Pharisaic Judaism. The power of Pharisaism throughout the centuries continues through the vitality of Judaism (all subsequent forms of Judaism are derivative of Pharisaism), which alone of the religions of antiquity proved immune to the Christian gospel.[48]

As Paul's position began to prevail in the debate within the early church about whether Gentiles were to become full-fledged Jews or not, Jewish Christians, at least in the Diaspora, began eating, living, and worshiping with Gentiles, which, from the Jewish point of view, was an invitation to assimilation. "Jews in the church were on the way to losing their Jewishness and their solidarity with the people Israel, the more so as the church became increasingly Gentile in membership. The church, therefore, was not only stealing potential converts to Judaism; it was weakening the Jewishness of its Jewish members. To such a movement responsible Jews had to say no. The integrity of Israel and its fidelity to Torah was at stake."[49] It seems never to have crossed the minds of Christians that what the church called Jewish stubbornness was, from Israel's perspective, fidelity to Torah and Torah's Author. What the Jewish people were taught by their rabbis to deny was not Jesus, not Jesus' death, not even necessarily Jesus' resurrection, but rather a church which taught that Israel's covenant with God had been superseded, nullified, and replaced by a new covenant. To be Jewish was to remain faithful to the Torah.

During the First Roman War the Temple of Jerusalem was burned to the ground in 70 AD by Tacitus's troops. "The Jewish aristocratic class of priests, or Sadducees, was destroyed forever, and it was the scribal class of legal experts, or Pharisees, who inherited that vacuum of Jewish leadership."[50] They met at Yavneh, west of Jerusalem near the Mediterranean coast, to save Judaism, advocating religious fidelity to the Torah and the moral integrity of the Law, extending the lost Temple's rituals of purity into the Jewish home. "The home and its regular meals would be observed as once was the Temple and its sacrificial meals."[51] To this day, Jews remain faithful to this Pharisaic decision to follow the Law, to sustain its regulations and rituals as their faithfulness to God. The problem for Christian theology today is how to interpret, as Christians, this decision to choose the Torah instead of Jesus Christ as the gift of God. One way, of course, is the traditional Christian interpretation of the Jewish decision as unfaithfulness. As a result, God has rejected God's people and Christianity supersedes Judaism as the true heirs of God's promise to Abraham. However, Christians also have grounds for viewing the continuing validity of Judaism within their Christian perspective.

The core of a positive Christian theology of Judaism, which sees Judaism as a form of faithfulness to the God of Abraham and Sarah, is to affirm that Israel continues to be the chosen people of God even after Gentiles have been engrafted into that covenant promise to Abraham through Jesus Christ. This affirmation can be certified either through a one covenant or two covenant theory.[52] In the double covenant view, the distinctiveness of the two faith traditions is emphasized, including emphasis on the novelty of Christianity, although both covenantal traditions are seen as rooted in the Hebrew scriptures. The church and the synagogue remain as two distinctive successors of the Abrahamic covenant, but successors, nevertheless, of the one common covenant rooted in Abraham. "We should rather think of Judaism and Christianity as parallel paths, flowing from common memories in Hebrew scriptures, which are then reformulated into separate ways that lead two peoples to formulate the dialectic of past and future through different historical experiences."[53]

For many Jews and Christians, Judaism and Christianity remain two different religions, bearing different messages and different meanings in the service of the one God of the scriptures they share in common. "Christianity came into being as a surprising, unprecedented and entirely autonomous religious system, not as a child, whether legitimate or otherwise, of Judaism."[54] From this point of view, only when Christianity sees itself as the early church saw itself, as new and uncontingent, as a revision of the history of humanity from Adam onward, and not as a substitute or heir to Judaism, will they really see that they are alien to one another.[55] The Christian interpretation of Jesus is a new religion, a new covenant with the same God Jews and Christians worship. The Jewish God is also the Christian God; both worship one God who is the same God and the only God. Yet there is no inner connection that links Christianity and Judaism traditions of faith, nor needs there be one. The Jesus Christ of the Gospels surprises the Jew familiar with contemporary Judaism, overturning the Temple money changers, who enabled the most important rite in the Israelite cult, the daily whole-offering sacrifice which meant atonement for each and all Israelites throughout the year, and replacing it with the rite of the Eucharist.[56] "The only way for a believing Jew to understand Christianity is in Jewish terms, and the only way for a believing Christian to understand Judaism is in Christian terms."[57]

Although the two covenants are parallel in the sense that they derive from the choice of the one God, they are two distinct covenants, one of them not necessarily seen as a replacement, substitute, heir, or reaffirmation of the other, but as a new covenant with a new people, including some Jews who chose loyalty to Christ instead of the Torah, but mostly Gentiles who now know the same God known by the Jews. From this point of view, Israel, through its faithfulness to the Torah, has as much a place and a role to play in the meaning of salvation as do Christians, through their faithfulness to Christ. God has not abandoned God's people. Jews remain the people of the covenant, to which Christians are newcomers through a sheer act of grace, through a parallel but novel covenant.

There is, however, another perspective which sees an even more intimate connection between Judaism and Christianity than the theology of the double covenant. In the theology of the single covenant, Judaism is the root and trunk of which Christians are a branch (and in which there remains an asymmetrical relation). The covenant is the same, continuing, single Abrahamic covenant, not simply the same God, in both cases, but Christianity is the engrafting of Gentiles into that one covenant. To use a different analogy, Jews and Christians are brothers and sisters of the same household of faith. Or, to use a still different image, there are two forms of God's single covenant, one in the shape of the Torah, the other in the shape of Christ, but both are forms of a single reality. In this particular theory, Christianity is Judaism for Gentiles. It is Judaism for Gentiles in the sense that the God of the covenant who continues the covenant in Judaism now incorporates Gentiles into that single covenant through Jesus who is the Christ. Jesus as the Christ is God's covenant with Gentiles as the Torah is God's covenant with the Jews. But they are one covenant in two forms.

This is the perspective represented in a study catechism approved in 1998 by the Presbyterian Church (U.S.A.). It asks whether the covenant with Israel was an everlasting covenant. "Yes. With the coming of Jesus the covenant with Israel was expanded and confirmed. By faith in him Gentiles were welcomed into the covenant. This throwing open of the gates confirmed the promise that through Israel God's blessing would come to all peoples. Although for the most part Israel has not accepted Jesus as the Messiah, God has not rejected Israel. . . . The God who has reached out to unbelieving Gentiles will not fail to show mercy to Israel as the people of the everlasting covenant."[58]

Neither theory collapses the real differences between Christians and Jews about the meaning of Jesus for each community. The same messianic promise that makes it possible for Christians to believe Jesus is the Messiah makes it impossible for Jews so to believe. This is the fundamental theological question at the center of the difference between Jews and Christians about belief that Jesus is the Christ. The church rests on its faith that Christ has come, and that this is the redemption bestowed by God on humankind; Israel is not able to believe this, as Israel remains faithful to the covenant as the Torah. Martin Buber is utterly clear about the inability of Jews to accept the Christian claim. "We know more deeply, more truly, that world history has not been turned upside down to its very foundations—that the world is not yet redeemed. We sense its unredeemedness. The church can, or indeed must, understand this sense of ours as the awareness that we are not redeemed. But we know that this is not it. The redemption of the world is for us indivisibly one with the perfecting of creation, with the establishment of the unity which nothing more prevents, which is no longer controverted, and which is realized in all the protean variety of the world. Redemption is one with the kingdom of God in its fulfillment. An anticipation of any single part of the completed redemption of the world—for example of the redemption beforehand of the soul—is something we cannot grasp, although even for us in our mortal hours redeeming and redemption are heralded. But we perceive no caesura in history. We are aware of no center in history—only its goal, the goal of the way taken by the God who does not linger on his way."[59]

Likewise, Schalom Ben-Chorin makes the same argument: "The Jew is profoundly aware of this unredeemed character of the world, and he perceives and recognizes no enclave of redemption in the midst of its unredeemedness. The concept of the redeemed soul in the midst of an unredeemed world is alien to the Jew, profoundly alien, inaccessible from the primal ground of his existence. This is the innermost reason for

Israel's rejection of Jesus, not a merely external, merely national conception of messianism. In Jewish eyes, redemption means redemption from all evil. Evil of body and soul, evil in creation and civilization. So when we say redemption, we mean of the whole of redemption."[60] In anticipation of the eschatological twist which Christians give as their answer to this conundrum, he asks rhetorically, "So can there be an anticipation or 'advance payment' of redemption in some part-sectors, before the final, total and universal redemption of the world? Can the Redeemer himself have come into the world before the redemption of the world has become a real happening? This is the central question of Christian existence."[61]

Is Jesus that Messiah? Or is the Messiah still to come? Two different answers to this question constitute the core around which instincts, beliefs, and practices of these two traditions of faith are constructed. That is the central theological difference between Christians and Jews, in the first century and in the twentieth. Christians and Jews speak past each other on this most central argument between the family members within the household of Abraham. Jews hold the Messiah is an anointed human being who effectively brings to fulfillment the kingdom of God's justice and peace. If the Messiah has come, we will know it, for the swords will be made into plowshares. Not seeing this, the Jew remains waiting faithfully. Christians ought to acknowledge this as a faithful decision, indeed a faithful witness, for apart from our eschatological hope, we have no evidence whatsoever that Jesus qualifies as Messiah.

Christians see Jesus as the one whose efficacy has transformed us and through whom God continues to call for the eventual transformation of the world. He is our savior now and in the future. When fully established, his reign, which is now fragmentary, even perhaps only anticipatory, will be realized. Our christology is our confession of that faith, and it, too, is a faithful decision, indeed a faithful witness, to God's messianic age. "Christians must reformulate the faith in Jesus as the Christ in terms which are proleptic and anticipatory, rather than final and fulfilled. Jesus should not be said to fulfill the Jewish hopes for the coming Messiah, which indeed he did not. Rather, he must be seen as one who announced this messianic hope and who gave signs of its presence, but who also died in that hope, crucified on the cross of unredeemed human history."[62]

Note well, however, that both Jews and Christians await the kingdom, and they await the same kingdom, and they equally live by hope and anticipation. Whether the Messiah who will finally bring this Kingdom will be Jesus or another is finally an eschatological question, not a christological question proper (that is, restricted to incarnation and atonement). In this sense, for Christians christology is necessarily tied to eschatology. "Christianity, as much as Judaism, continues to live in a dialectic of fulfillment and unfulfillment."[63] But we will have to wait to let

the eschaton settle this inner-family or inter-mural dispute. We cannot settle it as a christological question. Then we will know who is right and who
is wrong about christological claims, if that is at all the kind of judgment
that will be appropriate in that time.

When the undisputed Messiah comes, will Jesus come again or will the
Messiah be another? If it is Jesus and if the returning Jesus as the risen
Christ resembles in any way the one portrayed in the Gospels, both as
pre- and post-resurrection, the answer will likely be, "What is it to you
now?" Put in another way, the question about which one of the family
members was right in this inter-familial argument, about who is "the
beloved son" (Isaac and Israel or Jesus and the Church)[64] will then have
become inappropriate, because it will be redundant. God's creation will
then be fulfilled. The kingdom will be here, and we will no longer have
anything to dispute. Indeed, I suspect that if we are still at each other's
throats, we will know that the Messiah still has not come, clearly for the
second, and perhaps even the first, time.

CHAPTER EIGHT

Is Jesus the Only Way, Truth, and Life?

Can one believe in the truth of the Christian faith, and still accept Islam, Buddhism, and Hinduism as authentic "way of life" or "pathways"? Does belief in Jesus Christ as the incarnation of God lead Christians to attempt to eliminate the "other religions" through conversion, or must one relativize one's beliefs to matters of sheer taste or habit in order not to see "the other" as an enemy or object to be assimilated? In an increasingly global village, Christians are forced to ask, "Is Jesus the only way, truth, and life?" "Is Christianity the one true religion?" or, "Are there many paths to the same goal?" "Does each way of life constitute a truth?" This chapter will examine four theological answers to these questions. I will begin with the three dominant perspectives on these questions along the current landscape, namely, exclusivism, inclusivism, and pluralism, and conclude with my own strategy, which I call confessional pluralism.

I. New Context and New Attitudes

Although the appropriateness of the category of "religion" for designating the various "pathways" or "faiths" or "ways of life" by which people construct their world is debated today among those engaged in academic religious studies programs, I will use the term "the religions" throughout this chapter, and mean by it the beliefs, values, and actions of a community related to a way of life directed toward a holistic perspective. The religions grow out of at least two basic assumptions. First, human existence is not given ready made; it has to be achieved through transformation. Second, religion is the means toward ultimate transformation.[1] Christianity usually has made a third assumption. Jesus Christ is the one, only, and final means toward ultimate transformation given by God for all humanity. He is the only way, truth, and life. Therefore, Christianity is the one true religion. All of the other religions are either false, idolatrous, or mere preparation for Christian faith. This third assumption has been deeply challenged in much of the Christian world today.

One reason for this challenge is our *increasing awareness* of other cultures as significant players on the world scene. The gradual ascent of other cultures on the world scene at the beginning of the new millennium makes us take account of these renewed political, military, and economic centers of power. Religion is intimately tied to the resurgence of these cultures. Although some theories of secularization in the late 1960s presumed religion was dead, we have discovered a new vitality to the religions around the world. Fundamentalist forms of the religions have appeared in almost every country which has been forced to come to terms with the modern world.[2] In addition, we are aware of the increasing presence and power of the Mid-Eastern and Eastern religions in our own country. The media increasingly present the religions on the screen ("Seven Years in Tibet," "Kundun," and "Little Buddha") and in our news magazines ("Buddhism in America").[3]

Another reason is our *increasing contact* with adherents to a non-Christian religion. Beyond a vague awareness of the religions in the media, many Christians, through personal travel, encounter the world of temples and shrines where they observe the exotic practices of adherents. In many American cities, even small and mid-size towns, "foreign investments" in manufacturing or distribution enterprises are accompanied by new restaurants, groceries, retail stores, as well as places of worship. My wife teaches in a private high school with large numbers of Jewish, Muslim, Hindu, and Buddhist students; my two sons, Protestant Christians, were a distinct minority in this school when they attended in the 1980s. Many of our friends are practicing members of one of these living religions. Increasingly, Christian families welcome a Jew, Muslim, Buddhist, or Hindu as the mate of one of their children.

A third factor is our *increasing knowledge* of the practices and beliefs of unfamiliar religions through the liberal arts curriculum both of private colleges and state universities. Buddhism, Hinduism, Islam, Judaism, and Christianity together constitute around 71.4% of the world population. Christians make up 32.8%; Muslims, 19.6%; Hindus, 12.8%; Buddhists, 6%; Jews, .2%.[4] Throughout the last twenty-five years in academic circles there has been a plethora of books written and courses taught in colleges of liberal arts and departments of religious studies which have increased our knowledge of these religions. Large sections of books on the world religions can be found not only in larger chain book stores, such as Borders or Barnes & Noble, but even in run-of-the-mill bookstores in every suburban shopping mall.

How should Christians interpret these "living religions" of the world? If God is one, why is there not one religion? Are all the religions really one in some fundamental sense, or are they in the end incommensurate? Is there one, and only one, way to God? Is Jesus the only way, truth, and life? What perspective should Christians adopt toward the non-Christian religions?

There are two popular attitudes toward the plurality of religions which I consider to be mistaken in thinking about a Christian "theology of the world religions." The first one is that all religions are essentially the same. Deep down they share the same "essence." They are merely different paths leading to the same essential truth. The apparent differences between the religions are merely accidental, culturally conditioned elements of time and place. Behind or beneath all of these cultural accretions, however, there is a common "essence" shared by all the living religions. This common essence is an experience, an experience of the holy, or of mystical unity, or of righteousness as a cosmic demand, or of faith, or of attainment of emptiness. Alternatively, the common essence is what is attended to by this experience, such as God, or, to use apparently neutral language, Being Itself or Ultimate Reality. A recurring image shaping this attitude is of different paths leading to the sublime summit of Mt. Fuji, each religion a path winding its way up the mountainside to the same truth or goal at the top of the mountain.

This viewpoint is attractive to many Christians, especially those who believe in one God who is a God of love and who wills the salvation of all people. We might call this outlook the "school of common essence." It makes the distinction between the essential truth which all religions share in common and the nonessential practices and propositions which are distinctive to each of the religions. What the religions share in common is "religion." If we look deeply into the religions, we find an inner core which each shares with the other, an essential experience or a common insight or a shared truth in all of them.

There are some benefits to this attitude. It seems, at least at first blush, to be open-minded, tolerant, generous, even inclusive. It seeks to discover a common identity between all human beings, an identity which binds us all together and provides a basis on which to overcome our cultural barriers of division and conflict. When we discover, acknowledge, and act upon what we share as our common religious core, we will transcend the culturally constructed barriers of the concrete religions which lead to conflict. Although we may retain our religions because we are creatures of a variety of cultures, we can relativize them because we recognize that they all share a common essence of religious experience or devotion to an ultimate reality. Anyone who is tortured by the memory of what human beings have done to each other in the name of their particular religion surely will find this attitude attractive.

But there are some overwhelming liabilities to this strategy. Is there a common set of beliefs or practices among the religions? Obviously not. Is there, perhaps, some universal essence to all these religions? That possibility cannot be dismissed out of hand as merely modernist ideology. But if there is, what is this common essence? If it is a common religious experience, what is that experience? If it is a common object, what is that object? The problem is that advocates of a common essence cannot agree on whether it is a common experience or common object that all share, and if it is one or the other of these, what that common experience or object is. For instance, one finds different conceptions of it between Immanuel Kant (sense of moral oughtness), Frederick Schleiermacher (feeling of absolute dependence), Rudolf Otto (experience of the holy), Frederick Heiler (worship), Ernest Hocking (righteousness as cosmic demand), Paul Tillich (ultimate concern), Thomas Huxley (mysticism), W. C. Smith (faith), and John Hick (devotion to ultimate reality). In the end advocates of this strategy can only stipulate what the essence is, a stipulation which reflects their own religious or philosophical perspective, their own intuitions, their own idiosyncratic agenda. The fact that none can agree is compelling evidence that there is no one essence which the religions share in common.

It simply is not the case that all religions have the same fundamental experience and object or goal, no matter how general or abstract that experience or object or goal is conceived to be. The various religions differ not simply in concepts but on what the religion aims to accomplish. Ultimate transformation as Christian forgiveness of sins, Hindu moksa, and Zen Buddhist satori are not simply different terms pointing in the same direction; but are different directions. For example, Buddhists deny there is any goal of the salvation (restoration or fulfillment) of the soul or the self. Life is misery and decay and there is no ultimate reality to it or in it or behind it. The cycle of endless birth and rebirth continues because of desire and attachment to the unreal "self." Right meditation and deeds will end the cycle and achieve Nirvana, the Void, or nothingness. Contrast this with Christianity, where there is an Ultimate Reality and purpose to life, namely, God and salvation. The problem is the salvation of the soul or self through its restoration or reconciliation or fulfillment in God. Such salvation is possible only on the basis of divine grace. Thus, while Christians speak redemption as the grace of forgiveness and transformation, Buddhists speak of enlightenment, freedom from all illusion and distortion and openness to all that is as it is. "Enlightenment brings freedom from all the suffering that results from having wants that can never be permanently satisfied, from having aims that can never be permanently fulfilled, from having guilt about which nothing can be done. It leads to serene acceptance of what is, moment by moment, without anxiety or regret."[5] Each viewpoint may be authentic, and no utter incompatibility may be entailed necessarily in recognizing the authenticity of each, but they are not the same soteriological concepts.

Furthermore, the religions do not all agree on affirming God. There are religions which deny there is any Ultimate Reality whatsoever. For the three monotheistic faiths, God exists; for Buddhism, no God exists. It is, of course, possible that both are correct once it becomes clear what aspect or character of the world each is and is not affirming. But to claim that they are all really theists of some sort simply is not correct. When Christians talk of God and Buddhists of Emptiness, they are talking about two fundamentally different realities. God and Emptiness are radically different ideas, not two terms referring to the same underlying reality. Christians speak of an underlying reality, the reality that is somehow the cause of the finite or phenomenal world, whereas Zen Buddhists point to the final reality of that finite world itself.[6] Even if there is such a thing as religious experience as a distinct kind of experience, the experience may be seen as cosmic, acosmic, or theistic; that is, ultimacy found in the interrelatedness of the world, a depth beyond this world, or a personal reality intimately related to the world.[7] Different features of the totality of the world give rise to different features of reality. "To say that the Nothingness or Emptying realized by Buddhists is different from the God of whom the Bible speaks is not sacrilege."[8] Is the Real the personal God of the Judaic-Christian tradition or the impersonal ultimate of Vedanda and Buddhism?

The second popular but inadequate attitude is that all of the religions are relative. No one can say one religion is better than another. Each religion is limited, partial, incomplete, one particular way of looking at things, and therefore relative. To hold one religion better than another is narrowminded, offensive, and wrong. If one religion is better than another, it can only be better "for me" or "for them." But not one of them is rationally, morally, or pragmatically better than another one. The fact of plurality seems to imply not only relativity but relativism. The modern historical consciousness, one of the intellectual revolutions of the nineteenth century, causes us to recognize the historical and cultural context of all ideas and values. Everything humans are and produce is conditioned by their historical context and subject to the laws of historical development in particular times and places. Historical contexts are diverse and are always changing. Therefore everything humans do, including religion, is limited and changing, that is, it is relative to its context. The belief in one unchangeable truth is at best a benign illusion, at worst a mystifying and repressive ideology. The relativity of historical consciousness implies the claim that Jesus is the one and only way to God is relative to the historical development of Christianity.

Most of us are deeply shaped by this attitude today. It is one of the most recognized and articulate features of the postmodern world. Art is relative; judgments of beauty are merely matters of taste and preference. Politics is relative; it is merely a matter of where you were born whether you believe in democracy or dictatorship. Morality is relative; it is merely a matter of upbringing in the mores of the particular society in which you were raised. Every religious claim is relative, including the claim that Jesus is the only way to God. Within such a perspective it is impossible to make an argument even for the superiority of one religion over another, let alone the claim that one is universal, normative, and the final religion for all human beings. One can say all religions are equally true, or equally false, for that matter, but one claim is no more objectively truthful than the other, because all claims of truth and value are relative to the subjective preferences of individuals or, at best, the common framework of language within a particular community.

In accepting historical relativity, Christians have done much to increase their tolerance level for uncertainty, insecurity, and diversity in the postmodern world and to live more open-minded and creative lives in a pluralistic world. But, can many human beings live for very long on basis of thoroughgoing relativism? Does not complete relativism lead finally to cultural and moral nihilism? If so, few people, when push comes to shove, are willing to accept the claim that *everything* is merely a matter of taste or preference or linguistic convention within specific communities. What relativist is willing to claim that genocide, rape, incest, chattel slavery, or misogyny are merely relative matters of linguistic convention, social judgment, or taste of a particular culture? None of the neopragmatic relativists have much reserve about proclaiming the desirability, naturalness, or even finality of personal and political rights for every citizen of every society in the world as a criterion for judging cultures (although they do it with an engaging ironic twist).

Regardless of what kind of relativist the postmodern Christian is, most refuse to go with total relativism. As we make contextual, and therefore relative, judgments about these matters, we have some set of norms by which we make those judgments, which we believe has something to do with a world beyond our limited linguistic patterns of which we must take account. We make judgments about the religions, and these judgments entail notions about the way the world is and how the religions construct that world. For example, we can ask, Is Christianity true? Is

Buddhism true? Is Hinduism true? I may want to claim that Mormonism, paganism, the Rev. Moon, and New Age gnosticism might be true, or that they might tell us as Christians some true things about the world. Nevertheless, am I equally relativist about child sacrifice, or animal sacrifice, or about Satanism, Jonestown, or Branch Davidians, or about Fascism, Stalinism, Aryan Nation, or Al Qaeda? Most of us will not be relativist to the extent of arguing that all of these religions or quasi-religions are equally true simply because adherents are devoted with utter loyalty to them. We are willing to argue that some of them are truncated, one-sided, trivial, morally distorted, wrong, or even false.

The theological problem Christians must address in this new context with these new attitudes is what theological judgments they can make of the other religions and what is the theological basis for the judgments which they make. If religion is by its very nature pluralistic, that is, if "religion" is inseparable from "the religions," then the Christian must ask how she or he as a Christian is to understand the relationship of the religions. Such a question is not merely how Christians can learn to get along civilly with non-Christians, but how Christians are to understand the place of the other religions within the divine economy. A common pattern has emerged which distinguishes between exclusivism, inclusivism, and pluralism. I have adopted this pattern for the following discussion, evaluating the strengths and weaknesses of these three standard options from the point of view I describe at the end as confessional pluralism.

II. Exclusivism

The primary claim throughout the history of the church is that Christianity alone is the one true religion since it is the religion established by God in the unique saving event of Jesus Christ. God has graciously revealed the truth about Godself through Jesus Christ to the Apostles who have given this truth to the church through the Bible. No other religion is true because no other religion can be true. Jesus Christ is the *only* way for any human being to know God in a salvific way, and explicit faith in Jesus Christ is necessary for salvation, so Christians alone can obtain salvation.[9] Therefore, salvation is possible only in and through the church and its proclamation of Jesus Christ. This was the view of pre-Vatican II Roman Catholics and remains the view of Protestant fundamentalists and conservative evangelicals.

Exclusivist views, and especially conservative Protestant forms of it, depend on a set of assumptions which seem to require the exclusivist claim. Protestant exclusivists assume the primary frame of reference for evaluating the other religions is and can only be certain specific texts in the Bible.[10] Reason and human experience play no role in answering this theological question. Furthermore, a particular view of how the Bible determines our answer to this question is assumed. It is not the gospel or the kerygma of the New Testament which determines our theological answer, but specific texts which are assumed to be revealed answers to this specific question.[11] A handful of New Testament texts is selected as decisive and it is assumed these texts are to be interpreted in an exclusivistic way. In Mark 16:15-16, Jesus says to his disciples, "Go into all the world and proclaim the good news to the whole creation. The one who believes and is baptized will be saved; but the one who does not believe will be condemned." In John 14:6, speaking to Thomas, "Jesus said to him, 'I am the way, and the truth, and the life. No one comes to the Father except through me.'" In Peter's sermon in Acts 4:10, 12, where he is referring to "the name of Jesus Christ of Nazareth, whom you crucified, whom God raised from the dead," he says, "There is salvation in no one else, for there is no other name under heaven given among mortals by which we must be saved." John 3:16, 18 and Romans 10:9-15, among other texts, support "a consistent pattern of 'fewness' in redemption and 'wideness in judgment.'"[12] The Bible, also, gives clear reasons for its explicit exclusivism. Jesus is the only "God-man," the only mediator between God and humanity. Salvation is due to his sacrificial crucifixion. This occurred once and for all for all humankind. Therefore, Jesus is the only Savior because only he can be the savior of all humanity.

The Christian religion alone, therefore, is the one true religion. Non-Christians do not know salvation because they cannot know it. Inasmuch as salvation can be gained only through participation by faith in Jesus Christ, Christians must reject as false any teaching that the non-Christian religions are, can be, or even might be ways to salvation. Christians, therefore, must take up only a missionary obligation to all non-Christians. "If they die without knowledge of Jesus Christ, they perish."[13] Although there are some moderate evangelicals who hold a veiled trust that somehow God will give every good-willed pagan a second chance to hear about Jesus, either at the end of this life or in the next,[14] all exclusivists agree that without an encounter with Jesus Christ, salvation not possible. Thus, the claim is not only that Jesus Christ alone constitutes salvation (an ontological claim) but also that knowledge about this exclusive savior is required for salvation (an epistemological claim). "We conclude that 'name' refers to the focus of God's universal redemptive plan in the person and work of Jesus Christ, who must be the object of explicit faith by those who want to be saved. Peter does not appear to be referring to Jesus merely as the ontological ground of salvation—that is, as the sole source of atonement. Rather, he is indicating one must acknowledge Jesus explicitly before one can be saved."[15] If there is to be any dialogue, it is understood as indispensable to, a preparation for, or a version of evangelism. Dialogue is valid only as a means of proclamation and conversion to the one true religion.

The exclusivist claim cannot be dismissed out of hand simply because it offends postmodern relativistic sensibilities. The proclamation of God's work in Jesus Christ is the heart and power of the Christian message. Absolute loyalty to Jesus Christ is precisely what Christian faith has proclaimed throughout its history, beginning with the apostolic tradition and the New Testament. It is *possible* that Jesus of Nazareth might represent something so thoroughly surprising, so thoroughly exceptional and unique in history that he has no peers or analogues. "Pending the critical reflection necessary to determine otherwise, one must allow at least the possibility that Christian exclusivism's other claim to be appropriate to Jesus Christ could be critically validated."[16] The exclusivist claim must be subjected to theological analysis, not dismissed simply because "I don't like it." For the liberal Christian, the humanist, and the skeptic not to admit the possibility that the scandalous thing exclusivists claim is true is as arbitrary, as narrow-minded, and as ideological as the liberals' charge that exclusivists are being heard-hearted, mean, and arrogant. The exclusivist claim must be examined in light of the nature of the New Testament kerygma and in light of the Jesus Christ who is the subject of the church's faith.

The case against exclusivism is about as compelling, I believe, as a case in theology can be. To begin with, there is a variety of methodological questions which we must consider in evaluating the exclusivist claim. Given the strong appeal to scripture made by exclusivists, I will begin there. I counter the exclusivist claims about the exclusive role of scripture in answering our quandary by asking a series of rhetorical questions. Is the Wisdom and Word of God contained only in the Bible? Even if one adopts the classical Protestant *sola scriptura* as norm, does not one still have to ask what in the Bible is authoritative and how in answering our question? Is the authority of the Bible as the Word of God a half-dozen verses, or the Word of God as the proclamation of the love and mercy of God incarnate in Jesus Christ? Are not tradition, experience, and reason also avenues through which the Word or Wisdom of God is heard and, therefore, also criteria for answering our question? Even if one rejects this "quadrilateral" authority, do not tradition, experience, and reason, willy nilly, shape our hermeneutics of Scripture (what verses to chose and how to determine what they do and do not mean)? If not, why does John Sanders disagree so thoroughly with Ronald Nash—as evangelicals—on what the Bible teaches in the verses which Nash selects as definitive for our question?[17] Are the key passages for exclusivists part of the essential witness of the New Testament or the medium to convey a more basic claim about total commitment to Jesus Christ by his followers? Are these passages philosophical or theological doctrine about the relation of the religions, intending to negate all religions apart from Christ, or are they confessional language meant to affirm the importance of what God did in Jesus Christ in the Christian community and for the world? Finally, why do exclusivists usually ignore other biblical passages and other perspectives on the selected passages on our question, such as John 12:32, Acts 10:43, Romans 5:18, 1 Corinthians 15:22-28, 1 Timothy 4:10, 2 Peter 3:9, and 1 John 2:2, as well as the great christological hymns in Philippians and Colossians, which affirm the universal significance of Jesus Christ?

In addition to methodological questions, I also want to ask a pragmatic question. What are the consequences of the exclusivist answer? Is the exclusivist willing to follow out the implications of their position? Let me play a parlor game to test what is implied in the exclusivist viewpoint and to ask how far the particularist is willing to go to defend their position. Let me pose a thesis: "The only persons who are or can be saved are Christians who have been born again in Jesus Christ as the only way to salvation." This is, I believe, the claim of many North American evangelical exclusivists.[18] What are some of the implications of this claim? All humans who have lived from 1,000,000 BCE (or 10,000 BC [Creation Science] or 4004 BC [Archbishop Usher]) to 30 CE are eternally dammed. All non-Christians from 30 CE to the present, including all Jews and Muslims, are eternally dammed. In its extreme Protestant form, many, if not most, Christians (Roman Catholic, Eastern Orthodox, Russian Orthodox) from 30 AD to 1525 are lost because they have not had an evangelical born again experience. The conclusion is that the vast majority of all humanity from 1,000,000 BCE to the Protestant Reformation in the early sixteenth century is eternally lost because they did not confess Jesus as their Lord.

What shall we say about today?[19] Christians have increased as a proportion of the world population from one million of 181 million in 100 CE, to five million of 270 million in 1000 CE, to 1.7 billion of 5.2 billion in 1989 CE, so that 67.2% of all the world is non-Christian.[20] Further, 94.7% of all the world is non-Protestant. What do the exclusivists conclude from these data? All pre-Christians are lost; most pre-Protestant Christians are lost. Either 67% (non-Christians) or 95% of all humanity today (non-Protestants) will be lost. This conclusion does not seem to imply a God who is all-loving ("not willing that one should be lost") and who is all-powerful (will complete the inscrutable, infallible, and sovereign will). A batting average of .333 from Ken Griffy or Sammy Sosa is resounding success in a game where failure is more common than success. But a success rate of .075 percent of the world's population seems less than impressive for a loving and omnipotent God.

This brings me to the most telling objection to the exclusivist position: theodicy. *Exclusivism, in my opinion, is the extreme form of the problem of evil.* The problem has been stated most clearly by Schubert Ogden.[21] By establishing a double standard for obtaining salvation, exclusivism creates a form of the problem of evil to which there is, in principle, no solution. Exclusivists presuppose that there is a predicament that every human being faces, from the beginning, everywhere, and always: sin, or unfaith. All humans through Adam and Eve have forfeited the possibility of faith. Without election or prevenient grace, there can be no faith in God and, therefore, no salvation. So far, so good. However, the predicament of the vast majority of women and men is radically different from that minority who have become Christian. The vast majority of humanity has been and is trapped. Especially those prior to Jesus Christ, but also those who have not heard of Jesus today, are in double jeopardy. "Through no fault of their own, by far most human beings have been allowed to remain in their sin without any prospect of salvation."[22] They have no faith and are lost, but they also have no possibility of faith because they had not or have not heard about Jesus Christ. So, not simply as a consequence of their freedom and sin but also as a consequence of their *fate* (they were by sheer accident born at the wrong time and place), they are lost, abandoned by God to their own useless devices. "For in the nature of the case, it is not an evil that can be accounted for by any decision or agency other than God's own . . . specifically to God's abandoning them to their predicament instead of so acting as to liberate them from it, as God would have done for at least the few human beings who are in a position to become Christians."[23]

There is an alternative to this particular form of the theodicy problem. There are Calvinist versions of the theodicy problem. Stressing sovereignty and omniscience, some Calvinists teach those who did and do not know Jesus and therefore are not saved nevertheless either have not or would not have chosen him if freely given the choice, and therefore are rightly condemned to hell. "It is equally plausible philosophically that God knows that all individuals who never hear the gospel are individuals who would not believe if they were to hear the gospel."[24] The doctrine of divine omniscience seems to save God from indifference or malevolence. Some of these Calvinists go even farther. "God could conceivably desire all kinds of things to happen and still allow those things not to happen for some good reason, whether or not he chooses to reveal the reason to us."[25] It is not true that God is unjust. Since God defines justice and goodness, and predestines (or allows) the vast majority of humans to everlasting hell for God's own just and good reasons, some Calvinists seek to avoid the theodicy problem through the twin doctrines of omniscience and omnipotence.

If exclusivism is true, the vast majority of humanity is the victim of a double standard. Their freedom is useless (Arminian) or only apparent (Calvinist). Through no fault of their own they remain in sin and without any hope whatsoever. This is as true for the vast majority of humanity after Jesus as it was for all humanity before him. As Pinnock, an evangelical theologian, says of exclusivist views, they "present a God significantly lacking in mercy, and although they say that perspective is not their own fault since it is due to the way God has established the rules, the impression is pretty awful."[26] Perhaps there are other ways of thinking about the love and mercy of God in Jesus Christ than in the exclusivist way.

III. Inclusivism

Inclusivism is the claim that there are many ways to God but there is one norm by which the many ways can be constituted and known to be true. While there is truth in the other religions, no other religion can be true in the same sense in which Christianity is true. What truth there is in the other religions is constituted by God's work in Jesus Christ. The truth in the other religions is established by Christ and measured by him as the norm, and so they are included within the efficaciousness of the work of Christ beyond the church. The inclusivist move has been from *extra ecclesiam nulla salus*, "outside the church there is no salvation," to "without the church there is no salvation." "According to this answer, the possibility of salvation uniquely constituted by the event of Jesus Christ is somehow made available to each and every human being without exception and, therefore, is exclusive of no one unless she or he excludes her- or himself from its effects by a free and responsible decision to reject it."[27] Saved non-Christians belong to the essence of the church, the one salvation constituted by Jesus Christ. They are attached, linked, related to the church through implicit faith; they are Christians imperfectly, tendentially, potentially, latently, hiddenly, anonymously.

The inclusivist perspective does not include a positive view of the salvific significance of the other religions apart from Jesus Christ and the church. Grace is a sort of free-floating agency or power of Christ through the Holy Spirit beyond the church that touches individuals privately, either through some form of mystical awareness, or knowledge of truth, or moral earnestness through their following of their own conscience, or implicit faith exhibited by following the practices of their religion. Generally this view holds to the ontological necessity of Christ's work as redeemer (no one can be saved without it) but it questions the epistemological necessity of his work (awareness of his work in order to benefit from it). The watershed in contemporary inclusivism, which has become the official view of the Roman Catholic Church, is the Second Vatican Council's (1962-1965) "Declaration on the Relationship of the Church to Non-Christian Religions."[28]

Contemporary Roman Catholic inclusivism is primarily a christocentric inclusivism. Christ is the constitutive cause of the salvation effective in the other religions, and Christ is the final and complete goal of all the other religions. Whatever saving grace is present in the world religions has been caused by the event of Jesus Christ and moves inexorably toward him as their fulfillment. Christ is the final cause of God's universal salvific will, what God, from the beginning of time, had in mind in offering grace to humankind. Jesus Christ, then, is the end product of the entire process of universal revelation and grace. What has been realized in Christ is carried in and through the church. The church is his permanent, visible, sacramental presence in the world. Missionary work is important, not because the church is an island of salvation in the midst of perdition, but in order to aid others to become more fully aware of and thus more committed to what they already are, children of God in Jesus Christ.

The major representative of christocentric inclusivism in Roman Catholicism is Karl Rahner (1904-1984).[29] In trying to solve the problem of holding together the two principles of the necessity of Christian faith and the universal salvific will of God, he says that all people must somehow be capable of being members of the Church in a real and concrete sense. "If it be true that the man who is the object of the Church's missionary endeavor is or can be already prior to it a man who is on the way toward salvation and finds it in certain circumstances without being reached by the Church's preaching, and if it be true at the same time that the salvation which he achieves is the salvation of Christ, because there is no other, then it must be possible to be not only an anonymous 'theist,' but also an anonymous Christian."[30] In accepting himself or herself, the person is accepting Christ as the absolute perfection and guarantee of their anonymous movement toward God by grace.[31]

The liberal Protestant version of inclusivism is more *theocentric* at its core.[32] A non-Christian who is saved is saved because God is the kind of God whom Jesus Christ has clearly revealed God to be: a loving, gracious, forgiving, and merciful God toward all God's children. Since God desires to save all humankind, since God acts on this desire, and since God is sovereign ruler of the world, God's will ultimately will be fulfilled in all the creation through the Spirit of God. There is no person, no history, no culture, no religion that is outside God's creation and providence. "What it does mean is that all yearnings for God, all attempts to know and love God, however right or wrong, appropriate or inappropriate, happen within God's providence."[33] Grace is offered to all peoples through a concept of creation, specifically, through explicit doctrines of general revelation and divine providence. Grace is not an extrinsic addition to human nature; grace is a part of nature and infuses all human beings. It is part of the psychological human structure, the moral consciousness, the practices of the religions. Human beings are spirit, infinitely open to infinite mystery, the Ultimate, the Real, the Transcendent, Ultimate Reality.[34] In all human acts of knowing and loving, and especially in our moral and religious consciousness, humans are reaching out to the Infinite. There is a transcendental, common, general revelation of God the creator and providential ruler built into our very nature as human beings.

Increasingly there is a christocentric version of inclusivism among evangelical Protestants. By the mid-1990s, one conservative evangelical estimated that "higher than 50 percent" of evangelical denominational and mission leaders and college and seminary professors held this view.[35] Clark Pinnock and John Sanders are two of the key representatives of this perspective among current Protestant evangelicals.[36] An earlier advocate of such a view was Sir Norman Anderson, a British evangelical, who claimed it is only through Christ that anyone can come to a personal knowledge of God and only through his life, death, and resurrection that anyone can come to an experience of salvation.[37] He applied this claim, however, to the pre-Christian era. When the Israelites realized they were sinners and turned in repentance and faith, they were saved because they were *anticipating* (and so expressing saving faith in) the redemption which was finally made effective in Christ. Their knowledge was deficient but their forgiven status was identical with ours. Believing Jews under the old dispensation, therefore, enjoyed salvation through the saving work of Christ "(dated, of course, according to the calendars of men, but timeless and eternal in its divine significance)."

What about those today who have never heard the gospel? There is a way in which the efficacy of the one atonement is made available to those who have never heard about it. Although God saves only through Jesus who is the propitiation for our sins, Anderson asks, rhetorically, might it not be true of the followers of some other religion that the God of all mercy has worked in their hearts by the Spirit, bringing them to a realization of their sin, to repentance, and to throwing themselves on the mercy of God and being saved by the propitiation accomplished in Christ? Romans 10:12-18 says everyone who calls upon the name of the Lord will be saved. May it not be that ones who realize their sin and throw themselves sincerely on the mercy of God are redeemed by Christ because Christ died for all? If in this world persons have, at the prompting of the Spirit, thrown themselves on the mercy of God, that mercy will already have reached them, on the basis of the propitiation which has been made once and for all and they will be justified. A few evangelicals, such as Gabriel Fackre and Donald Bloesch, hold to the notion of the evangelization of the unevangelized after death,[38] and others, like Pinnock, propose that only those who had faith in God during their earthly life, and therefore were believers, even though not Christians, after death will encounter the reality of God's grace in Jesus Christ and know the fullness of salvation.[39]

What are the strengths of inclusivism? I have long argued in my classes, and not facetiously, that for most Christians, hell is for people other than oneself and one's loved ones. The closer we are to the ones we love, even if they have forthrightly rejected faith in Christ, the harder it is for us to consider hell as their eternal fate. The broader our human concerns and commitments are, the more we will revise our theology to make certain that all are included in the love and destiny of God. Inclusivism is one way to do this while maintaining the finality of Christianity. Inclusivism is not merely an "ethics of civility," or a culture of dialogue, but is an effort by Christians as Christians to look upon other religions as possible ways of salvation. It is a theology of the other religions which takes seriously the Christian idea that the God of Jesus Christ is a God of universal love, mercy, and redemption. Although it defines the love of God by Jesus Christ who constitutes the salvation of God, it does not restrict the love of God to an encounter with Jesus. It is an attractive way for many Christians to retain the Christian claims to finality while including all of humanity into the work of Christ.

But there are some major weaknesses in this perspective. The primary one is that inclusivism is still an exclusivist position. It is inclusive and even universal to the extent that it includes others within the claims of the Christian religion, but non-Christians are still included into the Christian religion as the only grounds of their salvation. "For it, too, there not only is but can be only one true religion, in the sense that Christianity alone can validly claim to be formally true."[40] Although Christ has universal significance, Christ is still definitive or normative for all the other religions, the *norma normans non normata*, the norm above all other norms. Inclusivism continues to insist Christ must be proclaimed the fullest revelation, the constitutive savior of whoever is saved. To move beyond this point toward pluralism is to jeopardize the distinctiveness, the superiority, and the finality of Christ and of Christianity. "The universal perspective that one thinks one has is really a particular view that ends up distorting other particulars in order to include them in its 'universal' embrace."[41] In the end, inclusivism remains a form of Christian imperialism to the extent that it does not permit the other religions to define truth in the way they understand the truth, and eliminates their truth by making its truth and effectiveness dependent on the Christian truth.

IV. Pluralism

The inclusivist perspective is an attempt to provide a more positive assessment of the other religions. However, for inclusivists Jesus Christ remains the norm by which we must judge any truth in the non-Christian religions. They maintain Christ as constitutive of all truth and the measure of the truth of all the other religions. There are, however, theologians who as Christians ask, "Is there only one true religion?" and they answer, "No." There are many true religions. They go beyond the fact of plurality to pluralism, a theological doctrine which goes beyond inclusivism. Pluralists claim not only that the other religions *might* be true, or are *constituted* as true by Jesus Christ, but that they are true on their own. John Hick (b. 1922) has been the most notable advocate of this viewpoint today. "I have suggested . . . that the spiritual and moral fruits that reflect a right relationship to the ultimate transcendent reality we call God are as evident in Jewish, Muslim, Hindu, and Buddhist lives as in Christian lives. . . . The non-Christian world relations are more than 'premessianic' preparations for Christian conversion. They are different but, so far as we can tell, equally authentic spheres of salvation/liberation, through which the universal presence of the Real, the Ultimate, the Divine is mediated to human beings."[42] Other religions are true; there is salvation in other religions. Christianity is one of the true religions among a plurality of true religions. It is one of many ways to the center, one religious stream flowing to the Real, one religion among many religions leading to Ultimate Reality.

In his early formulation, as we noted above, Hick claimed that "the universe of faiths centers upon God, and not upon Christianity or upon any other religion. . . . This must mean that the different world religions have each served as God's means of revelation to and point of contact with the different streams of human life."[43] In his later formulations, however, Hick recognized the problem of using the term God, a distinctly Christian concept, therefore, he reformulated his theocentric view of the other religions by referring to the Ultimate Reality or the Real which appears under different faces or masks in the various religions. Furthermore, all religions aim to achieve human goodness in terms of concern for others, kindness, love, compassion, honesty, and truthfulness. Insofar as they succeed in achieving this transformation, they are salvific in the sense that they move from self-centeredness to recentering in the Ultimate, the Real, the Transcendent final source and ground of everything as variously thought and experienced in the different religions.[44] The key inclusivist claim, then, is not only that there *can* be but that there *are* several true ways to God. Pluralism asserts a new theological claim about the plurality of religions. It is itself an independent claim which is an alternative to exclusivism and inclusivism. At least some other religions are true.

The basis for a Christian theological form of pluralism is a particular concept of God. People worshiping in church, synagogue, mosque, and temple are worshiping the same one Ultimate Reality and not different G(g)ods. Adonai, Allah, Rama, and Krishna are different names for the same ultimate being or ultimate reality. For anyone who believes in God there are three logical possibilities: 1) there are many g(G)ods; 2) there is one community that worships the one true God while others worship false gods or idols; and 3) there is one God, maker and sovereign Lord of all, the Really Real, who in its infinite fullness exceeds all our imaginations, the one Ultimate Reality, whom/which the devout in all religions *in fact* worship.

The foundation of the pluralistic claim, then, is that we live in a theocentric universe, and that a truly theocentric universe requires the kind of God described in the third logical possibility. God is infinite, mysterious, incomprehensible, and universal love. There are many ways to God, many communities of salvation, for such a God has no one special, favored way in which to achieve salvation. "They are all forms of the same fundamental human transformation from self-centeredness to a recentering in the ultimately Real as variously thought and experienced within the different ways of being human that constitute the great religious cultures of the earth."[45] The universe and its religious truth and salvation centers on Ultimate Reality, the Real (which Christians call God), not upon Christianity or the church or even Jesus Christ. There is a galaxy of faiths, and God is the sun of the galaxy. The different world religions have each served as one of God's means of salvation.

Furthermore, there are many mediators of this salvation and Jesus Christ is one of them. Jesus is not God, at least in the sense of the traditional Christian doctrine of the incarnation, but is rather the Christian's living contact with the one, universal, transcendent Ultimate Reality. In his presence, Christians are brought into contact with the one Really Real. He is our sufficient, effective, and saving point of contact with God. However, Christians can revere Christ as the one through whom they have found salvation without denying other points of saving contact between God and humanity. Thus, there can be intense loyalty to Jesus Christ and his cause by Christians, but this loyalty is not such that they can take the further step of placing him in a constitutive, normative, or exclusive position in regards to the other religious figures as the only way to God. Other religions are as effective and true a path to God as is Christianity.

How do we know that the religions are all alike as being one path among many to the goal of knowledge of God? It is important to recognize that pluralism is not complete relativism. No pluralist claims that all religions are equally true. Pluralists claim that some religions are true and some are false, or some are better paths than others, on the grounds that some empirically are more effective means of ultimate transformation than are others. Pluralists claim that the major living world religions are true, but no pluralist makes the indiscriminate claim that all are equally true; that Islam, Buddhism, Hinduism, Shinto, Mormon, Unitarian, paganism, Moon, New Age, Wicca, Scientology, People's Temple, Branch Davidian, Fascism, and Satanism are all equally true religions. Pluralists judge the truth of a religion by its fruits. A religion can be judged to be true when it passes the pragmatic test of truth. True religions are salvific, and they are salvific when they achieve an actual transformation from natural self-centeredness to a new orientation centered in Ultimate Reality manifested in fruits of spiritual, moral, and political change. "They are all forms of the same fundamental human transformation from self-centeredness to a recentering in the ultimately Real as variously thought and experienced within the different ways of being human that constitute the great religious cultures of the earth."[46] The various true religions in fact work in accomplishing their goal of salvation or enlightenment at least with equal success. "If we define salvation as an actual human change, a gradual transformation from natural self-centeredness (with all the evil that flows from this) to a radically new orientation centered in God and manifested in the 'fruit of the Spirit,' then it seems clear that salvation is taking place within all of the world religions."[47] Many religions are true insofar as they succeed in fulfilling the need for ultimate transformation. When they produce good fruits, namely, an ultimate transformation, they successfully lead their adherents to the one true God and are therefore true.

Here, however, is the rub. If one religion can be better than another, or even can be false, one has to apply some norm by which to judge it as true or false, better or worse, profound or trivial. It may be helpful for pluralists to move from a christocentric to a theocentric norm because the move seems to be less imperialistic in its claims. *But, among the many world religions, and not merely outside them, theocentric and pragmatic views of God and truth are at least as controversial a claim as are christocentric views!* Theism of any sort, whether Yahweh, or Allah, or trinitarian theism, or process theism, or classical Western theism, or a Neoplatonic view of God is a presupposition only of the three great monotheistic faiths, and these theistic faiths are as socially and culturally located as any of the alternative views.

Another way to put this point is to say that in the dialogue among the religions, any form of theocentrism *begs the question* for our side. It assumes the Christian—or at least monotheistic—view of reality as the true and normative view. The pluralist's theocentric view of reality is as distinctive to a certain kind of liberal Christian theology as the exclusivist's and inclusivist's christocentric view of reality is distinctive to more conservative strands of Christian theology. Furthermore, pragmatic brands of truth ("by their fruits you shall know them"), which take the virtues of the "fruits of the Spirit" in the New Testament or the "humane virtues" of modern liberal culture to be the proper pragmatic criteria of truth, are as culturally located as other versions of truth. To be blunt about it, *pluralism, willy nilly, is as imperialistic as exclusivism and inclusivism.* To claim that the other religions not only might be true but are true because they are, when judged by their fruits, *in fact* true paths to the one Ultimate Reality is as much a "tribal" (liberal) Western Christian claim as are exclusivism and inclusivism.

When John Hick claims all religions which seek Ultimate Reality are true, he speaks from a Christian, or at least monotheistic assumption. All pluralists have a set of philosophico-theologico-moral norms which, under the camouflage of the category of universal human experience, or by means of a universal theory of a common essence, or a common object of devotion, sneak in their own Christian version of the absolute and of soteriology, all of which is as much an imposition on the devotees of the others religions as it is to tell them they need to be saved by Jesus. "It is time to recognize that the metaphysics of universal ground is in fact an abstract expression of the biblical understanding of creation and hence not a neutral basis for dialogue among all the great religions."[48] Positing a numenal reality which one calls "the Real" or "Ultimate Reality" available to the philosopher is as offensive to the Vedantist or Buddhist who hold to impersonal ultimates as to call the reality God. Hick has a Platonic or neo-Platonic Christian view of Ultimate Reality, which is, to be sure, one of the historic Christian views of God. His idea of judging the truth or falsity of the religions by their fruits is both a Christian criterion and a Christian set of virtues. Pluralists pretend to a neutrality they do not have and impose supposedly neutral judgments that are covertly Christian. It is what John Cobb calls "the scholarly imperialism of defining others in Christian terms."[49]

How would you, the reader, respond to a Buddhist dialogue partner who proclaimed, "Christianity is a true religion because when Christians claim they have achieved salvation, they are making, unbeknownst to them, the implicit claim that they have achieved authentic Buddhahood. All true religions lead to Buddhahood and to Nirvana. Christianity is one of the many paths which lead to true Buddhist enlightenment and Nirvana. This is the accurate and adequate understanding of Christian symbols, language, experience, and practice"? As a Christian, I am willing to talk with Buddhists at great lengths to discover what we do and do not share in common, and to enrich my own Christian identity with Buddhist insights. But to be asked to accept the claim that I am really in essence a Buddhist and only a Christian "by name" and by "incomplete understanding" will not wash. I would expect a Buddhist to make precisely the same response. In a less hypothetical situation, I recall the day some students came to my theology class dazed and outraged by a Muslim student in one of their missiology classes who accused them face to face of being "heretics" and "infidels" because as Christians they did not worship Allah and follow the Koran. The claim that one is religious and theistic according to liberal instead of conservative definitions of religion and God is no less imperialistic in its claims than are exclusivism and inclusivism.

In the various dialogues to date among scholars and participants of the various religions, it has yet to be established that the religions are all alike, not only in their techniques for ultimate transformation, but even more fundamentally in their presuppositions about the nature of the human problem and in their goals which the religion tries to achieve. It may turn out to be true that the religions are *formally* alike: religious people are all practitioners who want to live in accord with reality. But they are *materially* (and so in reality) radically different. As Schubert Ogden says, "I have more and more found myself agreeing with the observation of Clifford Geertz that 'what all sacred symbols assert is that the good for man is to live realistically; where they differ is in the vision of reality they construct.'"[50]

V. Confessional Pluralism

Although there is some truth in each of these three predominant options, which I will discuss below, I think in the end all three make strong claims that we cannot uphold. Regardless of whether we exclude all religious people except Christians from God's salvation, or embrace all of them, through inclusivism or pluralism, I think all three claim to know more than we can know. Human beings are finite, contextual creatures, products of specific communities and so limited to the perspectives of their communities. We think, understand, and act as creatures of our contexts.[51] There is no woman or man who can stand above their concrete community (or complex of communities) to see everyone and everything from a universal, objective, transcendent point of view to know the truth or falsity of other religions. There is no "God's eye view" of anything. Christians can think and speak only as Christians, even when thinking about the other religions. There is a Jewish or Christian or Muslim or

Buddhist or scientific or secular or humanistic or atheistic perspective on this question, but no transcendent one. We do not know with certainty what God's view or way is on this question; even that claim itself is made within a particular postmodern Western Christian point of view. All we can do is make a claim about how we might answer this question from a Christian point of view.

Although we cannot say the other religions *are* true, we can say as Christians the other religions *can* be true or *may* be true, or even that they *are* true from a *Christian point of view*. Such a claim is not an imperialistic claim. It entails the recognition that every approach to our question can come only from a perspective, from the point of view shaped by the symbols, myths, and traditions within the "language game" of a context and a confession. The most we can do is to show how the other religions might be, or even how they are, from a Christian point of view. We might say something like this: if one begins with Christian presuppositions, with a certain set of Christian symbols and doctrines, Christians can say this or that about the other religions from their own point of view. I call this stance confessional pluralism.

I want to distinguish between, and affirm, a weak and strong form of confessionalism. In the weaker form, confessionalism supports a form of thoroughgoing relativity. It recognizes not only the fact of plurality but the truth of relativity, the truth about the contextuality our language, epistemology, and social reality, if not about ontology. Confessionalism represents an effort to undo imperialism, to recognize our lack of finality and absoluteness, to affirm modesty about theological claims. But there is a stronger form of confessionalism I also want to affirm. It affirms a kind of universalism which is, I think, compatible with confessionalism. Confessionalism can make, in its stronger form, claims about the universal significance of Christ as the icon and incarnation of God as creator and redeemer of the whole world. As confessionalism, it recognizes and affirms that all the religions can and do make universal claims about reality and about their way of life. Although none of these claims have to be absolute or exclusive, they are a confessional set of claims about the universal significance of the perceptions and insights of the particular religions. Christian confessionalism can make claims about the universal significance of Jesus Christ, and it can make claims about how the other religions can be, might be, or even are true from the Christian point of view.[52]

I will illustrate what a theology of the other religions might look like from the point of view of confessional pluralism. A confessionalist can argue the other religions can be true, might be true, or even are true, because the doctrine of the triune God introduces a pluralist principle into our thinking about God and the world. Pluralism is not only a philosophical assertion of the ontological priority of manyness. The concept of the triune God posits the grounds of interrelationship and plurality within the very idea of God. "Just as the experience of and belief in the Trinity affirms a radical, irreducible pluralism within the Godhead so too does it ground a similar pluralism as the very stuff and dynamic of finite reality."[53] Furthermore, the distinct character of each of the persons of the trinity supports a Christian affirmation a plurality of the world, including the religions. The "first person," the creator and providential ruler of the entire world and all of its creatures, creates and lures all creatures to the fulfillment of the purposes of God. The "second person," the Sophia or Logos of God, is incarnate in all of the creation, including the many religions, and so works to transform all of the creation into the divine image. The "third person," the Spirit ("the Lord and Giver of Life"), works creatively and redemptively in all the cultures, including the religions of the world, to bring the creation to its spiritual fulfillment. Christians affirm that God loves all the world, and, as sovereign judge and redeemer, will bring all of the creation to God's reign in God's own way and time. Although Jesus Christ does not constitute this salvation, Jesus Christ represents and re-presents the salvation which is offered by God to all human beings simply as human beings.[54] He decisively re-presents God's love present implicitly to all human beings. The divine love and power is always present everywhere, so all of the religions might be true insofar as they achieve true humanity as understood from the Christian perspective.

Any or all of these claims, however, are perspectival and confessional to the core. They make sense only within the Christian "story," the Christian "language game," or the Christian "construction of reality." They are a *Christian* theology of the other religions. There is no other way to approach the question of the truth (or falsity) of the other religions but from such a confessional perspective. The history of religions may describe the history and function of the various religions, but when historians address the question of the truth of the religions, the historian has become a theologian, whether that theology be Christian, secular, humanistic, agnostic, or whatever. The "answers" offered in the preceding paragraph arise from, are confined to, and are defined by a Christian way of looking at God and the world. If the Christian perspective is true in any sense of the term, we can say there might be or even is truth in the other religions for the reasons suggested above. But it is a judgment arising from, informed by, and geared toward the perspective of the Christian view of reality.

Finally, as a confessional pluralist I want to suggest there is truth in the other three viewpoints. I would include within confessional pluralism some features of the three standard positions of exclusivism, inclusivism, and pluralism. Confessionalism is pluralistic in the same way that no one religion, including Christianity or the Christian kerygma, is the final or absolute truth, nor is it the only way, truth, and life. It is one way among the great ways and can itself can be enriched and transformed by the truths of the other great religions. Also, confessionalism can be exclusivist—I prefer here the term particularist—in the sense that exclusivism maintains a central element of the Christian kerygma. Jesus Christ is the normative, decisive, definitive way for Christians to know and to say what they say about God and the world, including the many religions. When a Christian claims that "Jesus Christ is Lord," she or he is claiming that "there is no other name" which defines the problem for or provides the answer to the quest of the religious life. If we can take the exclusivist claim confessionally, Christians make an exclusive claim about Jesus Christ in the sense that they claim that Jesus Christ is Lord, that the way, the truth, and the life are defined for Christians only in relation to him as the life and work of God for our salvation.

There are, to be sure, real dangers in any sort of particularist claim. "The mistake arises when we take language which is deeply contextual, that is, confessional, and in the case of Paul probably also liturgical, and turn it into objective assertions of a quasi-scientific form that give us information about the eternal fate of non-Christians."[55] The error of exclusivism is that it promotes arrogance and idolatry by claiming to know that God has abandoned the majority of all humanity to a fate of eternal punishment unless they come to know Jesus Christ.

In the light of this theodicy problem, it seems to me there is truth, also, to be affirmed in the inclusivist viewpoint. The love, grace, and mercy of God, incarnate and represented in Jesus Christ, pervades the whole creation. My discussion of this above shows how christological claims entail, or can entail, the inclusivist view. In the end, pluralism is also true. Its truth is that it affirms, not simply acknowledges, the variety of paths offered in the various religions. Even though it cannot make its affirmation of the truth of the other religions from some transcendent point of view, pluralism is true, I believe, as long as one recognizes that this is a Christian affirmation based on theological perceptions focused on their triune view of God. The truth offered in each of the three predominant perspectives can be affirmed as long as one recognizes that the affirmations are confessional claims being offered as a Christian theology of the various religions.

Whether any of the four viewpoints described in this chapter represent God's truth about the fate of the other religions we do not know because we cannot know. The limits are our limits to certainty about our claims, not a limit on God's purposes and power to transform human life. Confessional pluralism is the case I make for how Christians might answer the question of whether Jesus is the only way, truth, and life; that is, how Christians might answer the question of the truth of the many religions. My final conviction, however, is summarized by Robert Bellah. "As to the fate of non-Christians, as well as of those who lived before Christ, the only Christian thing to say is that that is in the hands of God, or, to put it more colloquially, God can deal with that."[56]

Endnotes

Preface

1. Anatole France, "The Procurator of Judea," *Our Heritage of World Literature.* Revised Edition. Eds., Stith Thompson and John Gassner (New York: Henry Holt and Company, 1958), 800-806.

2. Ibid., 806

3. John Meier, *A Marginal Jew: Rethinking the Historical Jesus,* Volume 1 (New York: Doubleday, 1991), 7.

4. Dietrich Bonhoeffer, *Letters and Papers from Prison* (New York: Macmillan, 1953), 162.

Chapter One

1. Jaroslav Pelikan, *Jesus Through the Centuries: His Place in the History of Culture* (New Haven: Yale University Press, 1985).

2. There are four recent books on the portrayal of Jesus in the movies: Roy Kinnard & Tim Davis, *Divine Images: A History of Jesus on the Screen* (New York: Citadel Press, 1992); Lloyd Baugh, *Imaging the Divine: Jesus and Christ-Figures in Film* (Kansas City: Sheed and Ward, 1997); W. Barnes Tatum, *Jesus at the Movies: A Guide to the First Hundred Years* (Santa Rosa, CA: Polerbridge Press, 1997); and Clive Marsh and Gaye Ortiz, eds., *Explorations in Theology and Film* (Oxford: Blackwell, 1997).

3. James Edwards, "Who Do Scholars Say That I Am?" *Christianity Today,* March 4, 1996, 20.

4. John Dominic Crossan, "Our Own Faces in Deep Wells: A Future for Historical Jesus Research," in John Caputo and Michael Scanlon, eds., *God, the Gift, and Postmodernism* (Bloomington, IN: Indiana University Press, 1999), 284.

5. Mark Allen Powell, *Jesus as a Figure in History: How Modern Historians View the Man from Galilee* (Louisville: Westminster John Knox, 1998), 50.

6. Cicero, *De Divinatione* 2:28, quoted in E. P. Sanders *The Historical Figure of Jesus* (New York: Penguin Books, 1993), 143.

7. Powell, 184.

8. William Hamilton, *A Quest for the Post-Historical Jesus* (New York: Continuum, 1994), 19.

9. Ibid., 72. "There is no Jesus as he really was. What we find, wherever we look, is always fiction, and usually ideology."

10. Ibid., 73.

11. Ibid., 282. Another postmodern study of Jesus, this time based more on the contemporary apocalyptic imagination than on the literary imagination, although his book "is closer to [Hamilton's] than any other," is Thomas J. J. Altizer's *The Contemporary Jesus* (Albany, NY: SUNY, 1997). "This book is an attempt to bring together the worlds of New Testament scholarship and imaginative [apocalyptic] vision." xi.

12. Albert Schweitzer, *The Quest of the Historical Jesus* trans. by W. Montgomery (London: A. & C. Black, 1910); (New York: The Macmillan Co., 1950), reissued with a new introduction by James M. Robinson, 1968.

13. Crossan, "Our Own Faces in Deep Wells," 282-310.

14. David Frederick Strauss, *Life of Jesus Critically Examined* (1835-36), ed. by Peter Hodgson (Philadelphia: Fortress Press, 1972).

15. Joseph Ernst Renan, *Life of Jesus* (1863) (Amherst, NY: Prometheus, 1991). For an account of the significance of Renan and his influence on the modern cinematic pictures of Jesus, see Charlotte Allen, *The Human Christ: The Search for the Historical Jesus* (New York: Free Press, 1998), chapter 8.

16. For a critique of the bourgeois character and agenda of the modern quest of the historical Jesus, including the third phase, see Dieter Georgi, "The Interest in Life of Jesus Theology as a Paradigm for the Social History of Biblical Criticism," *Harvard Theological Review* 85 (1992), 51-83; Helmut Koester, "The Historical Jesus and the Historical Situation of the Quest: An Epilogue," in Bruce Chilton and Craig Evans, eds., *Studying the Historical Jesus* (New York: E. J. Brill, 1994), 535-45; and Helmut Koester, "The Historical Jesus and the Cult of the *Kyrios Christos*," *Harvard Divinity Bulletin* 24 (1995), 13-18. For a reply, see John Dominic Crossan, "Our Own Faces in Deep Wells."

17. James Robinson, *A New Quest of the Historical Jesus* (London: SCM, 1959), 28. See also pp. 32, 37.

18. Ibid., 109.

19. Rudolf Bultmann, *History of the Synoptic Tradition* (New York: Harper & Row, 1963).

20. Ernst Kasemann, "The Problem of the Historical Jesus," *Essays on New Testament Themes* (London: SCM Press, 1964), 15-47.

21. Robinson, 69.

22. Ibid., 70.

23. Gunther Bornkamm, *Jesus of Nazareth* (New York: Harper & Row, 1960).

24. Ibid., 13.

25. Ibid., 53.

26. Ibid., 67.

27. Ibid., 77.

28. Ibid., 188.

29. For a collection of this material, see Robert Miller, ed., *The Complete Gospels:*

Annotated Scholars Version (San Francisco: HarperSanFrancisco, 1994). See also, Bart Ehrman, ed., *After the New Testament: A Reader in Early Christianity* (University Press: Oxford, New York, 1999), esp. 144-92, 235-308.

30. Marvin Meyer, "Introduction," *The Gospel of Thomas: The Hidden Sayings of Jesus* (San Francisco: HarperSanFrancisco, 1992), 16.

31. Ibid., 9.

32. Ibid., 10, 12.

33. For an audio series which summarizes many of the themes of the Jesus Seminar, see "The Search for Jesus: Modern Scholarship Looks at the Gospels," tapes of a symposium sponsored by the Resident Associate Program of the Smithsonian Institution, published by the Biblical Archeology Society (1994), and featuring lectures by Stephen Patterson, Marcus Borg, and John Dominic Crossan.

34. See E. P. Sanders, "Jesus: His Religious Type," *Reflections,* Winter-Spring, 1992, 4-12.

35. Marcus Borg, *Meeting Jesus Again for the First Time* (San Francisco: HarperSanFrancisco, 1994), 15. See, also, Marcus Borg, *Jesus: A New Vision* (San Francisco: Harper Collins, 1987), Part One, especially chapter 3. One of the major advocates of the charismatic Jesus is Geza Vermes. "The representation of Jesus in the Gospels as a man whose supernatural ability derived, not from secret powers, but from immediate contact with God, proves him to be a genuine charismatic, the true heir of an age-old prophetic religious line. Geza Vermes, *Jesus the Jew: A Historian's Reading of the Gospels* (Philadelphia: Fortress Press, 1973). 69. See also pp. 13, 79, 223.

36. Ibid., 15, 31-32.

37. Ibid., 49.

38. Ibid., 53.

39. Ibid., 69.

40. Ibid., 81.

41. For a nuanced discussion of the relation of Jesus to first century Cynicism, see John Dominic Crossan, *The Birth of Christianity: Discovering What Happened in the Years Immediately After the Execution of Jesus* (San Francisco: HarperSanFrancisco: 1998), 333-335.

42. John Dominic Crossan, *Who Killed Jesus? Exposing the Roots of Anti-Semitism in the Gospel Story of the Death of Jesus* (San Francisco: HarperSanFrancisco, 1995), 48.

43. Crossan, *The Birth of Christianity,* 325-26.

44. Ibid., 325-337.

45. John Dominic Crossan, *Jesus: A Revolutionary Biography* (San Francisco: HarperSanFrancisco, 1994), 101; see also *Who Killed Jesus?* 48.

46. Koester, "The Historical Jesus and the Cult of the *Kyrios Christos.*"

47. John Hayes, *Son of God to Superstar: Twentieth-Century Interpretations of Jesus* (Nashville: Abingdon Press, 1976), 16. Also, Elaine Pagels, "The Gnostic Jesus and Early Christian Politics," (Tempe, AZ: Department of Religious Studies, 1982), 2.

48. *The Gospel of Thomas: The Hidden Sayings of Jesus,* tr. Marvin Meyer (San Francisco: HarperSanFrancisco, 1992). A new "harmony" of all of these "apocryphal" texts is available in *The Secret Gospels: A Harmony of Apocryphal Jesus*

Traditions, ed. and trans. R. Joseph Hoffmann (Amherst, NY: Prometheus Books, 1996).

49. Sanders' *Historical Figure of Jesus* can be interpreted not only as a summary of his work for a more general audience but also as an implicit critique and response to the Jesus Seminar.

50. Leander Keck, "The Second Coming of the Liberal Jesus," *Christian Century,* August 24-31, 1994, 784-787.

51. Luke Timothy Johnson, *The Real Jesus: The Misguided Quest for the Historical Jesus and the Truth of the Traditional Gospels* (San Francisco: HarperSanFrancisco, 1996), chapters 1-2.

52. Ben Witherington III, *The Jesus Quest: The Third Search for the Jew of Nazareth* (Downers Grove: InterVarsity Press, 1995).

53. Robinson, *A New Quest of the Historical Jesus,* 28. See also pp. 32, 37.

54. Johnson, *The Real Jesus,* 46.

55. Crossan, "Our Own Faces in Deep Wells," 283-85.

56. For two brief summaries of "consensus" portraits of Jesus, see Paula Fredriksen, *From Jesus to Christ: The Origins of the New Testament Images of Jesus* (New Haven: Yale, 1988), 127-130, and E. P. Sanders, *The Historical Figure of Jesus,* 10-11.

57. For a summary of this argument, see Ben Witherington III, *Jesus the Sage: The Pilgrimage of Wisdom* (Minneapolis: Fortress Press, 1994). See also his *The Jesus Quest: The Third Search for the Jew of Nazareth* (Downers Grove: InterVarsity Press, 1995), 185ff.

58. Rudolf Bultmann, *Theology of the New Testament,* vol. 1 (New York: Scribners, 1951), 33. Italics in the original.

59. Alister McGrath, *Christian Theology: An Introduction* (Oxford: Blackwell, 1994), 326.

60. Powell, 183.

61. Ibid., 88.

62. Ibid., 85.

63. Francis Schussler Fiorenza, "Christian Redemption between Colonialism and Pluralism," in Rebecca Chopp and Mark Taylor, eds., *Reconstructing Christian Theology* (Minneapolis: Fortress, 1994), 295.

64. Pagels, 6. In addition to the Nag Hammadi texts, see Robert Miller, ed., *The Complete Gospels* (San Francisco: Harper Collins, 1994), *The Lost Gospel of Q: The Original Sayings of Jesus* (Berkeley: Ulysses Press, 1996), Marvin Meyer, *The Gospel of Thomas: The Hidden Sayings of Jesus* (San Francisco: HarperSanFrancisco, 1992), Richard Valantasis, *The Gospel of Thomas* (New York: Routledge, 1997), and R. Joseph Hoffmann, ed., *The Secret Gospels: A Harmony of Apocryphal Jesus Traditions* (Amherst, NY: Prometheus Books, 1996).

65. There are some explicit advocates for the replacement of "catholic" Christianity by "gnostic" Christianity. Karen King, upon hearing the suggestion from John Dominic Crossan that such a transformation of Christianity could occur, says, "As I might well suggest we do." "The Jesus Summit: The Historical Jesus and Contemporary Faith," VCR, Episcopal Cathedral Teleconferencing Network,"

Chapter Two

1. Richard Swinburne, *The Coherence of Theism* (Oxford: Clarendon Press, 1977), 2. See also his *The Christian God* (Oxford: Clarendon Press, 1994) 125: "there exists necessarily and eternally a person essentially bodiless, omnipresent, creator and sustainer of any universe there may be perfectly free, omnipotent, omniscient, perfectly good, and a course of moral obligation."

2. For an extended discussion of this claim, see my *The Transforming God: An Interpretation of Suffering and Evil* (Louisville: Westminster John Knox, 1997), chapters 1-5.

3. See John Cobb's discussion in Stephen Davis, ed., *Encountering Evil: Live Options in Theology* (Atlanta: John Knox Press, 1981), 172-73.

4. David Cunningham, *These Three Are One: The Practice of Trinitarian Theology* (Blackwell, 1998), viii: "By the late eighteenth century it was possible to write theological accounts of the Christian faith in general, and of its understanding of God in particular, with little or no reference to the doctrine of the Trinity." See, specifically, the work of Theodore Jennings and Stanley Hauerwas.

5. See, for example, Theodore Jennings, *Beyond Theism: A Grammar of God-Language* (New York: Oxford University Press, 1985); William Placker, *Unapologetic Theology: A Christian Voice in a Pluralistic Conversation* (Louisville: Westminster/John Knox Press, 1989), and *Narratives of a Vulnerable God: Christ, Theology, and Scripture* (Louisville: Westminster John Knox, 1994); Stanley Hauerwas and L. Gregory Jones, eds., *Why Narrative: Readings in Narrative Theology* (Grand Rapids: William B. Eerdmans, 1989), esp. "Introduction: Why Narrative?"

6. Regina Schwartz, *The Curse of Cain: The Violent Legacy of Monotheism* (Chicago: University of Chicago Press, 1997). See, also, Carol Delaney, *Abraham on Trial: The Social Legacy of Biblical Myth* (Princeton, NJ: Princeton University Press, 1998).

7. Ibid., 17.

8. H. Richard Niebuhr, *Radical Monotheism and Western Culture* (New York: Harper & Brothers, 1943), 37.

9. Ibid., 58.

10. The following account of the christological controversy depends upon resources drawn from many sources: Richard Norris, ed., *The Christological Controversy* (Philadelphia: Fortress, 1980); Jarsolav Pelikan, *The Christian Tradition: A History of the Development of Doctrine, Vol. 1, The Emergence of the Catholic Tradition* (100-600) (Chicago: University of Chicago Press, 1971); J. N. D. Kelly, *Early Christian Doctrine* (New York: Harper & Row, 1959); Catherine Mowry LaCugna, *God For Us: The Trinity and Christian Life* (San Francisco: HarperSanFrancisco, 1991); A. C. McGiffert, *A History of Christian Thought, Vol. 1* (New York: Charles Schribner's, 1932); Justo Gonzalez, *A History of Christian Thought, Vol. 1* (Nashville: Abingdon, 1970); Wiliston Walker, *History of the Christian Church* (New York: Scribners, 1959); William Placker, *A History of Christian Thought: An Introduction* (Philadelphia: Westminster, 1983); Richard Rubenstein, *When Jesus Became God: The Epic Fight over Christ's Divinity in the Last Days of Rome* (New York: Harcourt Brace, 1999); A. H. M. Jones, *Constantine and the Conversion of Europe* (New York: Collier,

1962); Durmont Lane's *The Reality of Jesus* (Mahwah, NJ: Paulist, 1975), and finally, my notes from my teacher, J. Bruce Behney's "History of Doctrine" classes he taught at United Theological Seminary in the early 1960s.

11. Placker, *A History of Christian Thought*, 68.

12. Norris, *The Christological Controversy*, 6.

13. Rubenstein, *When Jesus Became God*, 4.

14. Pelikan, *Jesus Through the Centuries*, 5.

15. Robert Gregg and Dennis Groh, *Early Arianism—A View of Salvation* (Philadelphia: Fortress, 1981), 77.

16. Ibid., 9.

17. Ibid., 99.

18. Ibid., 53.

19. Ibid., 83.

20. Ibid., 116.

21. Ibid., 67.

22. Ibid., 43.

23. Ibid., 29.

24. Ibid., 78.

25. Ibid., 79.

26. Ibid., x.

27. Ibid., 59.

28. Ibid., 63.

29. Ibid., 64.

30. Rubenstein, *When Jesus Became God*, 9.

31. Gregg and Groh, 171.

32. Ibid., 177.

33. Ibid., 179.

34. Ibid., 180-81.

35. Ibid., 193-94.

36. Rubenstein, *When Jesus Became God*, 9.

37. Athanasius, "Orations Against the Arians," in Norris, 91.

38. Maurice Wiles, *Archetypical Heresy: Arianism Throughout the Centuries* (New York: Oxford University Press, 1996), 32.

39. Rubenstein, 169.

40. Ibid., 182.

41. Wiles, 35.

42. Rubenstein, 206.

43. Placker, *History of Christian Thought*, 78.

44. Rubenstein, 98.

45. LaCugna, 9.

46. Rubenstein, 228-29.

47. Apollinaris of Laodicia, "On the Union in Christ of the Body with the Godhead," in Norris, 104.

48. Ibid., 109.

49. His great critics were the Cappadocians, toward the middle and end of the fourth century, who stressed the need for a human soul and psyche in Christ. At

this point they stand in line with the *anthropos*/word school of Antioch. The Council of Constantinople in 381 CE ratified Nicea on Arius and condemned Apollinaris.

50. Paul Tillich, *Courage to Be* (New Haven: Yale University Press, 1952).

51. "The church is not bound to make human sin the last and most serious form of evil, or to see Christ's redemptive work simply as the forgiveness and removal of sin. . . . The demonic has replaced sin as the decisive form of evil and therefore as the decisive arena for Christ's victory—or impotence." Arthur McGill, *Suffering: A Test of Theological Method* (Philadelphia: Westminster Press, 1982), 52.

52. Daniel Migliori, *Faith Seeking Understanding* (Grand Rapids: Eerdmans, 1991), 149.

53. Ibid.

54. Ibid.

55. George W. Stroup III, "Christian Doctrine: I: Chalcedon Revisited," *Theology Today* XXXV (April 1978), 63-64.

56. Thomas Oden, *The Living God: Systematic Theology*, Volume One (San Francisco: Harper & Row, 1987), 292.

57. Ibid., 113.

58. For a more extended discussion of this point, see my *The Transforming God: An Interpretation of Suffering and Evil*, especially chapter 2, where I discuss some of the implications and attempted modifications of the classical idea of omnipotence.

59. Robert Jenson, *The Triune Identity* (Philadelphia: Fortress Press, 1982), and Ted Peters, *God as Trinity: Relationality and Temporality in Divine Life* (Louisville: Westminster John Knox Press, 1993).

60. Jurgen Moltmann, *The Crucified God: The Cross of Christ as the Foundation and Criticism of Christian Theology* (New York: Harper & Row, 1974), 201.

61. Ibid., 243, 245.

62. Ibid., 247.

63. Jurgen Moltmann, *Jesus Christ for Today's World* (Minneapolis: Fortress, 1994), 37-38.

64. Moltmann, *The Crucified God*, 229, 243.

65. Ibid., 243.

66. LaCugna, 21.

67. Ibid., 4

68. Ibid., 14.

69. Ibid., 149.

70. Ibid., 216.

71. Ibid., 225.

72. Ibid., 229.

73. Ibid., 378.

74. Ibid., 382.

75. Ibid., 383.

76. Ibid., 400.

77. Ibid., 388.

78. Ibid., 389.

79. Ibid., 391.

80. Ibid., 394.
81. Ibid., 399.

Chapter Three

1. For a Reformed understanding of evangelical identity, see Bernard Ramm, *The Evangelical Heritage* (Waco: Word, 1973), chapters 1-4.

2. "Distinct from both the Catholic and classical Protestant views is the revivalist stress on the turning point experience of conversion or the double turning points of conversion and baptism in the Holy Spirit." Bradley Hanson, *Introduction to Christian Theology* (Minneapolis: Fortress, 1997), 246-47.

3. James Davison Hunter, *American Evangelicalism: Conservative Religion and the Quandary of Modernity* (New Brunswick: Rutgers University Press, 1983), 3. See also Alister McGrath, *Evangelicalism & the Future of Christianity* (Downers Grove, IL: InterVarsity Press, 1995), 53.

4. For a pietistic understanding of evangelical identity, see, also, Donald Bloesch, *The Evangelical Renaissance* (Grand Rapids: Eerdmans, 1973).

5. Hunter, 7; see also Bloesch, chapter 3; see also John Gerstner, "The Theological Boundaries of Evangelical Faith," in Wells and Woodridge, eds., *The Evangelicals* (Nashville: Abingdon Press, 1975), 25; see also Henry Knight III, *A Future for Truth: Evangelical Theology in a Postmodern World* (Nashville: Abingdon Press, 1997), 18; see also McGrath, 55-56.

6. Hunter, 9.

7. McGrath, 57.

8. Ibid., 66.

9. Douglas Jacobsen and Frederick Schmidt, "Behind Orthodoxy and Beyond It: Recent Developments in Evangelical Christology," *Scottish Journal of Theology*, Vol. 45, 515-541.

10. Ibid., 519.

11. Ibid., 520.

12. See, for instance, the discussion between Pinnock and liberal theologian Delwin Brown in *Theological Crossfire: An Evangelical/Liberal Dialogue,* eds. Delwin Brown and Clark Pinnock (Grand Rapids: Zondervan, 1990), Part Four, Sections 7 and 8.

13. Jacobson and Schmidt, 522-24.

14. Ibid., 527.

15. Pinnock, *Theological Crossfire,* 145. Pinnock says again, "In fact, I think Jesus was not just radically unique but *metaphysically different* from all other beings," in Stephen Davis, ed., *Encountering Jesus: A Debate on Christology* (Atlanta: John Knox Press, 1988), 74. This same focus on ontological instead of functional language is affirmed by Douglas Webster, *A Passion for Christ: An Evangelical Christology* (Grand Rapids: Academie Books, 1987), 41.

16. See Daniel Migliori, *Faith Seeking Understanding: An Introduction to Christian Theology* (Grand Rapids: Eerdmans, 1991), chapter 4.

17. Jerry Walls, "What Is Doctrinal Pluralism?" *Quarterly Review,* 4 (Winter, 1984), 53-54.

18. Thomas Oden, *Agenda for Theology* (New York: Harper & Row, 1979), 34, 115. See also his *Requiem: A Lament in Three Movements* (Nashville: Abingdon Press, 1995), 23, 113, 130.

19. Oden, *Requiem,* 139.

20. Ramm, chapters 1-4.

21. Bloesch, chapter 3.

22. There are some evangelical christologies which do address more directly the christological question. These tend to be shaped by the contemporary question of beginning a christology from above or from below. Most of these do not like to begin either from above or below because they want to avoid the pitfalls toward "heresy" implied in one or the other beginning point. They prefer a middle ground. However, it is very difficult to be clear about what this middle ground is that avoids these pitfalls.

23. Bloesch, 143.

24. Below I will suggest an alternative interpretation of this startling omission, viz., that what is constitutive of North American evangelical faith is such a distinctive form of Christianity in the modern world in contrast to the orthodox faith of most Christians throughout the history of the church that it indeed, in fact and in practice, constitutes a distinctive form of christology that implicitly denies, or at least modifies or neglects, creedal christology. So the formula and the official theology remain orthodox, but the piety and methodology for formulating christological claims departs significantly from orthodox christology. This interpretation may seem to be in conflict with the one I have offered so far, but I think it is not if I can be permitted the distinction between what is formally confessed at the creedal level and what stands at the heart of the piety of North American evangelical christology.

25. McGrath, 66.

26. Garry Wills, *Under God: Religion and American Politics* (New York: Simon and Schuster, 1990), 21, 388.

27. Richard Coleman, *Issues of Theological Conflict: Evangelicals and Liberals* (Grand Rapids: Eerdmans, 1972), 61.

28. James Boice, *The Sovereign God* (Downers Grove, IL: InterVarsity, 1978).

29. J. I. Packer, *Knowing God* (Downers Grove, IL: InterVarsity, 1973), 17-72.

30. John Wesley, "The Almost Christian," *John Wesley's Sermons: An Anthology,* eds. Albert Outler and Richard Heitzenrater (Abingdon Press, 1991), 62-68; see also his "The More Excellent Way," 512-21.

31. Webster, *A Passion for Christ,* 21.

32. "Wesley, in the final analysis, although drawn to the Moravians through their mysticism, was eventually driven to the Moravians because their synthesis emphasized the one thing that he wanted most and that mysticism alone could not promise: assurance." Robert Tuttle, *John Wesley: His Life and Thought* (Grand Rapids: Francis Asbury Press, 1978), 224. See also his *Mysticism in the Wesleyan Tradition* (Grand Rapids: Francis Asbury Press, 1989). Tuttle contrasts Wesley's evangelical sense of the primacy of grace and of faith as assurance to the mystical sense of blind obedience involving the dark night of the soul, their sense of the

annihilation of the self, and their development of the Christian life in terms of human effort.

33. Glenn Chesnut, *Images of Christ: An Introduction to Christology* (Minneapolis: Seabury Press, 1984), chapter 4.

34. Henry Nelson Wieman, *The Wrestle of Religion with Truth* (New York: Macmillan, 1928); Bernard Meland, "The Mystic Returns," *Journal of Religion* 17 (1937), 146-60; and his "The Faith of a Mystical Naturalist," *Review of Religion* 1 (1937), 270-78; and his *Modern Man's Worship* (New York: Harper, 1934).

35. See, for example, Sallie McFague, *The Body of God: An Ecological Theology* (Minneapolis: Fortress Press, 1993), and Rosemary Ruether, *Gaia and God: An Ecofeminist Theology of Earth Healing* (San Francisco: HarperSanFrancisco, 1992).

36. Albrecht Ritschl, *History of Pietism in the Lutheran Church of the 17th and 18th Centuries*, 2 vols, (1884). See, also, F. E. Stoeffler, *The Rise of Evangelical Pietism* (Leiden: Brill, 1965); and James Stein, *Philip Jakob Spener: Pietist Patriarch* (Chicago: Covenant Press, 1986).

37. "Modernization and Urbanization," *Encyclopedia Britannica*, Volume 24, 15 Edition, 1985, 255-266.

38. Hunter, 6.

39. "Modernization and Urbanization," 256.

40. Ibid., 259.

41. Franklin Baumer, *Modern European Thought: Continuity and Change in Ideas, 1600-1950* (New York: Macmillan, 1977), 27-28.

42. For a brilliant socio-historical account of the rise and character of modernity, see Stephen Toulmin, *Cosmopolis: The Hidden Agenda of Modernity* (New York: Free Press, 1990).

43. Knight, 37-40.

44. Ernst Cassirer, *The Philosophy of the Enlightenment* (Boston: Beacon Press, 1951), chapter 1.

45. Edward Farley and Peter Hodgson, "Scripture and Tradition," in Hodgson and King, eds., *Christian Theology: An Introduction to Its Tasks* (Philadelphia: Fortress, 1982), 46ff.

46. Bernard Meland, "Liberalism, theological," *Encyclopedia Britannica*, Volume 13 (1968), 1020-1022.

47. Ibid., 1020.

48. Ibid., 1021.

49. Hunter, 4, 15.

50. Ibid., 17.

51. Christian Smith, *American Evangelicalism: Embattled and Thriving* (Chicago: University of Chicago Press, 1998), chapter four.

52. Hunter, 27-48. For his study of what has happened to evangelicals since the 1980s, see James Davison Hunter, *Evangelicalism: The Coming Generation* (Chicago: University of Chicago Press, 1987).

53. For an earlier form of my argument, see my "What Liberals and Fundamentalists Have in Common," in Marla Selvidge, ed., *Fundamentalism Today: What Makes It So Attractive?* (Elgin: Brethren Press, 1984), 85-89.

54. For an eighteenth-century version of this evangelical theme, see John

Wesley, "The Witness of the Spirit I," and "The Witness of the Spirit II," *John Wesley's Sermons*, 145-156 and 393-404.

55. For a clear statement on the authority of reason and experience in theology as a key distinguishing mark of liberal theology, see Brown and Pinnock, 36, 56.

56. Delwin Brown and Sheila Greeve Davaney, "liberalism: USA," *The Blackwell Encyclopedia of Modern Christian Thought*, ed. Alister McGrath (Oxford: Blackwell, 1993), 325.

57. Smith, 103.

58. Martin Kahler, *The So-Called Historical Jesus and the Historic, Biblical Christ* (Philadelphia: Fortress Press, 1964; original, 1892).

59. Mark Allen Powell, *Jesus as a Figure in History: How Modern Historians View the Man From Galilee* (Louisville: Westminster John Knox, 1998), 19.

60. Walls, 59.

61. David Morgan, "Sallman's Head of Christ: The History of an Image," *The Christian Century* (October 7, 1992), 868. For a longer discussion, see his *Icons of American Protestantism: The Art of Warner Sallman* (New Haven: Yale University Press, 1996), and his *Visual Piety: A History and Theory of Popular Religious Images* (Berkeley: University of California, 1998).

62. It is important to acknowledge here that there is a recent cadre of evangelical theologians who have moved toward a new postmodern narrative methodology and content in their christological claims. See, for example, Henry Knight III, *A Future for Truth* (Nashville: Abingdon, 1997), chapter 8. The work of Gary Dorrien and William Placker are two other current examples.

63. Harold Bloom, *The American Religion: The Emergence of the Post-Christian Nation* (New York: Simon & Schuster), and Philip Lee, *Against the Protestant Gnostics* (New York: Oxford University Press, 1978).

64. Hunter, 65.

65. Paul Holmer, "Contemporary Evangelical Faith," in Wells and Woodbridge, *The Evangelicals*, 85.

66. Gary Dorrien, *The Remaking of Evangelical Theology* (Louisville: Westminster John Knox, 1998), chapter 1.

67. Robert Bellah, et. al., *Habits of the Heart: Individualism and Commitment in American Life* (Berkeley: University of California Press, 1985), 122.

68. Harold Bloom, *The American Religion*, chapter 2.

69. Ibid., 27.

70. Ibid., 40.

Chapter Four

1. For an extended discussion of my understanding of the terms modern and postmodern, and my reasons for locating liberation christologies within the postmodern context, see my essay, "Postmodernism: Intellectual Velcro Dragged Across Culture?" *Theology Today*, 51/4 (January, 1995), 524-538, especially 528-31 on "liberationist postmodernism." For a definitive essay on liberal theology, see Bernard Meland, "liberalism, theological," in *Encyclopedia Britannica*, 14th Edition, Volume 13, 1020-22; see also Delwin Brown and Sheila Greeve Davaney,

"Liberalism: USA," in Alister McGrath, ed., *Blackwell Encyclopedia of Modern Christian Thought,* (Oxford: Blackwell, 1993), 325-30; Kenneth Cauthen, *The Impact of American Religious Liberalism* (New York: Harper & Row, 1962); Henry P. Van Dusen, *The Vindication of Liberal Theology* (New York: Scribners, 1963); David Roberts and Henry P. Van Dusen, eds., *Liberal Theology: An Appraisal* (New York: Scribners, 1942); L. Harold DeWolf, *The Case for Theology in Liberal Perspective* (Philadelphia: Westminster Press, 1949); and Lloyd J. Averill, *American Theology in the Liberal Tradition* (Philadelphia: Westminster Press, 1967); Gary Dorrien, *The Making of American Liberal Theology* (Louisville: Wesminster John Knox, 2001). For important definitions of postliberal theology, see Sheila Greeve Davaney and Delwin Brown, "postliberalism," in *Blackwell Encyclopedia of Modern Christian Thought* 453-56; William Placker, *Unapologetic Theology: A Christian Voice in a Pluralistic Conversation* (Louisville: Westminster John Knox, 1989); Terrence W. Tilley, *Postmodern Theologies: The Challenge of Religious Diversity* (Maryknoll: Orbis, 1995); and William Placker, "Postliberal Theology," in David Ford, ed., *The Modern Theologians: An Introduction to Christian Theology in the Twentieth Century,* Volume II (Oxford: Blackwell, 1989).

2. John Macquarrie, *Jesus Christ in Modern Thought* (Philadelphia: Trinity Press International, 1990), 8.

3. Ibid., Part Two, 175-335.

4. John Hick, *The Metaphor of God Incarnate: Christology in a Pluralistic Age* (Louisville: Westminster John Knox Press, 1993), 109.

5. Donald Baillie, *God Was in Christ: An Essay on Incarnation and Atonement* (New York: Charles Scribners, 1948), 114, 117.

6. Ibid., 125.

7. Ibid., 129.

8. Ibid., 131.

9. Hick, 110.

10. Clark Pinnock and Delwin Brown, *Theological Crossfire: An Evangelical/Liberal Dialogue* (Grand Rapids: Zondervan, 1990), 173.

11. John Cobb, in Stephen Davis, ed., *Encountering Jesus: A Debate on Christology* (Atlanta: John Knox Press, 1988), 65-66.

12. For a detailed summary of Whitehead's metaphysical scheme, see Victor Lowe, *Understanding Whitehead* (Baltimore: Johns Hopkins, 1962); an excerpt from this can be found in Delwin Brown, Ralph James, and Gene Reeves, eds., *Process Philosophy and Christian Thought* (Indianapolis: Bobbs Merrill, 1971), "Whitehead's Metaphysical System," 3-20. The most significant application of Whitehead's philosophy to Christian theology can be found in John Cobb, *A Christian Natural Theology: Based on the Thought of Alfred North Whitehead* (Philadelphia: Westminster Press, 1965). Three very accessible books on Whitehead's philosophy and Christian theology are W. Norman Pittenger, *Process-Thought and Christian Faith* (New York: The Macmillan Co., 1968), Marjorie Suchocki, *God Christ Church: A Practical Guide to Process Theology,* New Revised Edition (New York: Crossroad, 1992), and C. Robert Mesle, *Process Theology: A Basic Introduction* (St. Louis: Chalice Press, 1993.

13. Cobb, "Critique by John B. Cobb, Jr.," *Encountering Jesus,* 64.

14. David Griffin, *A Process Christology* (Philadelphia: Westminster Press, 1973), 206.

15. Pinnock and Brown, 169.

16. John Cobb's major christological statements can be found in John Cobb, *Christ in a Pluralistic Age* (Philadelphia: Westminster Press, 1975); John Cobb and David Griffin, *Process Theology: An Introductory Exposition* (Philadelphia: Westminster Press, 1976); John Cobb, *Beyond Dialogue: Toward a Mutual Transformation of Christianity and Buddhism* (Philadelphia: Fortress, 1982); and John Cobb, "Christ Beyond Creative Transformation," in Stephen Davis, ed., *Encountering Jesus: A Debate on Christology* (Atlanta: John Knox, 1988).

17. Cobb, *Christ in a Pluralistic Age*, 64.

18. In *Process Theology: An Introductory Exposition*, Cobb uses the phrase "the creative love of God." "The creative love of God, insofar as it is incarnate, is Christ," 95.

19. Cobb, *Christ in a Pluralistic Age*, 72.

20. Ibid., 76. See, also, Cobb and Griffin, 98.

21. Cobb and Griffin, 99.

22. Ibid., 117.

23. Ibid., 139. See, also, "Christ Beyond Creative Transformation," 145-46.

24. *Process Theology: An Introductory Exposition*, 105.

25. Cobb, *Christ in a Pluralistic Age*, 142.

26. "Christ Beyond Creative Transformation," 150.

27. Ibid., 153.

28. Ibid., 157.

29. David Griffin, *A Process Christology* (Philadelphia: Westminster Press, 1973). For David Griffin, the requirements for an adequate answer to the question about incarnation is liberal to the core, as he goes beyond Baillie's model of the paradox of grace to even more typically liberal themes. These include: 1) the immanence of God in the world, which underscores the continuity between God and the world (one might even speak of his liberal christology "as an attempt to carry the doctrine of the incarnation to its logical conclusion," although he does not go as far as Thomas Altizer goes in proclaiming the death of God in radical secularization); 2) the importance of ontology (or metaphysics), which seeks to provide a coherent and universal picture of the world within which to set all talk about God and Jesus Christ; and 3) an implication of points one and two, viz., that no special interruption of the normal course of events is intrinsic to the christology. See, especially, chapter 9.

30. Ibid., 213.

31. Ibid., 216.

32. Ibid., 218.

33. Ibid., 231-232.

34. On this last point, see Carter Heyward, "Jesus of Nazareth/Christ of Faith: Foundations of a Reactive Christology," in Susan Thistlethwaite and Mary Potter Engel, eds., *Lift Every Voice: Constructing Christian Theologies from the Underside* (San Francisco: Harper Collins, 1990), 196.

35. For an extensive discussion of a variety of meanings of postmodernism,

including cultural postmodernism, liberative postmodernism, deconstructive postmodernism, and late modernism, see my essay, "Postmodernism: Intellectual Velcro Dragged Across Culture?"

36. David Griffin, "Postmodern Theology as First-World Liberation Theology," Religion and the Postmodern Vision (Department of Religious Studies, University of Missouri-Columbia, 1991), 6.

37. Jon Sobrino, "Theological Understanding in European and Latin American Theology," *The True Church and the Poor* (Maryknoll: Orbis, 1984), 7-83.

38. Ibid., 37.

39. For another example of this location of liberation theology within the liberal tradition in the West, see Schubert Ogden, *Faith and Freedom: Toward a Theology of Liberation* (Nashville: Abingdon Press, 1989), chapter 1.

40. This is recognized quite explicitly by Wells and Woodbridge in their book on "the evangelicals." They include two chapters on black evangelicals in Part II of their book, "Who Evangelicals Are"; one by William Parnell, "The Religious Heritage of Blacks," and one by William Bentley, "Bible Believers in the Black Community." David Wells and John Woodbridge, *The Evangelicals: What They Believe, Who They Are, Where They are Changing* (Nashville: Abingdon Press, 1975).

41. Lewis Charles Harvey, "Black Christology: The History and Theology of Black Music," United Theological Seminary *Journal of Theology,* XCI (Spring 1987), 7.

42. Ibid., 8.

43. For another perspective on the role of music in the African American religious experience, see Robert Simmons, "Syncretism in Sacred Music: Corridor to Intentional Inclusiveness," United Theological Seminary *Journal of Theology,* XCVI (1992), 60-76.

44. James Cone, *A Black Theology of Liberation* Second Edition (Maryknoll: Orbis Books, 1986; first edition, 1970) and his *God of the Oppressed* (New York: Seabury, 1975).

45. Cone, *A Black Theology of Liberation,* 110.

46. Ibid., 112.

47. Ibid., 113.

48. Ibid., 118.

49. Ibid., 119.

50. Ibid., 120.

51. Ibid., 124.

52. Cone, *God of the Oppressed,* 110.

53. Ibid., 113.

54. Ibid., 120.

55. Ibid., 135.

56. See, especially, Jon Sobrino, *Christology at the Crossroads* (Maryknoll: Orbis, 1978), and *Jesus the Liberator* (Maryknoll: Orbis, 1993), and Leonardo Boff, *Jesus Christ Liberator* (Maryknoll: Orbis, 1987).

57. Jose Miguez-Bonino, *Doing Theology in a Revolutionary Situation* (Philadelphia: Fortress, 1975), chapters 1-2.

Chapter Five

1. James Wall,"Paradoxical Goodness," *Christian Century*, February 5-12, 1997, 115. For another critique of this movie, see Darby Kathleen Ray, *Deceiving the Devil: Atonement, Abuse, and Ransom* (Cleveland: Pilgrim, 1998), 26-27.

2. Wall, 116.

3. James Conn, *Christian Century*, "Letters to the Editor," July 16-23, 1997.

4. Elizabeth Johnson, *Consider Jesus: Waves of Renewal in Christology* (New York: Crossroad, 1995), 104.

5. Daphne Hampson, *Theology and Feminism* (Oxford: Blackwell, 1990), 51.

6. Anne Carr, *Transforming Grace: Christian Tradition and Women's Experience* (San Francisco: Harper Collins, 1988), 163.

7. Hampson, 53.

8. Johnson, 107.

9. Walter Abbott, S. J., ed. *The Documents of Vatican II* (New York: Guild Press, 1966), 536.

10. "Vatican Declaration on the Question of Admission of Women to the Ministerial Priesthood" (1976), section 27.

11. J. Kilmer Meyers, "Statement on the Proposed Ordination of Women to the 122nd Diocesan Convention, October 1971," in Jacob Needleman, A. K. Bierman and James Gould, eds., *Religion for a New Generation* (New York: Macmillan, 1973), 188-89.

12. Mary Daly, *Beyond God the Father* (Boston: Beacon Press, 1973), 19.

13. Hampson, 59.

14. Jacquelyn Grant, *White Woman's Christ and Black Woman's Jesus* (Atlanta: Scholars Press, 1989).

15. Carr, 158.

16. Grant, chapter 3. See also Johnson, 97-98.

17. Kathleen Sands, *Escape from Paradise: Evil and Tragedy in Feminist Theology* (Minneapolis: Fortress, 1994), 85.

18. Elaine Pagels, *The Gnostic Gospels* (New York: Vintage Books, 1979), and her article, "The Gnostic Jesus and Early Christian Politics." University Lecture in Religion at Arizona State University, Department of Religious Studies, 1982, 228.

19. Susan Cady, Marion Ronan, and Hal Taussig, *Sophia: The Future of Feminist Spirituality* (San Francisco: Harper & Row, 1988).

20. Carol Christ, *Laughter of Aphrodite: Reflections on a Journey to the Goddess* (San Francisco: Harper and Row, 1987).

21. Letty Russell, *Human Liberation in a Feminist Perspective—A Theology* (Philadelphia: Westminster, 1974).

22. Rita Brock, *Journeys by Heart: A Christology of Erotic Power* (New York: Crossroad, 1988).

23. Grant, chapter 4.

24. Brock, chapter 3.

25. Sands, 85, 115.

26. Hampson, 76.

27. For one effort to engage feminists and womanists in conversation, see Susan Thistlethwaite, *God, Sex, and Race: Christian Feminism in Black and White* (New York: Crossroad, 1991).

28. Grant, 220.

29. Carr, 161.

30. Ibid., 168-69.

31. Madelon Nunn, "Christology or Male-olatry?" *Duke Divinity School Review* 42/3 (Fall, 1977), 144.

32. Julie Hopkins, *Towards a Feminist Christology* (Grand Rapids: Eerdmans, 1995), 91.

33. Ibid., 220.

34. Ibid., 221.

35. Ibid., 212.

36. Carr, 161.

37. Pagels, *The Gnostic Gospels* (New York: Vintage Books, 1981).

38. Pagels, "The Gnostic Jesus and Early Christian Politics," 5.

39. Ibid., 8.

40. Brock., 66.

41. Ibid., 67.

42. See the opening paragraphs in "Biblical Wisdom and Current Theological Ferment," the Report of the Task Force on the Study of Wisdom, the Council of Bishops (October 31–November 4, 1994), *Circuit Rider,* March, 1995, 32.

43. "The seminaries and the Vatican can keep on defining orthodoxy largely for the passing on of the traditions through the ordained clergy. But we laity have always crossed our fingers behind our backs when they lay out what orthodoxy is. We know in our daily lives theology has to be much fresher and more flexible than the definitions of orthodoxy can ever be." Elizabeth Bettenhausen, quoted in *Circuit Rider,* May 1994, 14.

44. Thus, Donna Blackstock, Presbyterian Church USA: "an attack on women . . . It is spiritual rape. . . . The *Layman* is using terrorist tactics to achieve its purposes."

45. Heim, 340.

46. Catherine Keller, "Inventing the goddess," *Christian Century,* April 6, 1995, 341.

47. Rosemary Ruether, *Sexism and God-Talk* (Boston: Beacon Press, 1983), 57.

48. Ibid.

49. Ibid.

50. "Biblical Wisdom and Current Theological Ferment," 35, 36.

51. Keller, 341.

52. Denis Edwards, *Jesus the Wisdom of God* (Maryknoll: Orbis, 1995), 39-42.

53. Ibid., 42-43.

54. Sophia is also represented in the Apocrypha, especially Wisdom 7:25-26.

55. Ibid. Ruether also points out that although the female side of God was diminished by the adoption of the male Logos symbol, it was not altogether cut off. The figure of the Holy Spirit picks up many of the Hebraic traditions of the female Sophia and Hokmah (spirit), 59.

56. Edwards, 33-39.

57. Ibid., 58.

58. Most participants in the christological controversy identified Wisdom in Proverbs 8 with Christ. Jarsolov Pelikan, *Jesus Through the Centuries* (New Haven: Yale University Press, 1985), maintains "the basis for the fullest statement of . . . the divine in Christ as Logos was provided not by . . . John 1:1-14 but by Proverbs 8:22-31."

59. Ibid., 36.

60. Leo Lefebure, "The Wisdom of God: Sophia and Christian Theology," *Christian Century*, October 19, 1994, 953.

61. Ibid.

62. Keller, 341.

63. Rebecca Pentz, "Jesus as Sophia," *The Reformed Journal*, December 1988, 17-22, and "Can Jesus Save Women?" in Stephen Davis, ed., *Encountering Jesus: A Debate on Christology* (Atlanta: John Knox Press, 1988), 77-109.

64. Keller, 340.

65. Thomas Oden, *Requium: A Lament in Three Movements* (Atlanta: Abingdon, 1995), 30.

66. Ibid., 30-31.

67. One evidence that many Sophia advocates remain within the field of Hebrew and Christian texts is that Goddess worshipers have understandably not felt at home among Christian feminists; indeed, radical (that is, goddess or post-Christian or cultural) feminists tend to dismiss Sophia as a mere cosmic handmaid of Yahweh—the inner feminine of a dominant masculinity.

68. Elizabeth Johnson, *She Who Is: The Mystery of God in Feminist Discourse* (New York: Crossroad, 1993). See also Catherine LaCugna, *God For Us: The Trinity and Christian Life* (San Francisco: Harper San Francisco, 1991).

69. Susan Cady, Marian Ronan, and Hal Tausig, *Sophia: The Future of Feminist Spirituality* (San Francisco: Harper & Row, 1986).

70. Cf. "Jesus as Sophia," *The Reformed Journal,* Volume 38, December 1988, 17-22, and "Can Jesus Save Women?" in Stephen Davis, ed., *Encountering Jesus: A Debate on Christology* (Atlanta: John Knox, 1988), pp. 77-109.

71. See Elizabeth Schussler Fiorenza, *In Memory of Her: A Feminist Theological Reconstruction of Christian Origins* (New York: Crossroad, 1983).

72. Adela Yarbro Collins, "New Testament Perspectives: The Gospel of John," *Journal for the Study of the Old Testament* 22 (1982), quoted by Carr, *Transforming Grace*, 173-74.

73. Ibid., 20.

74. "Jesus as Sophia," 21-22.

75. See Barbara Zikkmund, "The Trinity and Women's Experience," *Christian Century* Vol. 104 (April 15, 1987), 354-56.

76. Johnson, *She Who Is*, especially chapters 7-9. For a sympathetic review by an evangelical Protestant, see Amy Plantinga Pauw, "Braiding a new footbridge: Christian wisdom, classic and feminist," *Christian Century,* November 17-24, 1993, 1159-1162.

77. Thomas Finger, "Holy Wisdom, Love So Bright: Sophia in Scripture and Worship," unpublished paper.

78. David Bauer, "Who Do You Say that I Am?" *Good News*, January/February, 1995, 24.

79. Ibid., 25.

80. Randy Petersen, "Wisdom's Feast or Gospel's Famine," *Good News*, July/August, 1990, 14.

Chapter Six

1. This story is an edited verbatim transcript of a story Edward Wheeler, a former colleague of mine at United Theological Seminary, told me one afternoon at a faculty meeting and retold on tape for use here.

2. Burton Mack, *Who Wrote the New Testament?* (San Francisco: HarperSanFrancisco, 1996), 158, 171.

3. John Dominic Crossan, *Who Killed Jesus?* (San Francisco: HarperSanFrancisco, 1995), 4.

4. Darby Kathleen Ray, *Deceiving the Devil: Atonement, Abuse, and Ransom* (Cleveland: Pilgrim Press, 1998), 5.

5. Ted Peters, *God—The World's Future: Systematic Theology for a Postmodern Era* (Minneapolis: Fortress, 1992), 202. This section of this chapter significantly draws on his chapter 7.

6. Jon Levenson, *The Death and Resurrection of the Beloved Son: The Transformation of Child Sacrifice in Judaism and Christianity* (New Haven: Yale University Press, 1993), 57.

7. Ibid., 59.

8. Frances Young, *Sacrifice and the Death of Christ* (Philadelphia: Westminster Press, 1975). See also Gerhard Von Rad, *Old Testament Theology,* Volume I (Harper, 1962), and Alan Richardson, "The Atonement Wrought by Christ," *An Introduction to the Theology of the New Testament* (New York: Harper, 1958), 215-241. See also Timothy Gorringe, *God's Just Vengeance: Crime, violence and the rhetoric of salvation* (New York: Cambridge University Press, 1996), Part II.

9. Young, chapter 1.

10. Ibid., chapter 3.

11. Ibid., chapter 4, especially 80-82.

12. Gorringe, 57.

13. Peters, 206n.

14. For selections from the early Christian Apologists and early Gnostic texts, see Bart Ehrman, *After the New Testament: A Reader in Early Christianity* (New York: Oxford University Press, 1999), 54-93, 146-92.

15. See, for example, Philip Lee, *Against the Protestant Gnostics* (New York: Oxford, 1987), and Harold Bloom, *The American Religion* (Simon & Schuster, 1992).

16. Rene Girard, *Violence and the Sacred* (Baltimore: Johns Hopkins University Press, 1977); *The Scapegoat* (Baltimore: Johns Hopkins University Press, 1986); and *The Girard Reader,* ed. James G. Williams (New York: Crossroad Herder Book, 1996). For discussions of Girard's theory, see Leo Lefebure, "Victims, violence and the sacred: The thought of Rene Girard," *Christian Century*, December 11, 1996, 1226-1229; Leo Lefebure, "Beyond scapegoating: A conservation with Rene Girard

and Ewart Cousins," *Christian Century*, April 8, 1998, 372-375; Raymund Schwager, *Must There Be Scapegoats: Violence and Redemption in the Bible* (New York: Harper & Row, 1987); and Walter Wink, *Engaging the Powers: Discernment and Resistance in a World of Domination* (Minneapolis: Fortress, 1992), 152-154.

17. Lefebure, "Victims, violence and the sacred," 1226.

18. Schwager, 7.

19. Lefebure, "Victims, violence and the sacred," 1226.

20. Girard, "The Surrogate Victim," *The Girard Reader*, 20-29.

21. Girard, "Sacrifice as Sacral Violence and Substitution," *The Girard Reader*, 71-93.

22. Girard, "The Bible's Distinctiveness and the Gospel," *The Girard Reader*, 145-176.

23. Girard, *The Girard Reader*, 282.

24. James G. Williams, "Glossary: Sacrifice," in *The Girard Reader*, 292-93.

25. Girard, *The Girard Reader*, 282.

26. Ibid., 272.

27. James G. Williams, *The Girard Reader*, 70.

28. Lefebure, "Beyond scapegoating," 375.

29. Girard, *The Girard Reader*, 184.

30. Gustav Aulen, *Christus Victor* (New York: Macmillan, 1966).

31. Gorringe, 139.

32. Shailer Mathews, *The Atonement and the Social Process* (New York: Macmillan, 1930).

33. Anne Carr, *Transforming Grace: Christian Tradition and Women's Experience* (San Francisco: HarperSanFrancisco, 1988), 174.

34. John Macquarrie, *Principles of Christian Theology* (New York: Scribners, 1977), 315.

35. Young, 86.

36. For a discussion of this distinction in modern ethics, see Lucius Gavin, *A Modern Introduction to Ethics* (Boston: Houghton Mifflin Company, 1953), chapter 16.

37. For a discussion of the development of the moral and legal theories which underlie the modern understanding and critique of these theories as they relate to the development and critique of atonement theories in the modern West, see Gorringe's book on divine vengeance.

38. Clark Pinnock, *Theological Crossfire* (Grand Rapids: Zondervan, 1990), 149.

39. Delores Williams, *Sisters in the Wilderness: The Challenge of Womanist God-Talk* (Maryknoll: Orbis, 1993), 161-167.

40. Ibid., 162.

41. See Jacquelyn Grant, "The Sin of Servanthood and The Deliverance of Discipleship," in Emilie Townes, ed. *A Troubling in My Soul* (Maryknoll: Orbis, 1993), 212-13.

42. Rosemary Ruether, *Introducing Redemption in Christian Feminism* (Sheffield: Sheffield Academic Press, 1998), 100.

43. Ibid., 50.

44. Ibid., 51, 50.

45. Ibid., 54.

46. For another feminist criticism of the moral theory of atonement, see Ray, 13-18.

47. Joanne Brown and Rebecca Parker, *Christianity, Patriarchy, and Abuse: A Feminist Critique* (New York: Pilgrim Press, 1990), 9.

48. Rita Brock, *Journeys By Heart: A Christology of Erotic Power* (New York: Crossroad, 1988), 55.

49. Ibid., 56.

50. My comments on Robert Letham's views are from his book, *The Work of Christ: Contours of Christian Theology* (Downers Grove, IL: InterVarsity Press, 1993), chapter 7.

51. Ibid., 136.

52. Ibid., 137.

53. Ibid., 138.

54. Gorringe, 232.

55. For a discussion of the point, see Ray, chapter 2.

56. Schwager, 146-57.

57. Gorringe, 237.

58. Schwager, 202.

59. Christine Smith, *Preaching as Weeping, Confession, and Resistance: Radical Responses to Radical Evil* (Louisville: Westminster John Knox Press, 1992), 158.

60. Ibid., 155.

61. Ibid.

62. Ibid., 156.

63. Ruether, 101, 102.

64. Smith, 158.

65. Quoted in Byron Stone, *Faith and Film* (St. Louis: Chalice Books, 2000), 91.

66. Karl Barth, *Dogmatics in Outline* (New York: Harper Torchbooks, 1959), 101.

67. "A Brief Statement of Faith," *The Constitution of the Presbyterian Church (U.S.A.), Part I: Book of Confessions* (Louisville: Office of the General Assembly, 1996), 275.

68. Macquarrie, 311-12.

69. C. J. Den Heyer, *Jesus and the Doctrine of the Atonement* (Harrisburg: Trinity Press, 1998), 106.

70. Schubert Ogden, *Is There Only One True Religion or Are There Many?* (Dallas: Southern Methodist University Press, 1992), 92.

71. Williams, 165; JoAnne Marie Terrell, *Power in the Blood: The Cross in the African American Experience* (Maryknoll: Orbis, 1998), 142.

72. Hopkins, 56.

73. Ibid., 58.

74. Tamez, 158.

75. Stone, 86-87.

76. Macquarrie, 320.

77. David Wheeler, *A Relational View of the Atonement* (New York: Peter Lang, 1989), 193.

78. Ibid., 192.

79. Jon Sabrino, *Christology at the Crossroads* (Maryknoll: Orbis, 1978), 201-202.

80. Ogden, 93.
81. Gorringe, 74-75.
82. Ibid., 246-47.
83. Terrell, 113.

Chapter Seven

1. Rosemary Ruether, *To Change the World: Christology and Cultural Criticism* (New York: Crossroad, 1983), 31.
2. Little discussion of the significance of the Holocaust for both Jewish and Christian appeared before the mid-1960s. One of the most important books both for Jews and Christians was Richard Rubenstein, *After Auschwitz: Radical Theology and Contemporary Judaism* (Indianapolis: Bobbs-Merrill, 1966). An excellent summary of the discussion through the mid-1980s is presented in Richard Rubenstein and John Roth, *Approaches to Auschwitz: The Holocaust and Its Legacy* (Atlanta: John Knox Press, 1987). For an excellent example of the exchange among Jewish theologians, see "Richard Rubenstein and Elie Wiesel: An Exchange," in *Holocaust,* eds. John Roth and Michael Berenbaum (New York: Paragon House, 1989), 346-369.
3. Norman Perrin, *Rediscovering the Teachings of Jesus* (New York: Harper & Row, 1976), 39.
4. For example, Geza Vermes, *Jesus the Jew: A Historian's Reading of the Gospels* (Philadelphia: Fortress, 1981); James Charlesworth, *Jesus' Jewishness: Exploring the Place of Jesus in Early Judaism* (New York: Crossroad, 1995); James Charlesworth, *Jesus Within Judaism: New Light from Exciting Archeological Discoveries* (New York: Doubleday, 1988); John Meier, *A Marginal Jew,* Volume 1, *Rethinking the Historical Jesus,* Volume 2, *Mentor, Message, and Miracle* (New York: Doubleday 1991, 1994); Frederick Murphy, *The Religious World of Jesus: An Introduction to Second Temple Palestinian Judaism* (Nashville: Abingdon, 1991); E. P. Sanders, *Jesus and Judaism* (Fortress, 1985); and E. P. Sanders, *Judaism: Practice and Belief* 63 BCE–66 CE (Philadelphia: Trinity, 1992).
5. James Sanders, *The Historical Figure of Jesus* (New York: Penguin Books, 1993), 222, 225.
6. Ibid., 37.
7. Ibid., 33-39.
8. Ibid., 216. For a detailed summary of the contention between Jesus and the Pharisees, see chapter 14.
9. Vermes, 29, 35.
10. "Pharisees," *The Harper Collins Bible Dictionary,* ed. Paul Achtemeier (San Francisco: HarperSanFrancisco, 1996), 842.
11 Clark Williamson, *Has God Rejected His People? Anti-Judaism in the Christian Church* (Nashville: Abingdon Press, 1982), chapter 1.
12. Gerald Sloyan, *Jesus in Focus: A Life in Its Setting* (Mystic, CT: Twenty-Third Publications, 1983), 26.
13. Ibid., 25.
14. Williamson, 103-4. See also his "Christ Against the Jews: A Review of Jon Sobrino's Christology," *Encounter* (Fall, 1979).

15. See Robert Erickson, *Theologians Under Hitler: Gerhard Kittel, Paul Althaus, and Emanuel Hirsch* (New Haven: Yale University Press, 1985). For Barth's position, see Eberhard Busch, *Karl Barth: His Life from Letters and Autobiographical Texts* (Philadelphia: Fortress, 1975).

16. One of the most recent studies of this question is provided by John Dominic Crossan, *Who Killed Jesus: Exposing the Roots of Anti-Semitism in the Gospel Story of the Death of Jesus* (San Francisco: HarperSanFrancisco, 1995). The immediate purpose of the book is to reply to Raymond Brown's *The Death of the Messiah*. All of the story is "prophecy historicized rather than history recalled." While the text tries to assert Jewish responsibility and Roman innocence, Brown argues this is "neither prophecy nor history but Christian propaganda, a daring act of public relations faith in the destiny of Christianity not within Judaism but within the Roman Empire. In a way this was history, not past history but future history," 159. The Roman political system was responsible for the arrest, trial, abuse, and execution of Jesus.

17. "Pharisees," *Interpreters Dictionary of the Bible,* Supplementary Volume, ed. Keith Crim (Nashville: Abingdon Press, 1976), 663.

18. Crossan, 147.

19. Ibid., 148.

20. Pinchas Lapide, *Jesus in Two Perspectives* (Minneapolis: Augsburg, 1985), 76.

21. Paul van Buren, *A Theology of the Jewish-Christian Reality, Part 2: A Christian Theology of the People Israel* (New York: Harper & Row, 1983), 268.

22. Lapide, *Jesus in Two Perspectives,* 66.

23. Crossan, 65.

24. Sanders, 218.

25. "Probably, some individual Pharisees bore a measure of responsibility for this, but in both cases the principle, and certainly the ultimate, guilt lay with the representatives of the political establishment—Herod Antipas and his supporters in Galilee, and the chief priests and Pilate in the capital," Vermes, 36.

26. Vermes, 37.

27. Crossan, 148.

28. Vermes, 16.

29. Crossan, 152.

30. Williamson, 38.

31. van Buren, 275.

32. Crossan, 159.

33. Sloyan, 139.

34. For two significant studies of the themes of scapegoat and abuse, see Jon Levenson, *The Death and Resurrection of the Beloved Son: The Transformation of Child Sacrifice in Judaism and Christianity* (New Haven: Yale University Press, 1993), and Rene Girard, *The Girard Reader,* ed. James Williams (New York: Crossroad Herder, 1996).

35. Crossan, 152.

36. Lapide, 39.

37. "Pharisees," *Interpreters Dictionary of the Bible* (Nashville: Abingdon, 1985), 663.

38. Dan Cohn-Sherbok, "The Resurrection of Jesus: A Jewish View," in *Resurrection Reconsidered,* ed. Gavin D'Costa (Oxford: Oneworld Publications, 1996), 188.

39. van Buren, 271.

40. Cohn-Sherbok, 195.

41. Pinchas Lapide, *The Resurrection of Jesus: A Jewish Perspective* (Minneapolis: Auguburg, 1983), 152-53.

42. Cohn-Sherbok, 191.

43. Ibid., 194.

44. Ruether, 32.

45. Ibid.

46. Daniel Migliori, *Faith Seeking Understanding: An Introduction to Christian Theology* (Grand Rapids: Eerdmans, 1991), 243.

47. Rubenstein, 264.

48. "Pharisees," *Interpreters Dictionary of the Bible,* 663.

49. van Buren, 274.

50. Crossan, 16.

51. Ibid., 17.

52. John Pawlikowski, "Christology, Anti-Semitism, and Christian-Jewish Bonding," in Rebecca Chopp and Mark Taylor, eds., *Reconstructing Christian Theology* (Minneapolis: Fortress, 1994), 262-265.

53. Ruether, 42.

54 Jacob Neusner, "How Judaism and Christianity Can Talk to Each Other," *Bible Review* (December 1990), 36.

55. Ibid., 35.

56. Ibid., 37.

57. Ibid., 38.

58. Question 37, *The Study Catechism, Full Version with Biblical References* (Louisville: Presbyterians for Renewal, 1998), 23.

59. Jurgen Moltmann, *Jesus Christ for Today's World* (Minneapolis: Fortress, 1994), 120-21.

60. Ibid., 121.

61. Ibid.

62. Ruether, 42.

63. Ibid., 41.

64. For a discussion of this theme, see Levenson, especially Part Three.

Chapter Eight

1. See, for example, Frederick Streng, *Understanding Religious Man* (Belmont, CA: Dickenson, 1969), chapter 1; Frederick Streng, Charles Lloyd, and Jay Allen, *Ways of Being Religious* (Englewood Cliffs, NJ: Prentice-Hall, 1973), Introduction; Robert Elwood, *One Way: The Jesus Movement and Its Meaning* (Englewood Cliffs, NJ: Prentice Hall, 1973), chapter 3; Robert Elwood, *Religious and Spiritual Groups in Modern America* (Englewood Cliffs, NJ: Prentice Hall, 1973), chapter 1.

2. See the massive study of fundamentalisms around the world coordinated by

Martin Marty and Scott Appleby, eds., *Fundamentalisms Observed* (The Fundamentalism Project, Volume 1 of five volumes) (Chicago: University of Chicago Press, 1994).

3. "Buddhism in America," *Time*, October 13, 1997, 72-81. There are 2,445,000 Buddhists and 4,349,000 Muslims in the United States. *Information Please Almanac,* 1998, "Religious Population of the World, 1998," www.infoplease.com/ipa/ A0001484.html.

4. *Information Please Almanac,* www.infoplease.com/ipa/A1001484.html.

5. John Cobb, *Transforming Christianity and the World: Beyond Absolutism and Relativism* (Maryknoll: Orbis, 1999), 155.

6. Ibid., 89.

7. Ibid., 114.

8. Ibid., 125.

9. Ronald Nash, *Is Jesus the Only Savior?* (Downers Grove, IL: InterVarsity, 1994), 11.

10. Ibid. "I see little to be gained by extending speculation beyond what God has chosen to tell us," 136.

11. Ronald Nash, "Restrictivism," in *What About Those Who Have Never Heard?: Three Views on the Destiny of the Unevangelized* eds. Gabriel Fackre, Ronald Nash, and John Sanders (Downers Grove, IL: InterVarsity Press, 1995), 107-139.

12. Dennis Ockholm and W. Gary Phillips, "A Particularist View: An Evidentialist Approach," in Ockholm and Phillips, eds., *Four Views on Salvation in a Pluralistic World* (Grand Rapids: Zondervan, 1995), 238. See also Nash, *Is Jesus the Only Savior,* 16-18.

13. Harold Lindsell, quoted in Paul Knitter, *No Other Name?* (Maryknoll: Orbis, 1985), 79.

14. Fackre, Nash, and Sanders, Gabriel Fackre, "Divine Perseverance," 71-95.

15. Ockholm and Phillips, 232-33.

16. Schubert Ogden, *Is There One True Religion, or Are There Many?* (Dallas: Southern Methodist University Press, 1992), 36.

17. See the exchange between them in Fackre, Nash, and Sanders, 62f, 140f.

18. "Evangelicals are Christian believers whose theology is traditional or orthodox as defined by the historic Christian creeds. They also take the Bible as their ultimate authority in matters of faith and practice, have had a religious conversion, and are interested in leading others to the same kind of conversion experience," Nash, *Is Jesus the Only Savior?*, 106.

19. *Information Please Almanac,* www.infoplease.com/ipa/A1001484.html.

20. Fackre, Nash, and Sanders, John Sanders, "Introduction," 9. The figures were taken from the *World Christian Encyclopedia,* cited in *World Evangelization* 16 (1989), 40.

21. Ogden, 50-52.

22. Ibid., 51.

23. Ibid.

24. Ockholm and Phillips, 270.

25. Nash, *Is Jesus the Only Savior?*, 135.

26. Pinnock, in Ockholm and Phillips, 144.

27. Ogden, 31.

28. "Declaration on the Relationship of the Church to Non-Christian Religions," *Documents of Vatican II* (New York: Guild Press, 1966), 660-668.

29. Karl Rahner, "Anonymous Christians," *Theological Investigations,* Volume VI (New York: Seabury, 1974), 390-398, and his "One Mediator and Many Mediations," *Theological Investigations,* Volume IX (Herder, 1972), 169-184; see also his *Theological Investigations* V, "Christianity and the Non-Christian Religions," and *Theological Investigations* XII, "Anonymous Christianity and the Missionary Task of the Church."

30. Rahner, "Anonymous Christians," 391-92.

31. Ibid., 394.

32. The early John Hick represented a theocentric view. See his *God and the Universe of Faiths* (New York: St. Martin's Press, 1973).

33. Wesley Ariarajah, *The Bible and People of Other Faiths* (World Council of Churches, 1985), 10.

34. Okholm and Phillips, John Hick, "A Pluralist View," 47f.

35. Nash, *Is Jesus the Only Savior?*, 107.

36. Ockholm and Phillips, Pinnock, "An Inclusivist View," 93-148; Fackre, Nash, and Sanders, 21-61; and John Sanders, *No Other Name: An Investigation into the Destiny of the Unevangelized* (Grand Rapids: Eerdmans, 1992).

37. Sir Norman Anderson, *Christianity and World Religions* (Downers Grove, IL: InterVarsity Press, 1984).

38. Fackre, Nash, and Sanders, 71-95.

39. Pinnock, in Okholm and Phillips, 148.

40. Odgen, 32.

41. Cobb, 76.

42. Ockholm and Phillips, Hick, "A Pluralist View," 127, 128.

43. John Hick, "'Whatever Path Men Choose is Mine,'" in ed. John Hick and Brian Hebblewaite, *Christianity and the Other Religions* (Philadelphia: Fortress, 1980), 182.

44. Ockholm and Phillips, Hick, "A Pluralist View," 43-44.

45. Ibid., 44.

46. Ibid.

47. Ibid., 43.

48. Cobb, 90.

49. Ibid., 150.

50. Ogden, 66.

51. For one of the most significant descriptions of the theological confessionalism reflected in the following discussion, see H. Richard Niebuhr, *The Meaning of Revelation* (New York: Macmillan, 1960), especially chapter 2.

52. Cobb, chapters 8-9.

53. Paul Knitter, "Key Questions for a Theology of Religions," *Horizons* 17 (1990), 94.

54. Ogden, chapter 4. (I copied these quotations from my notes, but have been unable to locate the exact reference.)

55. Robert Bellah, 425. (I copied these quotations from my notes, but have been unable to locate the exact reference.)

56. Ibid.

Bibliography

Aldredge-Clanton, Jann. *In Search of the Christ-Sophia: An Inclusive Christology for Liberating Christians*. Mystic, CT: Twenty-Third Publications, 1995.

Aldwinckle, Russell. *More Than Man: A Study in Christology*. Grand Rapids: Eerdmans, 1976.

Altizer, Thomas J., *The Contemporary Jesus*. Albany: SUNY, 1997.

Anselm. "Cur Deus Homo," in *St. Anselm: Basic Writings*. LaSalle, IL: Open Court, 1968.

Aulen, Gustaf. *Christus Victor: An Historical Study of the Three Main Types of the Idea of Atonement*. New York: Macmillan, 1966.

Baillie, Donald. *God Was in Christ*. New York: Scribners, 1948.

Barth, Karl. *Church Dogmatics*. Volume I, Part 2, pp. 1-221; Volume III, Part 4; Volume IV. Edinburgh: T. & T. Clark. 1956ff.

———. *The Humanity of God*. Richmond: John Knox, 1960.

Bartlett, Anthony. *Cross Purposes: The Violent Grammar of Christian Atonement*. Harrisburg, PA: Trinity Press, 2001.

Berkouwer, G. C. *The Person of Christ*. Grand Rapids: Eerdmans, 1954.

Bloesch, Donald. *Essentials of an Evangelical Theology*. Volume 2. San Francisco: Harper & Row, 1979.

———. *Jesus the Victor: Karl Barth's Doctrine of Salvation*. Nashville: Abingdon, 1976.

Bonhoeffer, Dietrich. *Christ the Center*. New York: Harper & Row, 1960.

Boff, Leonardo. *Jesus Christ Liberator: A Critical Christology for Our Times*. Maryknoll: Orbis, 1978.

Borg, Marcus J. *Meeting Jesus Again for the First Time: The Historical Jesus and the Heart of Contemporary Faith*. San Francisco: HarperSanFrancisco, 1984.

——— and N. T. Wright. *The Meaning of Jesus: Two Visions*. San Francisco: HarperSanFrancisco, 1999.

Bornkamm, Gunther. *Jesus of Nazareth*. New York: Harper & Row, 1960.

Borowitz, Eugene. *Contemporary Christologies: A Jewish Response*. New York: Paulist, 1980.

Braaten, Carl. *No Other Gospel! Christianity Among the World Religions*. Minneapolis: Fortress, 1992.

Brock, Rita. *Journeys of the Heart: A Christology of Erotic Power*. New York: Crossroads, 1988.

Brown, Joanne Carlson and Carole Bohn, eds. *Christianity, Patriarchy, and Abuse: A Feminist Critique*. New York: Pilgrim Press, 1989.

Brown, Raymond, *The Virginal Conception and Bodily Resurrection of Jesus*. New York: Paulist, 1973.

Brunner, Emil. *The Mediator*. Philadelphia: Westminster, 1947.

Bultmann, Rudolf. *Jesus and the Word*. New York: Scribners, 1934.

———. *Jesus Christ and Mythology*. New York: Scribners, 1958.

———. *Theology of the New Testament*. 2 Volumes. New York: Scribners, 1951.

Burns, Charlene. *Divine Becoming: Rethinking Jesus and Incarnation*. Minneapolis: Fortress Press, 2001.

Bussmann, Claus. *Why Do You Say? Jesus Christ in Latin America*. Maryknoll: Orbis, 1985.

Cady, Susan and Marian Ronan and Hal Taussig. *Wisdom's Feast: Sophia in Study and Celebration*. San Francisco: Harper & Row, 1989.

Charlesworth, James H., ed. *Jesus' Jewishness: Exploring the Place of Jesus within Early Judaism*. New York: Crossroad, 1996.

Chestnut, Glenn. *Images of Christ: An Introduction to Christology*. Minneapolis: Seabury, 1984.

Cleage, Albert. *The Black Messiah*. New York: Sheed & Ward, 1968.

Cobb, John. *Christ in a Pluralistic Age*. Philadelphia: Westminster, 1975.

———. and David Griffin. *Process Theology: An Introductory Exposition*. Philadelphia: Westminster, 1976.

Cone, James. *A Black Theology of Liberation*. Philadelphia: Lippincott, 1970.

———. *God of the Oppressed*. New York: Seabury, 1975.

Conzelmann, Hans. *Jesus*. Philadelphia: Fortress, 1973.

Cook, Michael J. *Mark's Treatment of the Jewish Leaders*. Leiden: E.J. Brill, 1978.

Cragg, Kenneth. *Jesus and the Muslim: An Exploration*. London: Allen & Unwin, 1985.

———. *Mohammed and the Christian*. Maryknoll: Orbis, 1984.

Crocket, William and James Sigountos, eds. *Through No Fault of Their Own: The Fate of Those Who Have Never Heard*. Grand Rapids: Baker, 1991.

Crossan, John Dominic, *The Birth of Christianity: Discovering What Happened in the Years Immediately After the Execution of Jesus*. San Francisco: HarperSanFrancisco, 1998.

———. *The Historical Jesus: Life of a Mediterranean Peasant*. San Francisco: HarperSanFrancisco, 1991.

———. *Jesus: A Revolutionary Biography*. San Francisco: HarperSanFrancisco, 1994.

———. *Who Killed Jesus?: Exposing the Roots of Anti-Semitism in the Gospel of the Death of Jesus*. San Francisco: HarperSanFrancisco, 1995.

———, Luke Timothy Johnson, and Werner Kelber. *The Jesus Controversy: Perspectives in Conflict*. Harrisburg, PA: Trinity Press, 1999.

Cullmann, Oscar. *The Christology of the New Testament*. Philadelphia: Westminster, 1959.

Cunningham, David S. *These Three are One: The Practice of Trinitarian Theology*. Malden, MA: Blackwell, 1998.

Daly, Mary. *Beyond God the Father*. Boston: Beacon, 1973.

Davies, Alan, ed. *Anti-Semitism and the Foundations of Christianity*. New York: Paulist, 1979.

Davis, Stephen, ed. *Encountering Jesus: A Debate on Christology*. Atlanta: John Knox, 1988.

D'Costa, Gavin, ed. *Christian Uniqueness Reconsidered: The Myth of a Pluralistic Theology of Religions*. Maryknoll: Orbis Books, 1990.

Den Heyer, C. J. *Jesus and the Doctrine of the Atonement*. Harrisburg, PA: Trinity Press, 1998.

DeVries, Dawn. *Jesus Christ in the Preaching of Calvin and Schleiermacher*. Louisville: Westminster John Knox, 1996.

Dillistone, F. W. *Christian Understanding of the Atonement*. Philadelphia: Westminster, 1968.

Douglas, Kelly Brown. *The Black Christ*. Maryknoll: Orbis, 1994.

Drake, H. A. *Constantine and the Bishops: The Politics of Intolerance*. Baltimore: Johns Hopkins University Press, 2000.

Driver, John. *Understanding the Atonement for the Mission of the Church*. Scottsdale, PA: Herald, 1986.

Driver, Tom. *Christ in a Changing World: Toward an Ethical Christology*. New York: Crossroad, 1981.

Dunn, James D. *Christology in the Making: A New Testament Inquiry into the Origins of the Doctrine of the Incarnation*. Grand Rapids: Eerdmans, 1996.

Dupuis, Jacques. *Who Do You Say That I Am?* Maryknoll: Orbis, 1994.

Ehrman, Bart D. *Jesus: Apocalyptic Prophet of the New Millennium*. New York: Oxford, 1999.

Fackre, Gabriel, Ronald Nash, and John Sanders. *What About Those Who Have Never Heard? Three Views on the Destiny of the Unevangelized*. Downers Grove, IL: InterVarsity, 1995.

Fiddes, Paul S. *The Creative Suffering of God*. New York: Oxford University Press, 1988.

Fitzmyer, Joseph. *A Christological Catechism: New Testament Answers*. New York: Paulist, 1982.

Forsyth, Peter. *The Person and Place of Jesus Christ*. London: Independent Press, 1946.

———. *The Work of Christ*. London: Hodder & Stoughton, 1910.

Fredriksen, Paula. *From Jesus to Christ: The Origins of the New Testament Images of Jesus*. New Haven, CT: Yale, 1988.

Fuller, Reginald. *Foundations of New Testament Christology*. New York: Scribners, 1965.

Funk, Robert, and the Jesus Seminar. *The Acts of Jesus: The Search for the Authentic Deeds of Jesus*. San Francisco: HarperSanFrancisco, 1998.

Funk, Robert, Roy Hoover, and the Jesus Seminar. *The Five Gospels: The Search for the Authentic Words of Jesus*. San Francisco: HarperSanFrancisco, 1993.

Geitz, Elizabeth. *Gender and the Nicene Creed*. Harrisburg, PA: Morehouse, 1995.

Gerrish, B. A. *Saving and Secular Faith*. Minneapolis: Fortress Press, 1999.

Gilkey, Langdon. *Message and Existence*. New York: Seabury, 1979.

Gogarten, Fredrick. *Christ the Crisis*. London: SCM, 1970.

Gonzalez, Justo. *A History of Christian Thought*. Volume I. Nashville: Abingdon, 1987.

The Gospel of Thomas: The Hidden Sayings of Jesus. New translation with introduction and notes by Melvin Meyer. San Francisco: HarperSanFrancisco, 1992.

Goulder, Michael, ed. *Incarnation and Myth: The Debate Continues*. Grand Rapids: Eerdmans, 1979.

Grant, Jacquelyn. *White Women's Christ and Black Women's Jesus: Feminist Christology and Womanist Response*. AAR Academy Series Number 64. Atlanta: Scholars Press, 1989.

Grey, Mary C. *Feminism, Redemption, and the Christian Tradition*. Mystic, CT: Twenty-Third, 1990.

Green, Joel and Mark Baker. *Recovering the Scandal of the Cross: Atonement in New Testament and Contemporary Contexts*. Downers Grove, IL: InterVarsity Press, 2000.

Green, Michael. *The Truth of God Incarnate*. Grand Rapids: Eerdmans, 1977.

Gregorios, P., W. Lazareth and N. A. Nissiotis, eds. *Does Chalcedon Divide or Unite? Towards Convergence in Orthodox Christology*. Geneva: World Council of Churches, 1981.

Griffin, David. *A Process Christology*. Philadelphia: Westminster, 1973.

Grillmeier, Alois. *Christ in the Christian Tradition. Volume 1: From the Apostolic Age to Chalcedon; Volume 2: From the Council of Chaldecon to Gregory the Great*. New York: Sheed&Ward, 1964.

Haight, Roger. *Jesus Symbol of God*. Maryknoll: Orbis Books, 1999.

Hall, Thor. *The Evolution of Christology*. Nashville: Abingdon, 1982.

Hamilton, William. *A Quest for the Post-Historical Jesus*. New York: Continuum, 1996.

Hardy, Edward, ed. *Christology of the Later Fathers*. Philadelphia: Westminster, 1954.

Harnack, Adolf. *What is Christianity?* New York: Harper & Row, 1957.

Hart, Thomas N. *To Know and Follow Jesus: Contemporary Christology in Focus*. New York: Paulist, 1984.

Hassnain, Fida. *A Search for the Historical Jesus: From Apocryphal, Buddhist, Islamic & Sanskrit Sources*. Bath, UK: Gateway Books, 1994.

Hayes, John. *Son of God to Superstar*. Nashville: Abingdon, 1976.

Hengel, Martin. *The Atonement: The Origins of the Doctrine in the New Testament*. Philadelphia: Fortress, 1981.

Den Heyer, C. J. *Jesus and the Doctrine of the Atonement*. Harrisburg, PA: Trinity, 1998.

Hick, John. *The Center of Christianity*. San Francisco: Harper & Row, 1968.

——— and Brian Hebblethwaite, eds. *Christianity and the Other Religions*. Philadelphia: Fortress, 1980.

———. *The Metaphor of God Incarnate: Christology in a Pluralistic Age*. Louisville: Westminster John Knox, 1993.

——— and Paul Knitter, eds. *The Myth of Christian Uniqueness: Toward a Pluralistic*

Theology of Religions. Maryknoll: Orbis, 1987.

———, Clark Pinnock, Alister McGrath, Douglas Geivett, and Gary Phillips. *Four Views on Salvation in a Pluralistic World*. Grand Rapids: Zondervan, 1996.

Holwerda, David. *Jesus & Israel: One Covenant or Two?* Grand Rapids: Eerdmans, 1995.

Hopkins, Julie. *Towards a Feminist Christology*. Grand Rapids: Eerdmans, 1994.

Horsley, Richard A. and John Hanson. *Bandits, Prophets, and Messiahs: Popular Movements at the Time of Jesus*. San Francisco: HarperSanFrancisco, 1985.

———. *Sociology and the Jesus Movement*. New York: Continuum, 1994.

———. *Archeology, History, and Society in Galilee*. Valley Forge, PA: Trinity Press, 1996.

Hunt, Anne. *What Are They Saying About the Trinity?* New York: Paulist, 1998.

Jenson, Robert. *The Triune Identity: God According to the Gospel*. Philadelphia: Fortress, 1982.

Johnson, Elizabeth. *Consider Jesus: Waves of Renewal in Christology*. New York: Crossroad, 1990.

———. *She Who Is: The Mystery of God in Feminist Theological Discourse*. New York: Crossroad, 1993.

Johnson, Luke Timothy. *The Real Jesus: The Misguided Quest for the Historical Jesus and the Truth of the Traditional Gospels*. San Francisco: HarperSanFrancisco, 1996.

Kahler, Martin. *The So-Called Historical Jesus and the Historic Biblical Christ*. Philadelphia: Fortress 1964.

Kasemann, Ernst. *Jesus Means Freedom*. Philadelphia: Fortress, 1972.

Kasper, Walter. *Jesus the Christ*. New York: Paulist, 1976.

Kaufman, Gordon. *Systematic Theology: An Historicist Perspective*. New York: Scribners, 1968.

Kelber, Werner. *The Jesus Controversy: Perspectives in Conflict: John Dominic Crossan, Luke Timothy Johnson*. Harrisburg, PA: Trinity, 1999.

Kelly, J. N. D. *Early Christian Doctrine*. 3rd Edition. San Francisco: Harper & Row, 1958.

Kierkegaard, Soren. *Philosophical Fragments*. Princeton: Princeton, 1962.

Knitter, Paul. *No Other Name? A Critical Survey of Christian Attitudes Toward the World Religions*. Maryknoll: Orbis, 1985.

Knox, John. *The Death of Christ*. New York: Abingdon, 1958.

———. *The Humanity and Divinity of Christ*. Cambridge: Cambridge, 1967.

Koester, Helmut. *Ancient Christian Gospels*. Philadelphia: Trinity, 1990.

Kung, Hans. *On Being a Christian*. New York: Doubleday, 1976.

———. *The Incarnation of God*. New York: Crossroad, 1987.

LaCugna, Catherine. *God For Us: The Trinity and Christian Life*. San Francisco: HarperSanFrancisco, 1991.

Ladd, George. *I Believe in the Resurrection of Jesus*. Grand Rapids: Eerdmans, 1975.

Lane, Dermot. *The Reality of Jesus: An Essay in Christology*. New York: Paulist, 1975.

Lapide, Pinchas. *The Resurrection of Jesus*. Minneapolis: Augsburg, 1983.

LeBeau, Bryan, Leonard Greenspoon and Dennis Hamm, eds. *The Historical Jesus Through Jewish and Catholic Eyes*. Harrisburg: Trinity, 2000.

LeDue, William. *Jesus Among the Theologians: A Study of Contemporary Christology.* Harrisburg, PA: Trinity, 2001.

Lee, Philip. *Against the Protestant Gnostics.* New York: Oxford University Press, 1987.

Letham, Robert. *The Work of Christ: Contours of Christian Theology.* Downers Grove, IL: InterVarsity, 1993.

Levenson, Jon. *The Death and Resurrection of the Beloved Son: The Transformation of Child Sacrifice in Judaism and Christianity.* New Haven: Yale University Press, 1993.

Lonergan, Bernard. *The Way to Nicea.* Philadelphia: Westminster, 1976.

Ludemann, Gerd. *What Really Happened to Jesus? A Historical Approach to the Resurrection.* Louisville: Westminster John Knox, 1995.

Luttenberger, Gerard. *Who Do You Say That I Am: An Introduction to Christology in the Gospels and Early Church.* Mystic, CT: Twenty-Third Publications, 1998.

Machovec, Milan. *A Marxist Looks at Jesus.* Philadelphia: Fortress, 1976.

Mack, Burton L. *Who Wrote the New Testament? The Making of the Christian Myth.* New York: Harper, 1995.

McGrath, Alister. *The Making of Modern German Christology: From the Enlightenment to Pannenberg.* New York: Blackwell, 1986.

McKnight, Edgar. *Jesus Christ in History and Scripture: A Poetic and Sectarian Perspective.* Macon: GA: Mercer University Press, 1999.

McGarry, Michael B. *Christology After Auschwitz.* New York: Paulist, 1977.

McGiffert, A. C. *A History of Christian Thought.* Volume I. New York: Scribners, 1932.

Mackintosch, H. R. *The Doctrine of the Person of Jesus Christ.* T. & T. Clark, 1912.

Macquarrie, John. *Jesus Christ in Modern Thought.* Philadelphia: Trinity Press, 1990.

———. *Christology Revisited.* Harrisburg, PA: Trinity Press, 1998

———. *Principles of Christian Theology.* New York: Scribners, 1977.

Martin, Ralph and Brian Dodd, eds. *Where Christology Began.* Louisville: Westminster John Knox, 1998.

Martin, Raymond. *The Elusive Messiah: A Philosophical Overview of the Quest for the Historical Jesus.* Boulder, CO: Westview, 1999.

Marxsen, Willi. *The Beginnings of Christology.* Philadelphia: Fortress, 1969.

———. *Jesus and Easter: Did God Raise the Historical Jesus From the Dead?* Nashville: Abingdon, 1990.

Mathews, Shailer. *The Atonement and the Social Process.* New York: Macmillan, 1930.

Meier, John. *A Marginal Jew, Volume One: Rethinking the Historical Jesus; Volume Two: Rethinking the Historical Jesus: Mentor, Message, and Miracles.* New York: Doubleday, 1991.

Mercadante, Linda. "Bess the Christ Figure?: Theological Interpretations of *Breaking the Waves.*" *The Journal of Religion and Film* 5 (No. 1 April, 2001): *http://www.unomaha.edu/~wwwjrf/bessthe.htm.*

Meyendorff, John. *Christ in Eastern Christian Thought.* Crestwood, NY: St. Valdimer's Seminary, 1987.

Miguez-Bonino, Jose, ed. *Faces of Jesus: Latin American Christologies.* Maryknoll: Orbis, 1983.

Miranda, Jose. *Being and the Messiah.* Maryknoll: Orbis, 1977.

Moltmann, Jurgen. *The Crucified God: The Cross of Christ as the Foundation and Criticism of Christian Theology*. New York: Harper & Row, 1974.

———. *History and the Triune God: Contributions to Trinitarian Theology*. New York: Crossroad, 1992.

———. *Jesus Christ for Today's World*. Minneapolis: Fortress, 1994.

Moule, C. F. D. *The Origin of Christology*. New York: Cambridge, 1977.

Nash, Ronald H. *Is Jesus the Only Savior?* Grand Rapids: Zondervan, 1994.

Niebuhr, R. Richard. *The Resurrection and Historical Reason*. New York: Scribners, 1957.

———. *Schleiermacher on Christ and Religion*. New York: Scribners, 1964.

Neill, Stephen. *Jesus Through Many Eyes: Introduction to the Theology of the New Testament*. Philadelphia: Fortress, 1976.

Nicholls, Bruce J. *The Unique Christ in Our Pluralistic World*. Grand Rapids: Baker, 1994.

Norris, Richard. *The Christological Controversy*. Philadelphia: Fortress, 1980.

O'Collins, Gerald. *Christology: A Biblical, Historical, and Systematic Study of Jesus*. New York: Oxford University Press, 1995.

———. *The Resurrection of Jesus Christ: Some Contemporary Issues*. Milwaukee, WI: Marquette, 1993.

———. *What are they saying about Jesus?* New York: Paulist, 1977.

———. *What are they saying about the resurrection?* New York: Paulist, 1978.

Ogden, Schubert. *Christ Without Myth*. New York: Harper, 1961.

———. *Is There Only One True Religion or Are There Many?* Dallas: Southern Methodist University Press, 1992.

———. *The Point of Christology*. San Francisco: Harper & Row, 1982.

Okholm, Dennis and Timothy Phillips, eds. *More Than One Way? Four Views on Salvation in a Pluralistic World*. Grand Rapids: Zondervan, 1995.

Ottati, Douglas. *Jesus Christ and Christian Vision*. Louisville: Westminster John Knox, 1996.

Pagels, Elaine. *The Gnostic Gospel*. New York: Vintage, 1979.

Pawlikowski, John. *Christ in the Light of the Christian-Jewish Dialogue*. New York: Paulist, 1982.

Pannenberg, Wolfhart. *Jesus God and Man*. Second Edition. Philadelphia: Westminster, 1977.

Patterson, Stephen and James Robinson. *The Fifth Gospel: The Gospel of Thomas Comes of Age*. Harrisburg: Trinity Press, 1998.

Patterson, Stephen. *The God of Jesus: The Historical Jesus and the Search for Meaning*. Harrisburg, PA: Trinity Press, 1998.

Pedraja, Luis. *Jesus Is My Uncle: Christology from a Hispanic Perspective*. Nashville: Abingdon, 1999.

Peelman, Achiel. *Christ is a Native American*. Maryknoll: Orbis, 1995.

Pelikan, Jaroslav. *The Emergence of the Catholic Tradition 100-600*. Chicago: University of Chicago, 1971.

———. *Jesus Through the Centuries: His Place in the History of Culture*. New Haven: Yale, 1985.

Perrin, Norman. *The Kingdom of God in the Teachings of Jesus*. Philadelphia: Westminster, 1963.

————. *Rediscovering the Teachings of Jesus*. New York: Harper & Roq, 1967.

————. *The Resurrection according to Matthew, Mark, and Luke*. Philadelphia: Fortress, 1977.

Phipps, William. *Was Jesus Married? The Distortion of Sexuality in the Christian Tradition*. New York: Harper & Row, 1970.

Pinnock, Clark. *A Wideness in God's Mercy: The Finality of Jesus Christ in a World of Religions*. Grand Rapids: Zondervan, 1992.

Pittenger, Norman. *Christology Reconsidered*. London: SCM, 1970.

————. *The Word Incarnate: A Study of the Doctrine of the Person of Christ*. Welwyn: Nisbet, 1959.

Pregeant, Russell. *Christology beyond Dogma: Matthew's Christ in Process Hermeneutic*. Philadelphia: Fortress, 1978.

Rahner, Karl. *Foundations of Christian Faith*. New York: Crossroad, 1978.

————. *Theological Investigations*. Volume 1, 4, & 5. New York: Seabury, 1974-76.

———— and Thusing. *A New Christology*. New York: Seabury, 1980.

Ramm, Bernard. *An Evangelical Christology: Ecumenic and Historic*. Nashville: T. Nelson, 1985.

Ray, Darby Kathleen. *Deceiving the Devil: Atonement, Abuse, and Ransom*. Cleveland: Pilgrim, 1998.

Recinos, Harold. *Who Comes in the Name of the Lord? Jesus at the Margins*. Nashville: Abingdon, 1997.

Ricci, Carla. *Mary Magdalene and Many Others: Women Who Followed Jesus*. Minneapolis: Fortress, 1994.

Riley, Gregory. *One Jesus, Many Christs: How Jesus Inspired Not One True Christianity, but Many*. San Francisco: HarperSanFrancisco, 1997.

Ringe, Sharon. *Wisdom's Friends: Community and Christology in the Fourth Gospel*. Louisville: Westminster John Knox, 1999.

Robinson, James. *The New Quest for the Historical Jesus*. London: SCM, 1959.

Roukema, Riemer. *Gnosis and Faith in Early Christianity: An Introduction to Gnosticism*. Harrisburg, PA: Trinity, 1999.

Rubenstein, Richard E. *When Jesus Became God: The Epic Fight over Christ's Divinity in the Last Days of Rome*. New York: Harcourt Brace, 1999.

Ruether, Rosemary. *Introducing Redemption in Christian Feminism*. Scheffield Academic Press, 1998.

————. *Sexism and God-Talk: Toward a Feminist Theology*. Boston: Beacon, 1983.

————. *To Change the World: Christology and Cultural Criticism*. New York: Crossroads, 1981.

Samuel, Vinay and Chris Sugden, eds. *Sharing Jesus in the Two Thirds World: Evangelical Christologies*. Grand Rapids: William B. Eerdmans, 1984.

Sanders, E. P. *The Historical Figure of Jesus*. London: Penguin, 1993.

Sanders, John, et. al. *What About Those Who Have Never Heard? Three Views of the Destiny of the Unevagelized*. Downers Grove, IL: InterVarsity Press, 1995.

Sanday, William. *Christologies Ancient and Modern*. New York: Oxford, 1910.

Schillebeeckx, Edward. *Christ, the Sacrament of the Encounter With God*. New York: Sheed & Ward, 1963.

————. *Christ: The Experience of Jesus as Lord*. New York: Seabury, 1980.

————. *Jesus: An Experiment in Christology*. New York: Seabury, 1979.

Schleiermacher, F. D. E. *The Christian Faith*. New York: Harper & Row, 1963.

Schoonenberg, Piet, *The Christ*. New York: Herder & Herder, 1971.

Schreiter, Robert, ed. *Faces of Jesus in Africa*. Maryknoll: Orbis Books, 1991.

Shussler Fiorenza, Elizabeth. *Jesus: Miriam's Child, Sophia's Prophet*. New York: Continuum, 1995.

Schwager, Raymund. *Jesus in the Drama of Salvation: Toward a Biblical Doctrine of Redemption*. New York: Crossroad, 1999.

Schwartz, Hans. *Christology*. Grand Rapids: Eerdmans, 1998.

Schweitzer, Albert. *The Quest for the Historical Jesus*. Baltimore: Johns Hopkins, 1998.

Sellers, Robert V. *The Council of Chalcedon*. London: SPCK, 1953.

———. *Two Ancient Christologies*. London: SPCK, 1940.

Sergio, Lisa. *Jesus and Woman*. London: Hawthorne Books, 1975.

Sloyan, Gerald. *Jesus in Focus: A Life in Its Setting*. Mystic, CT: Twenty-Third Publications, 1983.

Snyder, Mary. *The Christology of Rosemary Radford Ruether: A Critical Introduction*. Mystic, CT: Twenty Third, 1988.

Sobrino, Jon. *Christ the Liberator: A View from the Victims*. Maryknoll: Orbis, 2001.

———. *Christology at the Crossroads: A Latin American Approach*. Maryknoll: Orbis, 1978.

———. *Jesus the Liberator: A Historical-Theological Reading of Jesus of Nazareth*. Maryknoll: Orbis, 1993.

Soelle, Dorothy. *Christ the Representative*. Philadelphia: Fortress, 1967.

Song, Choan-Seng. *Jesus, The Crucified People*. New York: Crossroad, 1990.

Soulen, Kendall. *The God of Israel and Christian Theology*. Minneapolis: Fortress, 1996.

Stegemann, Ekkehard and Wolfgang Stegemann. *The Jesus Movement: A Social History of Its First Century*. Minneapolis: Fortress Press, 1999.

Stein, Robert. *Jesus the Messiah: A Survey of the Life of Christ*. Downers Grove: InterVarsity, 1996.

Sugirtharajah, R. S., ed. *Asian Faces of Jesus*. Maryknoll: Orbis, 1993.

Tamez, Elsa, ed. *Through Her Eyes: Women's Theology from Latin America*. Maryknoll: Orbis, 1989.

Terrell, JoAnne Marie. *Power in the Blood? The Cross in the African American Experience*. Maryknoll: Orbis, 1998.

Thangaraj, M. Thomas. *The Crucified Guru: An Experiment in Cross-Cultural Christology*. Nashville: Abingdon, 1994.

Thompson, John. *Modern Trinitarian Perspectives*. New York: Oxford University Press, 1994.

Tillich, Paul. *Systematic Theology*. Volume II. Chicago: University of Chicago, 1956.

Thielicke, Helmut. *The Evangelical Faith*. Volume 2, Part 2. Grand Rapids: Eerdmans, 1974.

Thistlethwaite, Susan and Mary Engle, eds. *Lift Every Voice: Constructing Theologies from the Underside*. San Francisco: Harper & Row, 1990.

Thurman, Howard. *Jesus and the Disinherited*. Nashville: Abingdon, 1949.

Tracy, David. *Blessed Rage for Order*. New York: Seabury, 1975.

Bibliography

Turner, H. E. W. *The Patristic Doctrine of Redemption: A Study of the Development of Doctrine During the First Five Centuries.* London: Mowbray, 1952.

Van Buren, Paul. *The Secular Meaning of the Gospel.* New York: Macmillan, 1963.

Vicedom, George, ed. *Christ and the Younger Churches: Theological Contributions from Asia, Africa, and Latin America.* London: SPCK, 1972.

Wahlberg, Rachel. *Jesus According to a Woman.* New York: Paulist, 1975.

Weaver, Walter and James Charlesworth, eds. *Earthing Christologies: From Jesus' Parables to Jesus the Parable.* Valley Forge, PA: Trinity, 1995.

Webster, Douglas. *A Passion for Christ: An Evangelical Christology.* Grand Rapids: Academie, 1987.

West, Thomas. *Jesus and the Quest for Meaning.* Minneapolis: Fortress Press, 2001.

Wildman, Wesley. *Fidelity with Plausability: Modest Christologies in the Twentieth Century.* Albany, NY: SUNY, 1998.

Williams, James. *The Bible, Violence, and the Sacred: Liberation from the Myth of Sanctioned Violence.* San Francisco: HarperSanFrancisco, 1991.

Williamson, Clark. *Has God Rejected His People?* Nashville: Abingdon, 1982.

Wiles, Maurice. *The Remaking of Christian Doctrine.* Philadelphia: Westminster, 1978.

Witherington, Ben III. *The Jesus Quest: The Third Search for the Jew of Nazareth.* Downers Grove, IL: InterVarsity, 1995.

Yoder, John. *The Politics of Jesus.* Grand Rapids: Eerdmans, 1972.

Young, Frances. *From Nicea to Chalcedon.* Philadelphia: Fortress, 1983.

———. *Sacrifice and the Death of Christ.* Philadelphia: Westminster, 1975.

———. *The Making of the Creeds.* Philadelphia: Trinity, 1991.

Young, Pamela Dickey. *Christ in a Post-Christian World: How Can We Believe in Jesus Christ when Those Around Us Believe Differently—or Not At All?* Minneapolis: Fortress, 1995.

Zannoni, Arthur E., ed. *Jews and Christians Speak of Jesus.* Minneapolis: Fortress, 1994.

Zeitlin, Irving M. *Jesus and the Judaism of His Time.* New York: Blackwell, 1988.

Index

Index

Index

Schleiermacher, Frederick 80, 85, 88, 93-6, 98, 192
Schmidt, Frederick 70, 220
Schweitzer, Albert 25-27, 30, 34-36, 83, 214
Scientology 206
scribes 169
Second Temple 166-7, 169, 174
Second quest 28-9, 36
Second Vatican Council 32, 118, 129, 195, 201
secularization 190
Septuagint 130
semantic revisionism 180-83
servanthood 123
"Seven Years in Tibet" 190
Seventh Day Adventists 87
"Sheilism" 87
Shinto 206
"Sleeping with the Enemy" 152
Sloyen, Gerald 169-70, 174, 234
Simmons, Robert 226
single covenant 184-86
Sirach 131
Skarsgaard, Stellen 115
Smith, Christine 158-9, 222, 232
Smith, W. C. 192
Sobrino, Jon 105-6. 111, 171, 226, 233-34
social location 111
social prophet 31
Society of Biblical Literature 25
Society of Christian Philosophers 44
Socrates 30
Soelle, Dorothy 45
sola scriptura 197
solidarity 159, 161, 183
Sojourner 125
Sophia 49, 101, 122, 124, 126, 128-38, 210
sophialogy 132-34
Sosa, Sammy 198
soteriology 16, 43, 47-8, 52-6, 59, 60-2, 74, 77, 88-9, 106-7, 110-11, 125, 127, 141, 193
Southern Baptist Convention 87
sovereignty 61
"Spitfire Grill" 159
Spirit 210
Stalinism 195
Stein, James 222
Stone, Byron 232
story 24, 60
Strauss, David 26, 214
Streng, Frederick 235
strong form of confessionalism 209

Stroup, George 219
subordinationism 48, 51-2, 54, 65
substance/substantialism 52, 54-60, 67, 72, 88, 93-4, 97-8, 103
substitutionary atonement/substitute 16, 70, 73, 120, 144, 149-57
Suchocki, Marjorie 224
Suetonius 9
suffering 15, 43-7, 59-63, 66-7, 116, 142, 144, 153-4, 157, 159, 161-3, 181
suffering God 62-63, 66, 155, 162
subjectivism 87-89
supersessionism 165
surrogacy 152-3, 157
Swinburne, Richard 217
synagogue 168, 170, 173-4, 176, 183, 205

T

Tacitus 9, 184
Talmud 168, 170
Tamez, Elsa 161, 232
Tatum, W. Barnes 213
Tauler, John 76
Temple 37, 168-72, 184-5
Terrell, Jo Ann Marie 163, 232-3
Tertullian 48, 51, 55
Teresa of Avila 76
theism 15-6, 44, 47, 61-6, 193, 206
Theissen, Gerd 29
theocentrism 205-7
theocentric inclusivism 201-2, 204
theodicy 199, 200, 211
Theodore 57-8
theopaschitism 63
Theophilus 174
Third quest 29-35, 39-40
Third Reich 171
Thirty Nine Articles 85
Thomas 127, 196
Thistlethwaite, Susan 228
thoroughgoing eschatology 26, 32
"Time to Kill, A" 152
Timothy, Book of 198
Tillich, Paul 11, 59, 192, 219
Torah 17, 168, 177-8, 183, 188
totalizing 45-7
Torrence, T. F 71.
Toulmin, Stephen 222
transformation 41-2, 62-3, 66-7, 123, 146, 159, 162-3, 187, 190, 192, 206, 208, 211
Trier, Lars von 115